MORAL PANICS AND
THE MEDIA

ISSUES in CULTURAL and MEDIA STUDIES

Series editor: Stuart Allan

Published titles

Media, Risk and Science
Stuart Allan

News Culture
Stuart Allan

Television, Globalization and Cultural Identities
Chris Barker

Cultures of Popular Music
Andy Bennett

Masculinities and Culture
John Beynon

Cinema and Cultural Modernity
Gill Branston

Violence and the Media
Cynthia Carter and C. Kay Weaver

Ethnic Minorities and the Media
Edited by Simon Cottle

Moral Panics and the Media
Chas Critcher

Modernity and Postmodern Culture
Jim McGuigan

Sport, Culture and the Media
David Rowe

Compassion, Morality and the Media
Keith Tester

MORAL PANICS AND THE MEDIA

Chas Critcher

OPEN UNIVERSITY PRESS
Buckingham · Philadelphia

Open University Press
McGraw-Hill Education
McGraw-Hill House
Shoppenhangers Road
Maidenhead
Berkshire
SL6 2QL
United Kingdom

email: enquiries@openup.co.uk
world wide web: www.openup.co.uk

and
Two Penn Plaza
New York, NY10121-2289, USA

First Published 2003
Reprinted 2006

A catalogue record of this book is available from the British Library

ISBN 0 335 20908 4 (pbk)   0 335 20909 2 (hbk)

Library of Congress Cataloging-in-Publication Data
Critcher, C.
  Moral panics and the media/Chas Critcher.
    p. cm. – (Issues in cultural and media studies)
  Includes bibliographical references and index.
  ISBN 0-335-20909-2 (HB) – ISBN 0-335-20908-4 (PB)
    1. Mass media–Moral and ethical aspects.   2. Mass media–Social aspects.
I. Title.   II. Series.

  P94.C75 2003
  175–dc21

                                                              2002074963

Typeset by Type Study, Scarborough
Printed in Great Britain by Bell & Bain Ltd, Glasgow

CONTENTS

SERIES EDITOR'S FOREWORD

The term 'moral panic' currently resonates across an array of popular and academic debates about a range of topics, from the prospect of human cloning to the influence of video games on young people. In the popular lexicon, the term often works as a kind of short-hand for public hysteria, by definition 'irrational', and is almost always held to be indicative of someone else's behaviour rather than our own. Amongst researchers, the term is more likely to be taken to signify a host of complex – and contradictory – social processes shaping public perceptions of an exigent threat to the 'moral order of society'. Shared across most of these different inflections of the term, however, is the assumption that the media play a crucial role in determining the characteristics of a moral panic. Where things get particularly interesting, of course, is at the point where different users of the term look for evidence to support their own preferred theory about how such panics occur and why.

Chas Critcher's *Moral Panics and the Media* is a thoughtful elucidation of this exciting area of enquiry. Not surprisingly, he elects to begin the discussion by examining what is arguably the most influential investigation to date, Stanley Cohen's (1973) classic study *Folk Devils and Moral Panics*. Critcher identifies on its pages an 'ideal type' of moral panic, which in his view provides a useful yardstick against which to assess different kinds of cases that have taken place since its publication. More specifically, it is his aim to recast the assumptions underpinning Cohen's model so as to further elaborate an alternative framework. Special attention is devoted, for example, to the efficacy of the media in the contested process of claims-making about the nature of any perceived threat to public morality, and the stages by which it unfolds. Over the course of several chapters, Critcher scrutinizes a number of case studies – ranging from HIV/AIDS to the 'rave' scene (including the use of ecstasy tablets by young people), video nasties, child abuse in the family and paedophilia – against a set of questions prompted by the gaps and silences indicative of previous approaches. In deliberating over the extent to which each case can be reasonably regarded as a moral panic, Critcher attends to the organizing imperatives involved with an eye to clarifying precisely what is at stake in theoretical and methodological terms. This is a provocative and timely book, one that promises to help initiate a paradigm shift in the study of moral panics.

The *Issues in Cultural and Media Studies* series aims to facilitate a diverse range of critical investigations into pressing questions considered to be central to current thinking and research. In light of the remarkable speed at which the conceptual agendas of cultural and media studies are changing, the authors are committed to contributing to what is an ongoing process of re-evaluation and critique. Each of the books is intended to provide a lively, innovative and comprehensive introduction to a specific topical issue from a fresh perspective. The reader is offered a thorough grounding in the most salient debates indicative of the book's subject, as well as important insights into how new modes of enquiry may be established for future explorations. Taken as a whole, then, the series is designed to cover the core components of cultural and media studies courses in an imaginatively distinctive and engaging manner.

Stuart Allan

LIST OF TABLES AND FIGURE

Tables

Figure

ACKNOWLEDGEMENTS

In an academic career spanning 30 years, this is the first book I have ever written on my own. I can't say I enjoyed the experience very much. I didn't mind the tedious search for references, the constant replanning or apparently endless redrafting, but the lack of feedback was debilitating. This has made me even more grateful to those who have supported the project. Stuart Allan, the series editor, made helpful comments and was properly stringent about length. Editorial staff at the Open University Press were diligent and patient. I would not have been able to include as much international comparison but for the help of academics outside the UK: Philip Jenkins (USA), Sean Hier (Canada), Chris Atmore (New Zealand) and Deborah Lupton and Paul Jones (Australia). They may have only answered an email or two but their advice was crucial. That I was subsequently able to track down references at all was down to the assiduous work of largely anonymous staff at Sheffield Hallam University Library and the British Lending Library. An earlier version of Chapter 4 appeared in *Leisure Studies* and a longer version of one section of Chapter 7 in *Journalism Studies*. I am grateful to the publishers (Taylor & Francis www.tandf.co.uk) for permission to reuse them.

For psychological support, I am grateful to Bob Franklin, Brian Tweedale, Dave Waddington and Kevin Williams, even though their concern was often couched in general terms: 'How is your back/bunion/book?' Practical support was provided by the Cultural Research Institute at Sheffield Hallam University. Russell Jackson did an invaluable early literature and newspaper search. Pam Hibberd, as ever, worked tirelessly on the book's manuscript, including composing the graph in Chapter 7. Her word-processing skills are exceeded only by her patience. Three cohorts of Hallam University students on my final year option helped clarify my thoughts.

Other debts are more personal. Val, Jo, Laura and Annie tolerated even more than usual piles of newspapers, an air of preoccupation and general crabbiness. Bob Pearson, though he didn't know it, provided relief in our weekly game of snooker where incompetence doesn't matter. My dog Suki on our late night walks demonstrated how to chase your own tail and pursue imaginary rabbits, though thanks to this book I already knew how.

This turned out to be a very serious book; its subject matter made it so. I have managed to keep my sense of humour, though it isn't always evident in the following pages. There aren't many laughs in moral panics.

Introduction
ORIGINAL THOUGHTS

The project

The idea for this book was prompted by a feature in the *Observer* newspaper on the Waterhouse inquiry. This was an investigation into a network of abusers of young boys in care in North Wales in the 1970s and 1980s. The article recounted in harrowing detail the evidence of the victims and how those in authority had ignored many opportunities to recognize their plight, not least because they were frequently themselves the abusers. The proceedings of the inquiry had little interest for the media. Most witnesses remained anonymous. The events had occurred a long time ago. Many of the abusers were in prison; some had died. All this contrasted with the ongoing furore over the Sex Offenders Act 1997 and the prospect of convicted **paedophiles** at large in the community. The article resonated with me for two reasons. One was that as a student I spent two summers as a volunteer in childcare homes. On both occasions, members of staff had been suspended amidst allegations of sexual abuse. The Waterhouse inquiry did not altogether surprise me. The other reason was that 20 years before I had been part of the team who produced *Policing the Crisis* (Hall et al. 1978), a study of **social reaction** to 'mugging' in the early 1970s. **Mods** and **Rockers**, mugging, paedophilia – I did not know what else to call any of these except a moral panic. However, little seemed to have been done to establish moral panic as a 'key sociological concept' (Thompson 1998: 142). In academic work, it was either used casually as a footnote to other concerns or derided as hopelessly old-fashioned. In the upmarket press it had become an ambiguous reference, nicely caught by an *Independent on Sunday* editorial

(21 December 1993) in the aftermath of the murder of 2-year-old James Bulger: 'Moral panic is one of those deflating phrases used by sociologists and other allegedly impartial students of human behaviour to condescend to excitements amongst the general populace'. For all these reasons, I became interested in whether it had stood the test of time, required revision or ought to be abandoned. I developed an undergraduate module on moral panics and made them the subject of my professorial lecture (Critcher 2000b), with the long-term aim of producing this book.

At first I naively thought that my aim was to 'prove' whether or not moral panics existed but came to realize that moral panic was not a thing but an abstract concept, a model of a process. The task then became to find if there were constancies in the model when applied to quite different examples. Any moral panic model became not an end but a means. Its usefulness lay as much in what it did not reveal about a given example as what it did. In sociological parlance, this is called an heuristic device, more specifically an **ideal type**. The concept of ideal type was originally developed by the great German sociologist Max Weber. In a typically dense essay on social science methodology, Weber argued that all social scientists used ideal types. These were not 'ideal' in the usual sense of desirable but ideal in the logical sense. To use Weber's own example, the perfect 'market economy' has never existed but we can construct what it would look like if it were carried to its logical conclusion. The ideal type gives us a yardstick against which to measure actual examples, so we can measure how and why they deviate from the ideal type: 'this mental construct cannot be found empirically anywhere in reality' (Weber [1904] 1949: 90). An ideal type 'has the significance of a purely ideal *limiting* concept with which the real situation or action is *compared* and surveyed for the explication of its significant components' (Weber [1904] 1949: 93, original emphasis). The ideal type is 'not a end but a means' (1949: 92), most useful 'as an heuristic device for the comparison of the ideal type and the "facts" ' (1949: 102).

Ideal types have not had a good sociological press. The logic behind them is flawed, Weber did not follow his own advice, hardly anyone else has found them useful, our understanding of sociological methods has moved on (MacRae 1974; Parkin 1982). All this may well be true but unhelpful. Just as I do not know what else to call reaction to paedophilia except a moral panic, so I do not know what else to call my use of moral panic except an ideal type. Others can debate its epistemological status. I am interested only in whether it works. I never set out to follow Weber's precepts; I had not read his essay in 30 years. It just turned out to be the most accurate account of what I ended up doing.

The structure

The nature of this enterprise is reflected in the structure of the book. Part I, The Models, outlines two 'ideal types' of moral panics. The first, based on the seminal work of Stan Cohen (1973), I define in Chapter 1 as a processual model. The second, derived from the more recent work of Erich Goode and Nachman Ben-Yehuda (1994), I define in Chapter 2 as an attributional model. These two models generate clusters of questions around their processes or attributes. These are designed to be applied to any case study of a possible moral panic. The question for me is not, 'Does this example prove that moral panics exist?' but 'How useful is it to apply moral panic analysis to this case?' I also consistently search for aspects of the case which are beyond the grasp of moral panic analysis alone. I aim to test out moral panic as an heuristic device not to argue for its theoretical validity. To achieve this, each case study has a uniform structure of four sections. It begins with a narrative reconstruction of how the issue developed. The two models are then applied to assess the approximation of the case to the ideal types. The third section 'beyond moral panics' considers features of the case study which moral panic analysis alone will not reveal. Finally, work from other countries on the same issue is compared to the British case.

Part II, The Case Studies, applies the models to a series of case studies: **AIDS** (Chapter 3), **rave/ecstasy** (Chapter 4), **video nasties** (Chapter 5), physical and sexual **child abuse** in families (Chapter 6) and paedophilia (Chapter 7). Except for paedophilia, I did not intend to undertake original research and so looked for case studies which were already well documented, preferably with some use of moral panic frameworks or terminology and comparable analysis from other countries. The resultant selection is not meant to be comprehensive or even representative but indicative. For reasons explained in Chapter 10, food panics do not qualify. Other potential case studies had to be left out. Football hooliganism was rejected as lacking international comparison, asylum seekers as occurring too late in the very long gestation of this book. Two minor moral panics – 'dangerous dogs' in 1992–93 and 'alcopops' in 1996–97 – were omitted on grounds of space and their uniqueness to Britain. Road rage, discussed by Lupton (2001), was another possibility. My selection of case studies is contingent in practice and open-ended in principle. There is every reason why other case studies should be used to develop the debate. Extending empirical material and modifying conclusions is an integral part of the intellectual exchange of social science.

Part III, The Implications, looks across the case studies. In Chapter 8, I outline the similarities and differences in the occurrence and nature of moral panics in those few countries where they have been documented, in an effort to contribute to comparative analysis. Chapter 9 considers what the study of moral panics can learn from media sociology and what media sociology can learn from moral panics. Chapter 10 evaluates the status of the original methods in the light of the case studies and criticisms made by others. The model is defended but revised in important detail. The final two chapters move beyond the confines of moral panic analysis. Chapter 11 tries to explain why childhood has come to be the predominant focus of modern moral panics, at least in Britain. In Chapter 12, I tentatively explore the compatibility of any form of moral panic analysis with two dominant themes in contemporary sociology: the theory of the **risk society** and the concept of **discourse**. An Afterword indicates the lines along which future moral panic analysis should now proceed. The logic of the book should be clear: outline the basic models, apply them to some case studies and draw some conclusions. This structure may also help those readers who wish to use the book for limited purposes, a specific case study or just one of the implications. There is meant to be an overall argument but some may wish to use only parts of it.

The objective

This approach begs many questions. In one argument, all accounts are equally valid. My 'social construction' of the issue has no privileged status. Without getting into all the complicated arguments about the nature of knowledge which lie behind the argument, I must firmly rebut it. Sociology, like all social science, can exist at all only on the basis that it must, in principle and at some stage, be possible to assess the accuracy of a statement, deduction or generalization about a social problem. This is intrinsically difficult and there will always be areas of doubt and uncertainty – if only because we do not have sufficient knowledge about the status of the problem to assess claims about it. But to acknowledge difficulty and complexity is far from accepting that the enterprise is impossible. If we cannot do that, it is difficult to see what is the point of analysing how social problems are constructed, except to engage in a stifling debate about the impossibility of knowing anything. On the purpose of analysing social problems, I am with Becker.

> What can social science contribute to understanding and solving any social problem? It helps in several ways: (1) by sorting out the different definitions of the problem; (2) by locating assumptions made by interested parties – assumptions belied by the facts; (3) by discovering

strategic points of intervention in the social structures and processes that produce the problem; (4) by suggesting alternative moral points of view from which the problem area can be assessed

(Becker 1966: 23)

My concluding argument is that a moral panic has three dimensions. It involves an identifiable process of definition and action. It marks the moral boundaries of society. It is also a set of discourses of various kinds and levels. Even if this conclusion is not accepted, I would still hope that this work has demonstrated what I set out to test: the value of moral panic models in tracing the similarities and differences between otherwise diverse social problems in quite different national contexts. If that proves to be the total sum of my achievement, I shall be content.

Further reading

Becker, H. (1966) Introduction, in H. Becker (ed.) *Social Problems: A Modern Approach*. New York: John Wiley.

Thompson, K. (1998) *Moral Panics*. London: Routledge.

Weber, M. ([1904] 1949) 'Objectivity' in social science and social policy, in M. Weber, *The Methodology of the Social Sciences*, trans. and edited by E.A. Shils and H.A. Finch. New York: Free Press.

Part I
THE MODELS

The sociologist may have to reconcile himself or herself to the fact that logical and systematic schemes are not invariably mirrored in the 'structure' of the social world. That structure contains a measure of contradiction, paradox and absurdity . . . the analytic possibilities of sociology can be realized only when there is an abundance of discrepant theories which no one theory can contain.

(Downes and Rock 1998: 4–5)

1 | MADE IN BRITAIN: THE PROCESSUAL MODEL OF MORAL PANICS

Introduction

The most common quotation about moral panics is the opening paragraph of *Folk Devils and Moral Panics*:

> Societies appear to be subject, every now and then, to periods of moral panic. (1) A condition, episode, person or group of persons emerges to become defined as a threat to societal values and interests; (2) its nature is presented in a stylized and stereotypical fashion by the mass media; (3) the moral barricades are manned by editors, bishops, politicians and other right-thinking people; (4) socially accredited experts pronounce their diagnoses and solutions; (5) ways of coping are evolved or (more often) resorted to; (6) the condition then disappears, submerges or deteriorates and becomes more visible. Sometimes the object of the panic is quite novel and at other times it is something which has been in existence long enough, but suddenly appears in the limelight. Sometimes the panic passes over and is forgotten, except in folk-lore and collective memory; at other times it has more serious and long-lasting repercussions and might produce such changes as those in legal and social policy or even in the way the society conceives itself.
>
> (Cohen 1973: 9)

This is commonly evoked as the self-explanatory core of Cohen's work.

The numbers, which do not appear in the original, seem to identify six stages in the development of a moral panic but his original analysis was more complex and ambiguous. In this extract the details of each stage are only baldly stated, significant actors are omitted and the relationship between the stages is unspecified. To explore this further, it is necessary to briefly recap the events Cohen was endeavouring to explain, the nature of his overall project and the key theoretical influences upon it.

Cohen: *Folk Devils and Moral Panics*

At Easter 1964 young people from London and the south-east of England gathered at the east coast resort of Clacton. Some were identifiable as Mods and some as Rockers. It was cold and wet. The young people were bored. Minor scuffles and incidents occurred. People milled about in irritation, shepherded by a few police. The weekend became 'unpleasant, oppressive and sometimes frightening' (Cohen 1973: 29). Monday's newspapers head-lined a 'terror' (*Daily Telegraph*) wrought by 'wild ones' (*Daily Mirror*), with 97 arrests. On Tuesday, feature articles purported to explain how antagonism between Mods and Rockers was turning violent. Editorials called for government action.

The next Bank Holiday was Whitsun in May. Local and national papers cited Mods and Rockers, threatening that other southern coastal towns – Brighton, Eastbourne and Margate – would be targeted. It was again wet and cold. Crowds gathered, as did police and journalists. Some minor incidents produced another crop of wildly exaggerated headlines and condemnatory editorials. Those appearing in court were often refused bail, fined heavily for quite trivial offences (mostly obstruction and threatening behaviour) or imprisoned for the more serious. All were castigated by magistrates. Local traders, residents and Members of Parliament (MPs) demanded tougher action. A whole new social problem had been defined. In April 1964 Parliament coincidentally passed a Drugs (Prevention of Misuse) Act, increasing penalties for possession, especially of amphetamines. Under pressure, the Conservative government introduced in July a Malicious Damage Act, increasing fines and compensation payments. Over the following two years, the Bank Holiday pattern was repeated. Chief Constables coordinated massive police operations. Young people approaching seaside resorts were turned back, moved on if they arrived and arrested if they showed resistance. After 1966 seaside gatherings declined, as the Mod youth culture started to bifurcate and the media lost interest.

This attracted the attention of a newly starting PhD student, Stan Cohen. He collected newspaper articles, was present at several seaside resorts during 1965, especially Brighton at Whitsun, held discussion groups, and conducted interviews with young people, journalists and local opinion leaders.

Folk Devils and Moral Panics was first published in 1972, based primarily on a transactional approach to **deviance**. This challenged social science orthodoxy, that deviance could be identified and explained as a form of rule-breaking. Becker (1963) and others insisted that deviance was not an attribute of an act but a category constructed in the course of interaction between the putative deviant and others, especially agents of social control. In Becker's (1963) famous formulation (cited by Cohen 1973: 12–13), society decides the rules and how to apply them. Deviance is created by those who mobilize sanctions and labels. The labelling process becomes the heart of what is meant by deviance. The consequences are serious for the offender. In Lemert's (1967) formulation, elaborated by Wilkins (1964), acts of 'primary' deviance which provoke labelling are less important than the 'secondary' deviance which follows, as the deviant behaves in ways which meet the expectations of the label.

Other important perspectives included early constructionist ideas from the USA on how social problems come to be defined in public arenas (Gusfield 1963). For the role of the media Cohen drew on British work, especially that on the 1968 Vietnam demonstrations (Halloran et al. 1970). Some influences on Cohen's work now seem dated. He relied quite heavily on Smelser's (1962) structural functionalist account of crowd behaviour, which has subsequently been damagingly criticized (Waddington et al. 1989). Disaster research had identified stages of public reaction, initially seven, which Cohen collapsed into four: warning, impact, inventory and reaction. The analogy with disasters now seems forced. Disasters do not jeopardize moral order or create folk devils.

We can now return to the three elisions of the first paragraph. The first was the detail of how each stage works, outlined in three main chapters in Cohen. The media are the focus of Chapter 2. Cohen argues that the nature of social reaction depends upon the kind of information available in the public arena, including what causes the deviance and what kind of person the deviant is. Since most people have no first-hand knowledge of deviants, they are reliant on the media. Understanding the role of the media becomes central.

> The student of moral enterprise cannot but pay particular attention to the role of the mass media in defining and shaping social problems. The media have long operated as agents of moral indignation in their own right: even if they are not self-consciously engaged in crusading or muck-raking, their very reporting of certain facts can be sufficient to generate concern, anxiety, indignation or panic. When such feelings coincide with a perception that particular values need to be protected,

the pre-conditions for new rule creation or social problem definition are present.

(Cohen 1973: 16)

As a consequence 'much of this study will be devoted to understanding the role of the mass media in creating moral panics and folk devils' (Cohen 1973: 17). They are particularly important in the early ('inventory') stage of social reaction, producing 'processed or coded images' (Cohen 1973: 30) of deviance and the deviants. Three processes are involved. First is *exaggeration* and *distortion*, of the seriousness of events, the numbers involved, the extent of violence and damage to property. Highly emotive language is used, mythical stories perpetrated and rumours reported as fact. Second is *prediction*, that such events will recur. Third is *symbolization* through language: the word 'Mod' comes to stand for a whole youth style and its deviant status.

In Chapter 3 Cohen looks at how the media, political actors and the public make sense of Mods and Rockers. Three themes emerge. The first is their *orientation*, an emotional and intellectual evaluation, where images of doom and prophecies of disaster symbolize moral and social decline. Second are *images* of who the deviants are and why they behave in this way, with indiscriminate labelling of youth as a whole. Third is *causation*, nominating a range of explanations, from youth boredom to the breakdown of common morality. The distinction between the deviant and the normal is exaggerated. 'Moral panics depend upon the generation of diffuse normative concerns while the successful creation of folk devils rests on their stereotypical portrayal as atypical actors against a background that is over typical' (Cohen 1973: 61).

Chapter 4 examines how the 'system of social control' reacts to Mods and Rockers. Yet again we have three aspects. There is **sensitization**, where any form of hooligan behaviour is blamed on Mods and Rockers. Events which would otherwise be ignored now attract attention. Second comes increased social control measures: **diffusion** from a local to the national arena, *escalation* of existing controls and *innovation* of new measures. The police and judiciary dominate social control. **Moral entrepreneurs**, who interest Cohen greatly, petition politicians – local councillors, individual MPs and eventually the government – to increase the powers of the police and courts.

The second problem with the opening paragraph is that it does not encompass the full range of actors in the drama. The first omission is the control culture, such as the police. They are not named at the stage of 'measures resorted to', much less in the initial definition and labelling of the problem group – in both of which they belong. The second omission is that of the folk devil. The opening paragraph does not say there has to be a folk devil, referring to the possibility of a 'condition or episode' as well as a group, but the general thrust of the argument emphasizes the centrality of the folk devil. The stereotypes, prophecies of doom and negative symbolization of the inventory create the conditions 'to allow for full-scale demonology and hagiology to develop; the information had been made available for placing the Mods and Rockers in the gallery of contemporary folk devils' (Cohen 1973: 44). The final omission is that of public opinion. Cohen carefully compares what his two samples say about Mods and Rockers compared with media portraits, which they generally accept, though much toned down. However, public opinion does not appear in the first paragraph or in any of the amplification sequences.

The third problem with the opening paragraph is whether Cohen wishes to imply the existence of stages at all. The continuous interaction between the media, moral entrepreneurs and the control culture, at times almost indistinguishable, confirms Cohen's resistance to a linear (staged) model of moral panics. He finally rejects the disaster model as 'linear and constant' since the models needed are 'circular and amplifying' (Cohen 1973: 24). A 'natural history' model of social problems is similarly rejected because its 'more or less fixed sequence' is 'too mechanistic' (Cohen 1973: 10–11). Cohen is less interested in stages than processes: not what happens in what order and why but how social reaction evolves and develops. However, this effort to identify processes at work within loosely defined stages produces a series of paragraphs and diagrams which are implicitly linear. For example, in his discussion of the dynamics operative within the control culture's reaction to moral panics he outlines a sequence in which there is '(i) *initial deviance* leading to; (ii) the *inventory* and (iii) *sensitization* which feed back onto each other so as to produce (iv) an *overestimation* of the deviance which leads to an *escalation* in the control culture' (Cohen 1973: 142–3, original emphases).

The summary of the deviancy amplification model again produces what looks remarkably like a sequential model: '[(i)] initial (social structural) problem; [(ii)] initial (deviant) solution); [(iii)] societal reaction (distorted) operation of control culture with exploitation and creation of stereotypes; [(iv)] increase deviance and polarization; [(v)] confirmation of stereotypes' (Cohen 1973: 199). Cohen does seem drawn to what is, despite feedback loops and symbiosis, a sequential model. His unique contribution was to provide both an elaborate account of the central processes in a moral panic and a model of its overall trajectory. Not based upon discrete stages, it is best termed *a processual model of moral panics*. This will become the first model to test against our case studies. But we must also briefly note an early and influential application and revision of the model in relation to a moral panic about mugging.

Hall et al.: *Policing the Crisis*

In 1972–73 there emerged in Britain what was either a new kind of crime or a new label for an old kind: mugging. Apparently first used by a police officer who described a murder in London in August 1972 as a 'mugging gone wrong', it attracted press attention, the *Daily Mirror* describing it as 'a frightening new strain of crime'. Coverage peaked first in October and November 1972 and second in March 1973, when three youths from Handsworth in Birmingham were given unusually long detention sentences for a vicious attack some five months earlier. By August interest had waned. The first wave of concern about mugging lasted just thirteen months.

Hall et al. (1978) analysed the significance of mugging. Their work has been variously interpreted as a major contribution to criminology, Marxist theories of the state, media studies, the analysis of racism and ethnic relations, and post-war political history, including a prescient account of the imminent nature of Thatcherism. We are concerned only with its application of the moral panic model. Early on, Hall et al. (1978: 16–17) cite Cohen's opening paragraph to demonstrate that mugging fitted it almost exactly, though they do not follow his model or terminology precisely. They demonstrated that the panic about mugging had little basis in any statistical increase in street robberies, though this was subsequently challenged by Waddington (1986). The 'mugging' label evoked negative connotations of young black males dangerously prone to gratuitous violence. The 'mugger' became a classic folk devil, symbolizing a crisis in law and order. The law was not changed but police activity increased, as did court sentences. Hall et al. (1978) sought to offer a more elaborate account than Cohen of the roles of the media and the state.

Hall et al. (1978) filled in the detail of newsmaking practices, which Thompson (1998: 68–9) argues to be their distinctive contribution. First, they stressed the media's dependence on official and authoritative sources. The media acted as secondary definers of the perspectives offered by such **primary definers**. Second, they revealed how the media translated such statements into a 'public idiom', familiar to their readers. Third, the media then fed back to primary definers media reactions as if they were public opinion. Fourth, the media overemphasized violence to justify extreme concern. Even this is to simplify a complex argument which concludes that the relations between primary definers and the media serve, at one and the same time, to define 'mugging' as a *public issue*, as a matter of *public concern*, and to effect an ideological closure of the topic . . . whose dimensions have been clearly delineated, which now serves as a continuing point of reference for subsequent news reporting, action and campaigns.

(Hall et al. 1978: 75–6, original emphases)

The British media inherited the term 'mugging', with its connotations of random violence, race and urban disintegration, from the USA. The label, Cohen's 'symbolization', did not follow the emergence of muggers as folk devils but preceded it. So did intervention by the control culture. The police were active against black 'muggers' long before they were termed as such. The court cases validating the panic were based on arrests made several months earlier, traceable to the deteriorating state of relations between black youth and the police. Thus instead of deviant action being followed by social reaction, the sequence was intervention revealing deviant action setting off social reaction. The activities of official agencies were not simply reactive. 'They do not simply respond to moral panics. They form part of the circle out of which "moral panics" develop' (Hall et al. 1978: 52).

Hall et al. (1978) go beyond reforming the moral panic model; they transform it. Cohen's 'societal control culture' maintaining a 'moral consensus' is replaced by the state struggling to maintain **hegemony** or ideological dominance. The moral panic about mugging is interpreted politically. Media and politicians interact to produce a signification spiral where the panic feeds off itself. In a process of convergence, 'deviant' activities from quite different sources (delinquency, social permissiveness, trade union politics, Irish republicanism) are seen as essentially similar in kind. Each is mapped against thresholds of unacceptability (permissiveness, legality and violence). In the 1970s this justified law and order as the foundation for a new hegemony.

Primary definers and signification spirals, the state and hegemony, convergence and thresholds are the conceptual means by which the moral panics model is theoretically appropriated into a Marxist theory of crime, the law, the state and ideology. A degree of incompatibility is acknowledged. 'The problem concerns the relation to our analysis – which is pitched at the level of the state apparatus and the maintenance of forms of hegemonic domination – of the phenomenon described earlier as a moral panic' (Hall et al. 1978: 221). The debate is resolved in favour of retaining 'notion of the moral panic' but redefining it 'as one of the key ideological forms in which a historical crisis is "experienced and fought out"' (Hall et al. 1978: 221). This is a radical recasting of the model. Jones (1997) has pointed out that 'hegemony is not merely "added" to Hall's revised moral panic paradigm

Table 1.1 Conceptual transformations in the processual model

Folk Devils	*Policing the Crisis*
Labelling	Signification
Moral entrepreneurs	Primary definers
Amplification	Signification spiral
Disproportionality of societal reaction (understood largely statistically)	Disproportionality of societal reaction (understood as ideological misrepresentation)
Societal control culture	State exercising hegemony
Discrete 'moral panics'	Convergence of multiple panics into crisis of authority
Moral consensus	Mobilization of consent
Public opinion	Reproduction of common sense

Source: adapted from Jones 1997

but is part of a wholesale transformation of Cohen's conceptual repertoire'
(Jones 1997: 12). His summary of the precise nature of those transformations is presented in simplified form in Table 1.1.

There are two interrelated limitations of this radical revision. The first is
whether, even if they are accurate, the assertions about mugging are in
anyway generalizable to other moral panics, such as the reaction to football
hooliganism which was in full flow in the early 1970s. The second limitation
is whether mugging was as historically momentous as is claimed, which
Sumner (1981) doubts. 'In so appropriating and translating "moral panic"
into "crisis of hegemony", Hall effectively erased its specificity' (Jones 1997:
13). *Policing the Crisis* was nevertheless important in the development of the
moral panics model. Others followed. From Golding and Middleton's
(1979) work on welfare to Pearson's (1995) edited collection on a range of
social problems (youth crime, drugs, lone parents, child abuse, mental illness
and crime), the concept of moral panic has been evoked. Some usages have
been careful and critical, others more cavalier. Almost all cite Cohen (1973)
and some Hall et al. (1978). Because it is more generally applicable, Cohen's
model rather than that of Hall et al. will be applied to the case studies.

Eliciting a model

In the first paragraph, in the disaster analogy and in the outline of deviancy
amplification can be found the basis of a model of how moral panics work.

The first paragraph will here be extended into a processual model of the moral panic with seven loosely defined stages. Each has been revised to incorporate omissions from the first paragraph and is followed by questions applicable to any case study.

One: emergence. At this point a form of behaviour comes to be perceived as a threat. There is a general apprehension that something is wrong and a narrower focus on imminent danger. The initially fragmented response prefigures sense-making processes dominant in the next stage. This is what the first paragraph defines as the moment when a 'condition, episode, person or group of persons emerges to become defined as a threat to societal values and interests'. The object of the panic may be new or long established.

- In what form does the 'problem' emerge?
- What is perceived as novel about it?
- Why and in what ways is it perceived as a threat to the moral or social order?

Two: media inventory. This is a preliminary explanation of the nature of the threat and those who pose it, articulated primarily through the mass media. Three strategies are involved: exaggeration/distortion, prediction and symbolization. The media become sensitized to apparently similar events. These more complex processes underlie the baldness of the opening paragraph: 'its nature is presented in a stylized and stereotypical fashion by the mass media'.

- Who or what is stereotyped?
- What kind of stereotype is involved?
- Is there an identifiable folk devil?
- What evidence is there of exaggeration, distortion, prediction and symbolization?
- Do the media become sensitized to the issue?

Three: moral entrepreneurs. Groups or organizations take it upon themselves to pronounce upon the nature of the problem and its best remedies. Cohen sees the 'moral barricades' being manned 'by editors, bishops, politicians and other right-thinking people'. They offer orientations (emotional and intellectual responses), images of the deviants and explanations of their causal explanations.

- Who are the significant moral entrepreneurs, whether groups or individuals?
- Do they lead, follow or operate alongside the media?
- What orientations, images and causal explanations are evident?

Four: experts. Though the opening paragraph suggests 'socially accredited experts pronounce their diagnoses and solutions', Cohen does not elaborate. No particular expertise was required to pronounce upon the state of youth. However, on some issues expertise may carry particular weight, affecting the way the media, especially upmarket papers and broadcasting, come to define the issue. So the distinctive contribution of experts remains identifiable.

- Who claims expertise about this problem?
- On what grounds do they claim expertise?
- Is such expertise accredited by the media?

Five: coping and resolution. The reaction of the media, moral entrepreneurs and experts contain ideas about the required measures. Current powers are exploited but, if deemed insufficient, demands for legal reform will follow. This is what is meant by the first paragraph's description of 'ways of coping are evolved or (more often) resorted to'.

- What solutions are advocated and by whom?
- Which measures are instigated and by whom?
- Are these innovations procedural and/or legal?
- In what ways are they effective and/or symbolic?

Six: fade away. The moral panics ends, as 'the condition then disappears, submerges or deteriorates and becomes more visible'. Cohen leaves open the possibility that the condition may re-emerge though serial recurrence is not specifically mentioned.

- When and why does the concern end?
- Does it or might it recur?
- What status does the problem subsequently have?

Seven: legacy. Cohen suggests that any moral panic may have 'little long-lasting effect' and become a 'footnote in history' or produce changes in social policy, the law or society's view of itself. As he suggests in his final chapter, Mods and Rockers, though now long forgotten, turned out to be one episode in a series of panics about youth in the 1960s and 1970s.

- What are the long-term effects of the issue?
- How is it related to previous or subsequent issues?

In appropriating Cohen in this way, there is a temptation to reduce the complexity of his analysis to a rather mechanical model of progression through inevitable stages. This would deny the symbiotic relationship between actors in a moral panic. Points two to five above, for example, are not in any simple sense linear: media, moral entrepreneurs, experts, public opinion, elites and the control culture reinforce each other's interpretations. Yet there is a kind of sequence implied in points one to five. As Cohen emphasizes about the deviancy amplification model, it is not an inevitable one.

> While it is true that each stage of the reaction appears to be a logical product of the prior one, the deviancy amplification model is a typical rather than an inevitable sequence. There are no overwhelming technical reasons why it should not be broken or at least re-routed at various points.
>
> (Cohen 1973: 173)

Each stage can be seen as essentially problematic, enabling or preventing progression through subsequent stages. Any potential moral panic may fail to follow, or be diverted away from, the next stage implied in the model.

In Part Two of the book, each case study will be tested against this model by asking the questions under each of these seven headings. As discussed in the introduction, the methodology of the ideal type provides a useful yardstick against which to assess different kinds of cases. We shall be as interested in discovering where and why it does not fit as much as where it does. This may tell us about the peculiarities of the case, the insufficiency of the model or both. Cohen's is not, however, the only extant model of moral panics. The alternative, from a quite different intellectual tradition, is reviewed in the next chapter.

Further reading

Cohen, S. (1973) *Folk Devils and Moral Panics*. St Albans: Paladin.

Hall, S., Critcher, C., Jefferson, T., Clarke, J. and Roberts, B. (1978) *Policing the Crisis: Mugging, the State and Law and Order*. London: Macmillan.

Thompson, K. (1998) *Moral Panics*. London: Routledge.

2

NOTES FROM A BIG COUNTRY: THE ATTRIBUTIONAL MODEL OF MORAL PANIC

Introduction

In the USA, debates about the kinds of issues called moral panics in the UK have been dominated by a distinctive approach called **social construction-ism**. Such work rarely cites the concept of moral panic. 'Scare' and 'panic' appear as descriptive terms – even sometimes in the titles of major works – but they are not substantial concepts. Goode and Ben-Yehuda (1994) seek to relocate moral panics within a social constructionist approach. The orig-inators of social constructionism are Spector and Kitsuse (1977). They crit-icized the assumption that sociology could define, measure, explain and prescribe remedies for social problems. Just as labelling theory had under-mined the conventional definition of deviance, so social constructionism denied that social problems were self-evident. If problems are socially con-structed (Blumer 1971), the task is to 'describe and explain the definitional process in which morally objectionable conditions or behaviors are asserted to exist and the collective activities which become organized around *those assertions*.' This requires focus on 'how those definitions and assertions are made, the processes by which they are acted upon by institutions, and how those institutional responses do or do not produce socially legitimated categories of social problems and deviance' (Spector and Kitsuse 1977: 72, original emphases).

Sociologists cannot decide whether such claims are justified by the 'objec-tive' status of the problem. Marxists (Agger 1993) and feminists (Gordon 1993) argued that it was possible and necessary to analyse structures of power and domination as objective conditions in society. Some critics

(Woolgar and Paluch 1985) suggested that constructionists had failed to appreciate the logic of their own position. If all attempts to analyse problems were simply social constructions, then logically this should apply to their own analyses as well. Others, sympathetic to the constructionist emphasis on interpretative processes (Best 1993), retained the attempt to assess the reality of claims made about social problems, producing 'contextual' rather than 'strict' constructionism. 'Contextual constructionists study claims-making within its context of culture and social structure' (Best 1993: 139). The position of Goode and Ben-Yehuda seems about right. 'To most sociologists, the strict constructionist approach simply makes no sense whatsoever' (Goode and Ben-Yehuda 1994: 100).

Whatever the school of constructionism favoured, its adherents have periodically attempted to model the process of social problem construction. Spector and Kitsuse (1977) advocate comparative and cumulative analysis which seeks to 'move from descriptions of specific cases to generalizations about the *type* of phenomenon in question' and to 'examine sequences of events, to seek the processual character of development' (Spector and Kitsuse 1977: 134). Preferring the term 'career' to 'natural history', they agree that social problems pass through key stages. Others before and since have made similar contributions, some of which are summarized in Table 2.1.

These models remain abstract, lacking vital detail or cumulative empirical evidence. The more substantial contribution of social constructionism, evident in Gusfield's (1981) 'strict' constructionist analysis of drunk driving or

Table 2.1 Stages in constructionist models

	Blumer (1971)	*Downs (1972)*	*Spector and Kitsuse (1977)*	*Peyrot (1984)*
Stage 1	Emergence	Pre-problem	Claims asserted and publicized	Mobilizing agitation
Stage 2	Legitimation	Discovery and optimism	Official agencies respond	Policy formation
Stage 3	Mobilization	Realization of costs	Claims makers dissent from solutions	Policy implementation
Stage 4	Official plan formation	Decline of public interest	Claims makers posit alternatives	Programme modification
Stage 5	Plan implementation	Post-problem		Reform agitation

Best's (1990) 'contextual' constructionist analysis of 'missing' children, has been to foreground the activity of claims making.

Claims making and the mass media

Claims making was fundamental to Spector and Kitsuse's original formulation. 'The notion that social problems are a kind of *condition* must be abandoned in favour of a conception of them as a kind of *activity*. We call this *claims-making activity*' (Spector and Kitsuse 1977: 73, original emphases). The study of social problems does not merely involve but is centred on 'accounting for *the emergence, nature, and maintenance of claims-making and corresponding activities*' (Spector and Kitsuse 1977: 75–6, original emphases). Analysis focuses on the agents, places, strategies and impacts of claims making. The agents of claims making are professionals of various kinds, political activists, grassroots and official agencies.

Almost anyone can become a moral entrepreneur, if they can access public arenas. Hilgartner and Bosk (1988) produce a long and indiscriminate list of these arenas, including fictional and factual media, the legal system, political institutions, pressure groups and professional organizations. Arenas have limited carrying capacity, producing constant competition for attention. To achieve prominence, issues must appear novel and dramatic, be opportune and have salience. Successful issues pass from one arena to another, gathering support from media, politicians and law enforcers. The crucial activity of **claims makers** is persuasion: 'claims making is a rhetorical activity' (Best 1990: 24). Claims makers seek to establish 'ownership' of a problem. They have to give it a name, establish it as a threat and advocate solutions, what Best (1990) calls 'grounds', 'warrants' and 'prescriptions'. If successful, the issue's appearance in public arenas will attract the attention of the public, whose concerns confirm the significance of the issue.

All this is useful. As later case studies will show, claims makers are very important in moral panics, more so than Cohen's allusions to moral entrepreneurs and experts indicate. Yet curiously, and quite unlike Cohen, constructionists persistently underestimate the role of the media in claims making. For Spector and Kitsuse (1977: 79) the media are important to claims making since they 'publicize and disseminate news about such activities (as well as participate in them)'. This apparent afterthought, that the media might make claims themselves, seems quite typical of initial social constructionist thinking. Fritz and Altheide (1987) have criticized this vagueness. Implying that the media have a role does not explain their significance. They advocate recognition of the importance of **news values**, effects on the audience and interaction between media. But media sociology seems to have passed the constructionists by. Goode and Ben-Yehuda have inherited this constructionist flaw, blind to the importance of the media while clear-sighted about claims making.

Goode and Ben-Yehuda: *Moral Panics*

Erich Goode and Nachman Ben-Yehuda published *Moral Panics: The Social Construction of Deviance* in 1994, some 20 years after the work of Cohen, to whom the book was dedicated. They are contextual constructionists. While the relationship between the social construction of a problem and its objective occurrence is problematic, it can still be established. Moral panics have observable effects upon moral values, as well as legal and social policy. Claims makers are fundamental to the process, especially in the form of social movements. All these are underpinned by tendencies towards collective behaviour, evident in the importance of rumour, urban legends, even hysteria or delusion. Such collective behaviour is fundamentally irrational, observable when societies experience, 'a kind of fever . . . characterized by heightened emotion, fear, dread, anxiety, hostility and a strong sense of righteousness' (Goode and Ben-Yehuda 1994: 31). Their perspective is cultural (the process of definition), political (organized interests) and psychological (collective behaviour). Their empirical case studies, in some ways the most impressive parts of the book, range across continents and centuries, from medieval witchcraft in Europe to drugs in 1980s Israel.

Moral panics are differentiated from both social problems generally and specific moral crusades. Social problems differ from moral panics in lacking folk devils, panicky reactions or wild fluctuations of concern. Moral crusades are initiated by moral entrepreneurs, using the issue as a vehicle for their own interests. To become a moral panic, a crusade has to mobilize a wider constituency with a variety of interests. The crusade is an organized agitation, the moral panic a contingent alliance of interests. Such distinctions reveal the essential common characteristics of moral panics, five defining 'elements or criteria' (Goode and Ben-Yehuda 1994: 33). Since these are the core of their attempt to specify the distinguishing attributes of moral panics, they require some detailed attention.

One: concern. Any moral panic involves a 'heightened level of concern over the behaviour of a certain group or category and the consequences that the behaviour presumably cause for the rest of society' (Goode and Ben-Yehuda 1994: 33). It must be 'manifested or measurable in concrete ways' such as 'public opinion polls, public commentary in the form of media attention, proposed legislation, social movement activity and so on' (1994: 33).

Two: hostility. Moral panics exhibit 'an increased level of hostility toward the groups or category regarded as engaging in the behaviour in question'. Members are 'collectively designated as the enemy, or an enemy, of respectable society' whose behaviour is seen as 'harmful or threatening' to the values, the interests and even existence of society, 'or at least a sizeable segment' of it. The threat must be attributed to 'a clearly defined group in or segment of the society' (Goode and Ben-Yehuda 1994: 33). Folk devils, constructed through a process of stereotyping, are essential to a moral panic.

Three: consensus. In a moral panic it is not enough for some agents to express concern and hostility; it must resonate in society so that 'there must be at least a certain minimal measure of consensus in the society as a whole – or in designated segments of the society – that the threat is real, serious and caused by the wrongdoing group members and their behaviour' (Goode and Ben-Yehuda 1994: 34). The consensus need not be universal or even national; it may be limited to some groups or some regions. But 'a substantial segment of the public must see threat in that condition for the concern to qualify as a moral panic' (1994: 35). Without such support, the moral panic will not develop. Alternatively, it may be forestalled by organized opposition to claims makers: 'in some moral panics, the opposing voice is weak and unorganized, while in others, it is strong and united' (1994: 35).

Four: disproportionality. This is the most fundamental characteristic since 'the concept of moral panic *rests* on disproportionality' (Goode and Ben-Yehuda 1994: 38, original emphasis). Disproportionality is evident where 'public concern is in excess of what is appropriate if concern were directly proportional to objective harm' (1994: 36). Disproportionality can be empirically demonstrated where statistics are exaggerated or fabricated, the existence of other equally or more harmful activities is denied or where concern is demonstrably out of line with measures of actual trends in allegedly deviant behaviour.

Five: volatility. It is proposed that 'by their very nature, moral panics are volatile; they erupt fairly quickly (although they may lie dormant or latent for long periods of time, and may reappear from time to time) and nearly as suddenly, subside' (Goode and Ben-Yehuda 1994: 39). A moral panic may build on previous ones but each episode cannot be sustained for long.

To exemplify the attributes, they examine two negative cases. AIDS was not a moral panic because it lacked disproportionality, its threat to health being a real one. Scares over health epidemics or food contamination are not moral panics because they lack folk devils as objects of hostility. The general case is that these five criteria must all be met for any case to be termed as a moral panic. This is in essence what we shall call an *attributional model of a moral panic*; cases lacking the attributes are not to be understood as moral panics.

The authors are equally interested in explanations of moral panics. They identify three. The first, the 'grassroots' model, argues that panics originate with the general public who exhibit 'a widespread, genuinely felt – if perhaps mistaken – concern' (Goode and Ben-Yehuda 1994: 127). Generalized anxiety focuses on an often mythical threat. In the second, 'elite-engineered' model, an 'elite group deliberately and consciously undertakes a campaign to generate and sustain concern, fear and panic on the part of the public over an issue that they recognize not to be terribly harmful to the society as a whole' in order to 'divert attention away from the real problems in the society', solving which would affect the elite's interests (1994: 135). The third 'interest group' model suggests that 'the exercise of power in the creation and maintenance of moral panics is more likely to emanate from the middle rungs of power and status than the elite stratum'. Organized interest groups, such as 'professional associations, police departments, the media, religious groups, educational organizations' (1994: 139) are more significant than elites in determining 'the content, direction or timing of panics' (1994: 139).

They reject the elite-engineered theory, preferring a combination of grass-roots and interest group theories. Without grassroots feeling, a moral panic has no foundation; without interest groups, it finds no expression:

> the grassroots provide fuel or raw material for a moral panic, organizational activists provide focus, intensity and direction . . . issues of morality provide the *content* of moral panics and interests provide the *timing* . . . Together, the two illuminate moral panics; interest groups co-opt and make use of grassroots morality and ideology.
>
> (Goode and Ben-Yehuda 1994: 43, original emphases)

They suggest asking three questions of any instance about its timing, when and why it started and ended; content, why this issue came to prominence; and target, why this particular group was singled out for attention. Goode and Ben-Yehuda share with Cohen an interest in when, how and why moral panics start and end; their impact upon institutions and the law; their apparent function, in times of rapid or unsettling social change, of reaffirming the basic moral values of society; and the recurrence of moral panics as typical of modern societies:

> we are not focusing on a single, brief, discrete episode lasting a few months or a year or two. We are, in fact, discussing a series of events – a

process . . . A close examination of the impact of panics forces us to take a more long-range view of things, to look at panics as a social process rather than as separate, discrete, time-bound events.

(Goode and Ben-Yehuda 1994: 229)

This stress on processes is not perhaps wholly compatible with an attributional model and is not the only contradiction in their work.

Goode and Ben-Yehuda make only limited attempts to trace general patterns in the construction of moral panics. Their definition is more about outcomes than the ways they are produced. Concentrating on claims makers, they are remarkably uninterested in other key actors. Consequently, they underestimate the role of the media. In the book's index there are 51 entries under mass media. Hardly any are theoretical or even analytical in nature; they are mostly evidential and descriptive. The media are largely incidental to the attributional criteria even though empirically central to moral panic narratives. For example, their analysis of the Israeli drugs panic of 1982 immediately acknowledges that the media played a 'crucially important' role. 'The media, both electronic and printed, provided the information which fuelled the panic; relevant media items were collected and filed' (Goode and Ben-Yehuda 1994: 186). Yet how and why they played this role is not discussed, whereas the moral vocabularies employed by various interest groups in constructing the panic are analysed in detail. The result is a conundrum: 'one is, of course, left puzzled about the dubious role the media played in helping this moral panic come about' (1994: 198). Thus, unlike Cohen, they do not emphasize the processes of newsmaking in the media. Both the strengths and weaknesses of a constructionist approach to moral panics are evident in the work of Philip Jenkins.

Jenkins: *Intimate Enemies*

Jenkins' (1992) book applies a contextual constructionist approach to a series of panics in Britain between 1974 and 1991: rape and violence against women, paedophilia and sexual abuse of children. Its empirical and analytical content will be covered in later chapters (6 and 7). Here we are concerned with his general orientation. Jenkins cites Cohen's opening paragraph but is otherwise uninterested in defining the process or attributes of a moral panic. The term is sometimes used quite loosely, as in his comment on child abuse in the 1980s that 'the intensity of public concern was more than sufficient to justify the term "*panic*"' (Jenkins 1992: 9, original emphasis). Jenkins' work parallels that of Goode and Ben-Yehuda by discussing theories of moral panics, trying to explain their timing, content and targets while refusing to see the media as active claims makers.

Jenkins discovers the key actors to be claims makers: individuals, such as MPs and moral entrepreneurs; issue-based pressure groups, especially on child protection; professionals such as doctors, social workers and the police; and social movements, especially Christian evangelists and feminists. This discredits the assumptions of elite engineered theories and supports interest group theory. He accepts the importance of **social anxiety,** a predisposition to panic among society as a whole. Issues of morality and permissiveness became highly sensitive in Britain as a result of its changing national identity in the world, the experience of black immigration and the pace of social change, especially around the family and sexuality. Cultural rather than economic issues came to dominate the political landscape. Anxieties about social change underwrote moral panics. Issues on which conservative opinion had lost ground were displaced onto more viable targets; homosexuality onto paedophilia, pornography onto child pornography, Satanism onto **ritual abuse.** The moral agenda distracted attention from the economic and political problems of Britain in the 1980s. The timing, content and targets of British moral panics thus become comprehensible.

The argument is highly suggestive until he discusses the media. They are descriptively central but theoretically marginal in his work. Jenkins agrees that the centralized structure and sensationalist tendencies of the British press affect their coverage of social problems but still denies that they can create moral panics: 'it is dubious if the media could create and sustain a campaign to demonize a group or individual if there was not already a constituency prepared to accept such a view' (Jenkins 1992: 21). He does not consider how the British press can act as a surrogate for public opinion. His view might have been different, had he used as his principal source the midmarket *Daily Mail* rather than the upmarket *Times.* In both Jenkins and Goode and Ben-Yehuda we find, compared with Cohen or Hall et al., much greater emphasis on claims making but lesser importance attached to the mass media. This is no accident; it reflects the two traditions from which the works emanate.

Two models, one project

Thompson (1998) sees a distinct difference in the way the concept of moral panic has been developed in the USA compared with Britain. In American sociology, he identifies 'a tendency to lose the initial theoretical cutting edge and to reject the earlier radical concern to disclose the processes of social control and ideological conflict involved in moral panics'. British sociology has tended 'to dispense with the concept on the grounds that it involves subjecting "representations" to the judgement of "the real" rather than concentrating on the operation of representational systems in their own right' (Thompson 1998: ix). While the American tradition has stressed the politics of social movements, the British tradition has emphasized social anxiety. This bifurcation has meant that 'some of the most useful contributions of each of these approaches have yet to be fully combined into an explanatory framework' (Thompson 1998: 16). He indicates the strengths and weaknesses of each position. American work delineates the roles of claims makers. However, the emphasis on the plurality of interests and social problems prevents recognition of 'the multiplicity or rapid succession of moral panics in a particular period' (Thompson 1998: 19). Relatedly, they underestimate the role of the mass media. Defining them as 'simply another middle range interest group' prevents explanation of 'the convergence or the linking by labelling of the specific issue to other problems' (Thompson 1998: 19). Thompson suggests that Jenkins concentrates on claims makers at the expense of the mass media and the wider political context. Hall et al. (1978) may have tied moral panic too closely to a Marxist approach but their decoding of media discourses of moral crisis is more convincing than anything to be found in the constructionist approach.

Thompson advocates offers a fusion of these two traditions. This is not an easy project. There are areas of substantive differences as well as commonality between the two schools. There is agreement around a number of general propositions. These can be summarized as the ideas that:

- Social problems are socially constructed and generally bear little relationship to the actual occurrence of the problem.
- Moral panics are the most extreme yet periodically recurrent form of social problem definition.
- Moral panics affect the legal framework of moral regulation and social control.
- Moral panics serve to confirm the moral/ideological boundaries of society.

Beyond this, there are significant differences of emphasis which can be summarized in tabular form (Table 2.2).

Overall, the British tradition is interested in moral panics because they produce social control outcomes emanating from the state, influenced by political elites and the media. The media not only are the place where debate occurs, but also actively shape and contribute to it. The result of the successful moral panic will be an ideological closure: the imposition of one definition and thus resolution of the problem. The American tradition is more

Table 2.2   British and American traditions of moral panic analysis compared

Issue	*British tradition*	*American tradition*
Prime interest	Outcomes of social control	Processes of social construction
Strategic site	Political institutions/ the state	Public arenas
Key definers	Political elites/media	Claims makers
Media role	Endorsing and amplifying primary definitions	Conduit for claims making
Form of public debate	Ideological closure	Claims making rhetoric

interested in the processes of social construction, how it is played out in public arenas, especially as influenced by claims makers. The media are only one public arena and exert little independent influence on the course of a moral panic. The successful moral panic validates the rhetoric of claims makers.

Such differences mean that the two models of moral panic are equivalent only descriptively. They quickly diverge when explanations of patterns are required. Mindful of this, we can still develop some questions derived from Goode and Ben-Yehuda under their five attributes, as follows.

Concern

- Who becomes concerned about this issue?
- How widespread is this concern?
- How is it expressed?

Hostility

- Who is defined as the enemy?
- What kind of threat do they pose?
- Is there a clear folk devil?

Consensus

- Does a clear consensus emerge about the seriousness, nature and sources of the threat?
- Who subscribes to this consensus?
- Is there any organized opposition to it?

Disproportionality

- What are claimed to be the dimensions and implications of the issue?
- Do these claims stand up to scrutiny?

Volatility

- How long does this episode last?
- How quickly does it develop and disappear?

To this we shall add some questions about claims makers.

Claims makers

- Who are the principal claims makers and counter claims makers?
- What are their motives and strategies?
- To what extent and why are they successful?

Some of these questions are similar to those derived from Cohen and others are different. In each case study both batteries of questions will be asked, following the outline of the basic narrative. As we accumulate answers to separate questions we shall be able to assess which, if any, of the processual and attributional models better explains the course of each issue, its key processes and agents. The status of the models across all of the case studies will be reconsidered in Chapter 10.

Further reading

Goode, E. and Ben-Yehuda, N. (1994) *Moral Panics: The Social Construction of Deviance*. Oxford: Blackwell.

Jenkins, P. (1992) *Intimate Enemies: Moral Panics in Contemporary Great Britain*. New York: Aldine de Gruyter.

Spector, M. and Kitsuse, J.L. (1977) *Constructing Social Problems*. Menlo Park, CA: Cummings.

Thompson, K. (1998) *Moral Panics*. London: Routledge.

Part II
THE CASE STUDIES

Essentially, a multiple-case (or multi-case) study occurs whenever the number of case studies exceeds one. The main argument in favour of the multiple-case study is that it improves theory building. By comparing two or more cases, the researcher is in a better position to establish the circumstances in which a theory will or will not hold. Moreover, the comparison may itself suggest concepts that are relevant to an emerging theory.

(Bryman 2001: 53)

3

UNHEALTHY PREOCCUPATIONS: AIDS

Introduction

In the five years between 1981 and 1986 a new, fatal and apparently uncontrollable disease appeared: AIDS. First discovered among gay men in San Francisco, it spread geographically across the world and socially among other vulnerable groups, such as intravenous drug users, and haemophiliacs, and finally into the population at large. Twenty years on, it is difficult to appreciate the shock of AIDS, the fears it induced and the views of homosexuality it revealed. In Britain political reaction and policy formation were more transparent and consistent than in many other countries, especially the USA. Such comparisons will be made later in the chapter. Our initial focus is on Britain using Berridge's (1996) authoritative account of the AIDS issue as comprising four phases.

The AIDS narrative

Policy 'from below', 1981–85

The first phase runs from 1981, when AIDS was first identified, to 1985, when a potential AIDS 'epidemic' was recognized. Early AIDS cases in the USA in 1980–82 had little impact in the UK. That changed in 1983 when the first AIDS patients arrived in London hospitals. A BBC *Horizon* television programme charting the spread of AIDS in New York's Greenwich Village confirmed the threat. Gay organizations like the Lesbian and Gay Switchboard alerted their constituency. First set up in 1982 to raise funds to support AIDS work, the Terrence Higgins Trust was reorganized in 1983 as a much more substantial organization. Clinicians and scientists – specialists in immunology, virology and genito-urinary medicine – signalled their concern. The Medical Research Council made its first grant for AIDS research in 1983. Gay representatives and clinicians were 'united by a need to press the urgency of the issue on government and by the lack of much by way of formal response at that stage' (Berridge 1996: 35).

Media interest, limited while the problem was apparently restricted to the gay community, was awakened by possible contamination of the blood supply. Berridge suggests that questions asked in Parliament attracted more government attention than previous lobbying. Despite evidence that AIDS could spread into the general population, government response remained low key. Then in 1985, the deaths from AIDS of the Chelmsford prison chaplain and of film star Rock Hudson were extensively reported in an 'outbreak of press panic' (Berridge 1996: 57). AIDS was assumed to be contagious. Measures of exclusion and isolation were advocated by some media columnists, politicians and right-wing pressure groups. Nurses, laboratory workers, home helps and the police felt vulnerable. Sections of the press developed their view of AIDS as a 'gay plague' visited for their sins upon sexual deviants, which 'established an agenda of prejudice and ignorance' (Beharrell 1993: 214), absent from television coverage (Miller and Beharrell 1998).

But there were countervailing influences. Gay and medical groups actively used the media to argue their case, a process Altman (1988) has termed 'legitimation through disaster'. The Terrence Higgins Trust 'quickly established itself as an authoritative source for the media' (Miller and Beharrell 1998: 84) and 'a small number of clinicians used their relationship with a handful of leading medical reporters to place pressure on key actors in government' (Miller and Williams 1998b: 130). They found an ally in the Chief Medical Officer of Health, Dr Donald Acheson. He established dialogue with the Terrence Higgins Trust, set up an Expert Advisory Group on AIDS and advised ministers of the gravity of the situation. His diagnosis was eventually accepted. In December 1985 Norman Fowler, Secretary of State for Social Services, announced a wide range of measures on AIDS, including funds for health authorities, a telephone advice line and a planned public information campaign. Politicians acted when AIDS threatened haemophiliacs, drug users, women and children, as well as gay men. While the number of actual cases remained small, statistical projections predicted a mass epidemic. Media coverage helped 'structure a response of fear and panic' (Berridge 1996: 99). Politicians had to act, however difficult and distasteful the issue. But a wider policy strategy was still required.

A national emergency, 1986–87

By 1986 'a mood of impending apocalypse gripped leading civil servants and politicians. AIDS became a policy issue of the highest priority, indeed it was a national emergency' (Berridge 1996: 81). Berridge argues that consolidating a public health approach required the support of key actors. Leading members of the cabinet were persuaded. Civil servants took medical expertise seriously. These influences outweighed those of downmarket newspapers and maverick individuals. The policy of an otherwise populist and moralistic governmental regime

> was not a draconian response. The collective public-health responses of quarantine, notification, screening which had been rejected at the 'expert' level in 1985, were also rejected at the political level. A policy consensus emerged which stressed a liberal middle-of-the-road type of approach. This was advice for safe sex, not no sex; it was, eventually, harm minimisation for drug users, not prohibition of drug use. It was the consensual strategy of health education, from which no one could dissent. This was not the 'New Right' reaction which some commentators have stressed.
>
> (Berridge 1996: 83)

In 1986–87 this policy was implemented though not without considerable internecine strife (Miller and Williams 1998a). Two national press adverts advocating 'safe sex' appeared in March and July 1986, though drug needle campaigns were delayed until 1988. In November 1986, Health Minister Fowler announced a new package of measures, especially a massive public information campaign. A leaflet would be delivered to every house with the slogan 'Don't die of ignorance'. Symbols of a tombstone and then an iceberg were developed for TV advertising. The campaign reached its apotheosis in February 1987 with 'AIDS week' on television, the outcome of high-level meetings between Fowler, the BBC and the Independent Broadcasting Authority, the regulator of commercial television. All four channels took AIDS as the theme for 19 hours of programming. Other government initiatives during 1986–87 included the revamping of the Health Education Council as the Health Education Authority, the establishment of national AIDS Trust and the funding of a new specialist AIDS ward at Middlesex Hospital, opened by Princess Diana.

Press reaction was variable and contradictory (Beharrell 1993, 1998). Some mid- and downmarket papers, notably the *Mirror* and *Today*, did not follow the 'gay plague' line. Even where a paper's editorials and columnists tried to blame gay men, feature articles and advice pages advocated safe sex, admitting a threat to heterosexuals denied elsewhere in the paper. Upmarket papers generally showed a 'greater sensitivity to the view points dominant amongst the health professionals and departmental officials' (Beharrell 1993: 228), the key news sources for specialist health correspondents (Miller and Williams 1993). Broadcasting adopted the mantle of social responsibility, embodied in AIDS week.

> In contrast to some sections of the national press, TV news displayed considerable support for the idea of a government health campaign (if not for the concrete form the campaign took) and an almost total accept-ance of the orthodox line on the risks of heterosexual transmission.
>
> (Miller and Beharrell 1998: 72)

Berridge (1992: 17) is quite clear that the ' "gay plague" presentation' was 'both historically and media-specific'. It occurred only in some papers and only before 1986.

The effects of the publicity campaigns were mixed, with some evidence of increased public awareness but little change in sexual behaviour. Public opinion seemed to favour a punitive reaction. A *News of the World* poll showed majorities in favour of compulsory testing and the isolation or even sterilization of the infected. A groundswell of public feeling was waiting to be tapped but there was nobody to exploit it. Otherwise powerful groups, such as the pro-family lobby inside the Conservative Party, were ignored. With the exception of the Chief Rabbi, the churches did not oppose the government strategy. The doctors' professional body, the British Medical Association, headed off members wanting compulsory testing of patients.

> Ultimately both the tabloid press and popular opinion were ineffective in policy terms. The furore over the 'gay plague' representations has tended to overlook their complete lack of policy impact. The official consensus formed around safe sex and harm minimisation, not around quarantine or anti-gay propaganda.
>
> (Berridge 1992: 22–3)

By mid-1987 attention was diverted by an impending general election in the UK. AIDS would never again assume such prominence as a public and policy issue.

Normalization and routinization, 1987–89

Initially AIDS was an anomaly over which nobody claimed jurisdiction. In the late 1980s this changed, producing what Berridge (1992) calls normal-ization (as a sexually transmitted disease), professionalization (by doctors) and institutionalization (into the health care system). Government expenditure on AIDS rose from between £1 million and £2 million in 1986 to £200 million by 1991. The voluntary sector was incorporated into provision of services such as hospices and counselling services, controversial among the increasingly marginalized gay community. AIDS was being redefined from a threatening epidemic to a chronic disease, amenable to palliative care. Estimates of its likely prevalence were revised downwards. The normalization of AIDS was evident in the culture as a whole through AIDS benefits, AIDS days and red ribbons. In soap operas and elsewhere, gay lifestyles were portrayed as more acceptable, even if Conservative Party opinion had its revenge in passing Clause 28 in the Local Government Act 1988, forbidding local authorities to 'promote' homosexuality. By the late 1980s AIDS, as an object of public policy, a target for medical services and an ever-present possibility for gay men, appeared to have been routinized. In the next decade the orthodoxy was challenged.

The repoliticization of AIDS, 1990–94

An upmarket newspaper, the *Sunday Times,* attacked AIDS policy in the early 1990s. It argued that the heterosexual spread of AIDS was a myth perpetrated by a gay conspiracy and that HIV did not automatically lead to AIDS. New ministers at the Department of Health were thought to be less sympathetic to the AIDS strategy. In November 1989 Labour peer Lord Kilbracken received a written parliamentary answer that only one person had been infected outside established risk groups. His subsequent attack on the AIDS 'myth', though endorsed by some mid- and downmarket papers, was largely discredited by expert opinion in upmarket papers (Beharrell 1993: 220) and ignored by television news (Miller and Beharrell 1998). In June 1992 emerged the story of a 24-year-old HIV positive man alleged to have knowingly infected several women. All the papers covered it but did not revise their established positions.

The liberal alliance behind the consensus attenuated. Gay groups had been more and more excluded, internally divided by those committed to the 'regaying' of AIDS as an issue of sexual politics. Yet the move to debunk the supposed AIDS myth did not succeed. Normalization continued. Obituaries of famous gay men from the media, notably the filmmaker Derek Jarman, Princess Diana's ministrations and characters in soap operas all demonstrated that AIDS had become part of the cultural landscape: no longer a mass threat, but part of everyday reality.

Applying the models

As Thompson (1998) suggests, AIDS did look like a moral panic, especially in its early phases. Weeks (1985) noted that AIDS had all the hallmarks of a panic: an emergent threat, the stereotyping of an outgroup with homosexuals as the folk devil, pronouncements about the decline of family life and sexual morality, and the advocacy of extraordinary measures. A 'generalised panic' (Weeks 1985: 46) about the 'gay plague' (Meldrum 1990) seemed to peak in 1983. Later, Weeks (1989, 1993) saw 1982–85 as the moral panic phase of AIDS, preceded by a period of dawning crisis and followed by one of crisis management. For the middle period, moral panic provides 'a valuable framework for describing the course of events' (Weeks 1989: 5). Others see the health education policy as evidence of a successful moral panic (Fitzpatrick and Milligan 1987), but Strong and Berridge (1990) argue that no phase of the AIDS crisis resembled a moral panic. Eldridge et al. (1997: 66) suggest that by 1985 'there was a clear case for the development of a moral panic' but the model cannot explain its subsequent failure to develop. The acid test is whether, or how effectively, the processual and attributional models can account for how and why AIDS did not become a moral panic.

Processual model

One: emergence: form, novelty, threat. The form was a potentially fatal blood transmitted disease. It was genuinely new and threatening, Berridge (1996: 2) emphasizing 'the novelty and shock of the arrival of the syndrome, the enormous sense of disorientation which it caused'. Initially threatening gay men and intravenous drug users, it eventually extended to haemophiliacs and heterosexuals, including women and children.

Two: media inventory: stylization and stereotyping; exaggeration, distortion, prediction and symbolization; sensitization; folk devil. All this was evident in some sections of the media who did try to create folk devils. Where gay men and intravenous drug users 'were already routinely portrayed as "deviant minorities"', there was a strong temptation 'to invest AIDS with the supernatural power to "seek out" stigmatized and marginalized groups' (Beharrell 1993: 214). The disease and the lifestyles associated with it were stylized and sensationalized. Its causes were distorted but exaggeration was not present and predictions about its spread were downplayed. Symbolization and sensitization were absent. Crucially, broadcasting and upmarket newspapers did not share the agenda of popular papers, whose own approach was inconsistent. There was not a single media agenda about AIDS or its victims.

Three: moral entrepreneurs: significant actors; relationship to media; orientations, images and causal explanations. These were conspicuous by their absence, whereas opposition was effective. Attempts by some newspapers to become primary definers of the AIDS issue failed partly because they were not supported by moralists or experts outside the media. Clergy, politicians, police officers and organized pressure groups remained reticent about the issue. Few were prepared to blame the victim.

Four: experts: who; grounds for claims; media accreditation. As an illness, AIDS was a medical issue. Eventually medical opinion prevailed. High in status and credibility, their expertise was not easy to dismiss. Specialist health correspondents in the media accepted their definitions as authoritative. Credibility as experts rather than lobbyists was also gained by gay pressure groups, especially the Terrence Higgins Trust. Expert opinion was clearly weighted against a moral panic.

Five: coping and resolution: proposed solutions, measures adopted; procedural/legal; effective/symbolic. In the case of AIDS the measures resorted to were precisely not those expected in a moral panic, such as compulsory testing or segregation of victims. The only new legislation created a crime of knowingly infecting others. Social control agencies did not increase powers nor was there any symbolic or physical segregation of folk devils. Measures were essentially informative and educative, aimed at both the homosexual and heterosexual population.

Six: fade away: timing, recurrence; subsequent status. AIDS faded as an issue once the crisis had passed and forecasts of an epidemic were revised. It did not disappear or become submerged; it was routinized as a policy issue, a media topic and a cultural theme. A steady increase in reported cases at the beginning of the twenty-first century may require new policies but they are likely to be within the established health education strategy. If it recurs as an issue, it will not be as a moral panic.

Seven: legacy: long-term effects; relationship to other issues. AIDS was essentially incorporated into existing methods for coping with sexually transmitted diseases, though it may well have had long-term implications for discourses about homosexuality.

The processual model confirms that AIDS was not a moral panic and explains precisely what was lacking. AIDS did not produce the required media unanimity, moral entrepreneurs or expert endorsement.

Attributional model

One: concern: among whom; how widespread; forms of expression. Concern was galvanized by groups opposed to a moral panic, such as doctors and gay organizations. Media opinion was uneven and divided, unsure whether there should be more concern or less. The government health education campaign of 1986–87 was premised on insufficient public awareness of the dangers of AIDS and too little preventive action to avoid it; they wanted to create the right kind of concern. Occasional polls suggested public support for draconian measures. Qualitative evidence (Kitzinger 1993) indicates that the public may have accepted some media definitions, those of television rather than the press. The degree and kind of concern are not that commensurate with a moral panic.

Two: hostility; enemy, threat, folk devil. While some sections of the press displayed clear homophobic tendencies, the attempt to portray gay men as legitimate targets of hostility seems largely to have failed. The contamination of the innocent, such as haemophiliacs, was occasionally attributed to those 'guilty' of homosexual or bisexual behaviour. Such views appeared unable to mobilize any latent antipathy towards homosexuals among the heterosexual population. Expert opinion obstructed the construction of a folk devil.

Three: consensus: clarity, among whom, organized opposition. There was no consensus within the media. A consensus implicitly antagonistic to a moral panic emerged in a nascent policy community which eventually converted government. Opposition to a moral panic, an effective alliance of gay organizations and medical experts, was organized and authoritative. The proponents of moral panic were, by contrast, isolated and fragmented.

Four: disproportionality: dimensions and implications; claims versus reality. A moral panic involves the exaggeration of a problematic condition or behaviour beyond what objective measures warrant. Berridge (1996) points out that the number of cases of AIDS in the UK remained small throughout the 1980s: 29 in 1983, 106 in 1984, 271 in 1985, and 610 in 1986. By April 1989 the total had reached 2000, of whom 1000 had died; by 1989 the cumulative total was 8000. In European terms this was a moderate level, higher than the Nordic countries but much lower than France, Spain or Italy (Berridge 1996: 1). Compared with deaths from heart disease or cancer, AIDS proved to be insignificant though the sense of an impending epidemic was real enough. More importantly, the roles of those involved in the debate were the opposite of a usual moral panic. Those seeing government policy as gay propaganda implied there was no serious threat to the heterosexual population. Conversely, the AIDS alliance saw government and public acknowledgement of the problem as insufficient. They wanted the problem understood in proportion when others thought it had already got out of proportion. The concept of 'disproportionality' does not work for AIDS.

Five: volatility: length; speed of emergence and decline. AIDS as an issue developed slowly and its routinization was incremental. There was no sudden eruption of concern, disappearing as fast as it appeared.

(Six): claims makers: principal claims and counter claims makers; motives and strategies; degree of success. The counter claims makers defined the issue almost before claims makers could operate. Claims makers were isolated and fragmented with no groups outside the media seeking to create a panic.

None of Goode and Ben-Yehuda's attributes applies even partially to the AIDS issue. The nature of the threat and its association with deviant life-styles had some potential for a moral panic which limited sections of the downmarket press sought to exploit. Yet without media unanimity or moral entrepreneurs, opposition proved effective. Victims were not successfully portrayed as agents of their own destruction. Concern and consensus focused on public health issues. Disproportionality was not an issue.

Kitzinger and Miller apply Cohen's stages to AIDS. That they do not fit they take to be a deficiency in the model. 'If reaction to AIDS is or was a moral panic, it was a moral panic manqué, and the reasons behind the fail-ure of the moral panic or the success of resistance need to be examined' (Kitzinger and Miller 1998: 222). In our view, the models are successful in indicating which conditions were absent and do begin to explain why. This is not to deny the appropriateness of further exploration of the precise pro-cesses involved (Miller et al. 1998). One of these, which moral panic analy-sis cannot deliver, is the configuration of political ideologies and cultural discourses around AIDS.

Beyond moral panics

In all the case studies, however much or little they approximate to the models, we shall encounter features which the models cannot incorporate because they are 'beyond' moral panic analysis. As Rocheron and Linné (1989: 412) have argued, 'the concept of "moral panic", especially when used in a reductionist manner, is neither specific nor sensitive enough to take account of the endemic nature of ideological conflicts over morality.' One interpretation (Beharrell 1993) views the outcome of such ideological debate about AIDS as the victory of a dominant (liberal, medicalized) perspective on AIDS over alternative (New Right) and radical (sexually liberationist) perspectives. A wider view situates AIDS as one dramatic instance of 'a con-tinuing discourse towards homosexuality' (Weeks 1993: 26–7).

Watney (1988), whose general critique of the whole moral panics model will be encountered in Chapter 10, stresses its inability to encompass the discourses constructed around AIDS, about the disease itself and the gay community's deviant sexuality.

> We are not living through a distinct coherent 'moral panic' concerning AIDS, a panic with a linear narrative and the prospect of closure. On the contrary, we are witnessing the ideological manoeuvres which 'make sense' of this accidental triangulation of disease, sexuality and homophobia.
>
> (Watney 1988: 60)

The family values (decency, respectability, masculinity) mobilized around AIDS cannot be revealed by the moral panic approach. Ultimately, for Watney, AIDS as a public issue is too deep-rooted to be interpreted in terms of ephemeral phenomena or as a displacement of other concerns, since at stake is 'the constant nature of ideological state supervision and non-state regulation of sexuality throughout the modern period, especially in matters concerning representation' (Watney 1988: 57). In this, Watney agrees with Weeks (1985, 1989, 1993) and Altman (1986) in the USA. He parts company by asserting that moral panic models are too narrow and superficial in scope. Asking whether or not or even why AIDS was not a moral panic does not seem a useful question. It omits more than it includes, particularly about the nature of discourses around homosexuality. The ideological and discursive particularity of the issue is lost with the application of a universal model.

International comparisons

AIDS was no respecter of national boundaries. 'AIDS was both global in its impact and implications and local in its manifestations and effects' (Weeks 1993: 25). National analyses concentrate either on policy or on the media, rarely on both. Since moral panic analysis requires tracing how an issue is constructed simultaneously in the media, other public arenas and among policy-makers, specific studies provide only part of the picture. Berridge's assessment of the impact of media reporting on policy has not been replicated elsewhere, even in the most documented case of the USA.

The USA: policy and media

All countries had a range of policy options:

• *repressive measures:* quarantine and compulsory testing

- *controlling measures:* mandatory reporting of cases, closure of gay bath-houses, blood screening, voluntary testing
- *preventive measures:* needle exchange schemes, public education pro-grammes, community groups, treatment programmes, research funding
- *protective measures:* anti-discrimination legislation.

The adoptions adopted, regionally or nationally, depended upon how and by whom the problem was defined.

In the USA an overall pattern is difficult to detect because there was simply no direction from government: 'the United States still does not have a national AIDS policy or a coordinated strategy for combating this public health threat' (Quam and Ford 1990: 44). Policy operated at the local level, though some signals emanated from a national government generally unsympathetic to welfare programmes and highly moralistic in outlook. Bayer and Kirp (1992b) have reviewed local policies. By 1983 AIDS was legally notifiable in every state and at-risk groups were asked not to donate blood. San Francisco closed its gay bathhouses in 1984 and other cities followed suit. In 1985 national controversy over the attempted exclusion from schools of children with AIDS provoked state laws prohibiting such discrimination. The federal government declared itself in favour only of voluntary testing, though it was made mandatory for the armed forces and immigrants. Increased pressure for quarantine was resisted by federal government but 12 states adopted such powers. Financial support for treatment and educational programmes had to come locally, federal support being minimal and dependent upon such programmes not being 'offensive'. Intravenous drug users were generally ignored in a 'policy of non-benign neglect' (Bayer and Kirp 1992b: 8).

Such local policies did not reflect homophobic opinion.

> The voice of AIDS hysteria, an aspect of broader American right-wing politics, never carried the day. In ideological terms, the story of AIDS is not a tale of conspiracy-building and witch-hunting of the kind urged by vocal extremists, but more a tale of consensus-building across professions, political ideologies, and sexual preferences.
>
> (Bayer and Kirp 1992b: 7)

The organizational strength of the gay community was a crucial factor, with evidence of 'the tremendous efforts made by gay men individually and in organizations to confront, struggle against, and at last conquer, the disease' (Quam and Ford 1990: 41). The media were initially hostile. Coverage in US magazines in the early years (1982–84) emphasized 'the deviant character of the victims rather than the problematic aspects of the disease itself' (Albert

1986: 135). Press coverage was criticized for 'single source reporting; favoring quotable sources; crediting conspiracies; lack of follow-up; focusing on controversy; and emphasizing entertainment value' (Check 1987: 989).

Television news coverage of AIDS on the three main American television networks has been exhaustively analysed. Colby and Cook (1991) argued that AIDS was not intrinsically an attractive issue for television. It primarily affected an 'unrepresentative' minority group and involved a range of taboo subjects (blood, semen, sex, death). There was also an anxiety to avoid scaremongering. Television networks commented upon but sought to dispel public fears of an epidemic: 'coverage of AIDS was not sensational: the networks attempted to reassure as much as they dramatized the story' (Colby and Cook 1991: 244). Conventional news practices ensured that early interest waned, despite increased rates of infection, unless a new development appeared, such as the death of Rock Hudson in 1985 or President Reagan's first speech on the issue in 1987. In government circles 'the policy agenda responded less to empirical indicators of the problem . . . or to the professional agenda . . . than to the media agenda' (Colby and Cook 1991: 244). The media agenda stressed the need for action but did not prescribe it. The consensus between professional and gay organizations was implicitly endorsed. As in the UK, the major tendencies in public debate did not favour a moral panic. This was also the trend in other developed nations.

Other countries: policy and media

The division of studies into a focus on either policy or media is evident in published work on other countries. For example, policy analysis for France (Steffen 1992) scarcely mentions the media, while analysis of French press coverage is not directly related to policy (Herzlich and Pierret 1989). National policies have been exhaustively analysed. One collection (Misztal and Moss 1990a) brings together studies of AIDS policies across the world (the USA, Brazil, France, Belgium, Germany, Italy, Poland, Australia, Africa); another (Kirp and Bayer 1992) is confined to the industrialized countries (the USA, Canada, Germany, Australia, Spain, the UK, France, the Netherlands, Denmark, Sweden and Japan). In no country does the response seem to have followed the model of a moral panic. The very longevity and complexity of the issue generally precluded rapid and crude response. Most seem to have followed four broad phases; initial doubt and uncertainty; the formation of incremental policy responses; implementation of specific measures; the eventual 'normalization' of AIDS within a medicalized framework. Within that common trajectory were quite different policy decisions.

The most extreme controlling measures involving compulsory quarantine were adopted in Cuba. The most punitive policies in industrialized countries were found in Sweden, the most liberal in the Netherlands and Denmark, while systematic denial of the problem was found in Japan, Italy and Spain (Kirp and Bayer 1992). Moerkerk and Aggleton (1990) divided European responses into four types: pragmatic, politically expedient, biomedical and belated. Britain came in the second group. Such differences are attributed to both longstanding characteristics of the national political culture and the balance of organizational interests in contemporary politics. Each national case presents a unique mix of such factors, with specific individuals and groups exerting influence at strategic moments.

Media coverage followed a similar pattern. When AIDS first appears, there is a tendency to view it as a gay plague. There is then alarm over the threat to the public at large and controversies over education campaigns or other policy measures. As policy develops and the threat of an epidemic recedes, the whole topic loses news value. Only exceptional events revive interest. The death of Rock Hudson reverberated internationally. Homophobic tendencies were evident. Reviewing studies of AIDS in the western media, Lupton (1994) identified

> a general neglect of AIDS while it seemed confined to gay men, contra-
> dictory and confusing coverage, the tendency of dramatic news to incite
> panic, the absence of certain groups in news accounts and the emphatic
> presence of others, the ability of prominent people to influence cover-
> age of AIDS regardless of their medical expertise or personal experi-
> ence, and an emphasis upon personalising the illness experienced.
>
> (Lupton 1994: 20)

Images predominated of 'homophobia, fear, violence, contamination, invasion, vilification, racism, sexism, deviance, heroicism and xenophobia' (Lupton 1994: 21). However, as AIDS spread during 1986–87, the 'discourse of risk' shifted from 'the specific and contained threat to reviled deviant out groups', to 'every individual, regardless of their sexual proclivities' (Lupton 1994: 65).

Just occasionally an event occurred which seemed to resemble a moral panic. Altman (1986: 189) suggests that the AIDS-related death of three Queensland babies in late 1984 provoked a local moral panic in that highly conservative Australian state. The death of two women in Japan in late 1986 and early 1987 provoked an outcry which finally moved a complacent government to action (Dearing 1992; Feldman and Yonemoto 1992). In early 1990 the Swedish media extensively reported the case of 'the HIV man' previously convicted of child abuse. Their calls for extreme measures of isolation and incarceration briefly resembled a 'situation of moral panic'

(Henriksson and Ytterberg 1992: 317). Locally important, such incidents were rare and affected policy minimally. More typical was the situation in France (Herzlich and Pierret 1989), where the press was initially attracted to the mystery of the disease, cited expert opinion, found labels associating it with homosexuality, used statistics cavalierly and emphasized, especially early on, the connection between infection and deviant sexual behaviour. In the summer of 1985, when infected blood supplies became a national issue, it all got out of control. 'The press was overexcited and panicked' (Herzlich and Pierret 1989: 1241). Overall the French press constructed a metadiscourse, as much about reactions to the disease as about the disease itself, which focused upon a foreign and strange 'other'. Yet all this had little effect on policy-making, directed by 'a process of alliance building between the gay associations and the world of the health professions' (Pollack 1990: 85). The 'major guarantor for consensus' was expert opinion. 'Given the symbolic power of their discourse, hardly any space was left for dissent in the public arena' (Pollack 1990: 85).

Overview

In no country where reaction has been documented did AIDS become a moral panic. It had some potential, in a genuinely novel threat associated with a marginal group, gay men, who might have been cast as folk devils. Popular journalists and columnists worked towards this goal but it was never realized. Upmarket newspapers and broadcasting organizations rejected this agenda, especially as it seemed likely to cause real panic. The combination of gay activism and medical authority directed perplexed governments towards public education policies. AIDS became a known quantity, medically and politically. The safe option was to defer to the experts. If there is a single reason why AIDS did not become a moral panic in any developed nation, this was it. As we shall see, this ceding of the definition of the problem and its remedies to established experts is not true of other issues. Moral panics, it would seem, flourish where anyone can be an expert.

Further reading

Altman, D. (1986) *AIDS and the New Puritanism*. London: Pluto.
Berridge, V. (1996) *AIDS in the UK: The Making of Policy 1981–1991*. Oxford: Oxford University Press.

Kirp, D.L. and Bayer, R. (eds) (1992) *AIDS in the Industrialized Democracies*: *Passions, Politics and Policies*. Montreal: McGill-Queen's University Press.

Lupton, D. (1994) *Moral Threats and Dangerous Desires: AIDS in the News Media*. London: Taylor and Francis.

Miller, D., Kitzinger, J., Williams, K. and Beharrell, P. (1998) *The Circuit of Mass Communication: Media Strategies, Representation and Audience Reception in the AIDS Crisis*. London: Sage.

Weeks, J. (1985) *Sexuality and its Discontents*. London: Routledge.

4

OUT OF THEIR MINDS: ECSTASY AND RAVES

Introduction

In five years 'raves' transformed the leisure lifestyles of Britain's youth. The details are complex, though the broad outline is clear: 'Making its public debut in this country in 1988 in the shape of "acid house" parties held in warehouses, fields and clubs, its illicit status quickly increased until it found its way into legal club venues in the 1990s as the "rave" scene' (Henderson 1993: 121). The narrative is well known (Shapiro 1999; Critcher 2000a) but the models have not previously been applied systematically to the issue. Its themes are clear but international comparison is sparse.

The rave/ecstasy narrative

The roots of rave, 1985–87

Acid house music, originally associated with LSD, had its roots in American club culture.

> Out of New York, Chicago and Detroit had come sounds that would change the world of popular music: garage, house and techno, three interlinked strands with similar premises – the use of technology to heighten perception and pleasure, and the release from mundane, workaday existence into fantastic visions of drama, vitality and joy.
>
> (Collin 1998: 24)

It influenced the 'Balearic beat' of clubs on Ibiza, where uninhibited and non-stop dancing had become the norm.

The second ingredient was ecstasy. This was the popular name for 3,4 methyledioxyampthetamine MDMA. First created in Germany in 1912 as a chemical preparation, it was developed in the USA in the late 1960s and prescribed for some psychiatric patients. Passing into the hands of drug dealers, its original nickname 'Adam' was rejected in favour of the more marketable 'ecstasy'. In 1985, after media scare stories, it was classified as a dangerous drug in the USA. Operating 'somewhere between LSD and amphetamine' (Henderson 1997: 4), ecstasy affects the brain, the experience of pleasure and bodily release in ways still not understood. A **Class A drug** in UK since 1977, it was imported from black gay clubs in New York in the early 1980s by followers of mystical sects and British musicians. Initially confined to the parties and clubs of 'Soho elite', it spread during 1985–86. A tablet cost £12–15 but its impact remained limited.

Rise and reaction, 1988–93

In late 1987, 'acid house was little more than an imported type of music with drug associations' (Thornton 1995: 158), but was soon introduced into London nightclubs. The first four months of 1988 saw adoption of the yellow smiley face logo, the emergence of drug argot and the donning of sporty clothes (Collin 1998). In January 1988, London Records issued volume 3 of *House Sounds of Chicago*, celebrating dance and drugs, covered by the February music press. By June *i-D* magazine was profiling this new subculture (Thornton 1995). Raves were located outside clubs. Early venues, disused warehouses in urban areas, attracted unwanted attention from the police. Rural spaces, such as aircraft hangars or barns, offered better cover. By the summer of 1988 raves were regular events, especially in the environs of the M25 orbital motorway around London. Entrepreneur Tony Colston-Hayter developed the Telephone Venue Address Releasing System. The rave venue was secret. Tickets were issued with a phone number for a computer message specifying the meeting point. Ravers there received a new message stating the actual venue. Police were outnumbered and powerless. An event could produce a profit of £50,000. Rave – a term borrowed from black America – was about to become 'the biggest youth subculture that Britain had ever seen' (McDermott et al. 1993: 250).

Henderson (1993: 121) stressed five essential characteristics of raves: larger than average venues; music with 120 or more beats per minute; ubiquitous drug use (ecstasy, amphetamine, LSD); distinctive dress codes;

extensive special effects (videos, lighting). Ecstasy was '*the* defining feature of Rave culture' (Merchant and McDonald 1994: 18, original emphasis). Its effects of energy, well-being and togetherness resonated with the new music. Thornton (1995: 15) cites estimates that by 1992 the UK club market had an annual turnover of £2 billion, with raves worth a further £1.8 billion. Academics studied sexual behaviour (Henderson 1993), the demographics of participants (Thornton 1995; Collin 1998) and their understanding of the risks involved in ecstasy consumption (Merchant and McDonald 1994). Rave diversified as it spread but ecstasy use remained common. 'The drug is central to the Rave Culture and the experience of one cannot be understood in isolation from the experience of the other' (Merchant and McDonald 1994: 28).

This development had not gone unnoticed by the media and the police. The *Sun* newspaper discovered rave in August 1998, initially marketing its own smiley T-shirt but became hostile when the drug connection was revealed by a raid on a boat party in November, the organizers of which were sentenced to lengthy jail terms. The BBC banned all records including the word 'acid'. The next turning point came in June 1989, when 11,000 flocked to Sunrise's Midsummer Night Dream Party at White Waltham airstrip in Berkshire. Tabloid reporters' lurid accounts of this new threat to youth appeared in the *Sun* and *Daily Mail*. The latter's 26 June 1989 editorial condemned 'acid house' as 'a facade for dealing in drugs', a 'cynical attempt to trap young people into drug dependency under the guise of friendly pop music events'. The 'stiffest penalties' were justified for 'those responsible for this gigantic exercise in hooking our youth on drugs' (cited in Collin 1998: 97).

The police were hostile but initially impotent. Bans on the grounds that raves lacked the licences required by the Public Entertainments Act 1982 failed when the organizers successfully argued that theirs were private functions. An obscure 1967 statute, the Private Places of Entertainment Act, required any private entertainment for profit to hold a licence but few local authorities had adopted it. In the summer of 1989, North West Kent police set up a Pay Party Unit. Within three months it had 60 staff and 30 computers, information on 5275 named individuals and 712 vehicles. It had monitored 4380 phone calls and made 257 arrests. The unit quickly came to understand the centrality of drugs to the rave scene but could not convince the authorities. 'When we started to tell MPs and the Home Office what was really going on, they wouldn't believe it. It was always denied by everyone, including the government' (Collin 1998: 107).

Pressure intensified when professional criminals organized 'security' at raves. The police had some success, galvanizing local authorities and persuading the telephone regulator to close the lines used by organizers, but became convinced that special measures were needed. Conservative back-bench MP Graham Bright sponsored the Entertainments (Increased Penalties) Act 1990, dubbed the 'Acid House Bill'. It increased penalties for unlicensed public entertainment to fines of £20,000, 6 months in prison or both. It 'heralded in quite Draconian measures' to quash the rave culture 'ranging from fines and confiscation of record decks and PA [public address] systems to the long-term imprisonment of rave organizers' (Merchant and McDonald 1994: 17). It was passed without opposition in July.

This effort at social control did not go uncontested. Tony Colston-Hayter founded and led the Association of Dance Party promoters to campaign against the 3 a.m. curfew on nightclubs. In February 1990 it organized 'Freedom to Party' rallies in Trafalgar Square, London and in Manchester but attendance was sparse and the effect minimal. Media hostility was reactivated by safety advice about ecstasy such as a 'raver's guide' published in Liverpool in 1992 (McDermott et al. 1993) and the 'safe dancing' campaign in Manchester a year later. In 1993 Home Secretary Michael Howard included rave as one of several new targets for a major new law.

Criminal Justice and Public Order Act 1994

This wide-ranging law encompassed action against terrorism and pornography, reform of the juvenile justice system, and clarification of police stop and search powers, as well as targeting raves and **New Age Travellers**. New offences – of 'trespassory assembly', 'aggravated trespass' and 'trespassing with intent to reside' – carried heavy fines and short prison sentences. The police were given powers to immediately require people to disperse and to seize, remove and destroy any vehicles left behind (Osgerby 1998). The legislation defined a rave as 'a gathering of a hundred or more persons, whether or not trespassers, at which music is played during the night', such music being 'that which is wholly or predominantly characterized by the emission of a succession of repetitive beats' (Henderson 1997: 11). Under Section 47, it became illegal to 'hold, wait for or attend a rave'; under Section 45 the police could arrest anybody refusing police instructions to leave a rave site; under Section 49 police could stop and redirect all traffic within five miles of a rave (Henderson 1997: 10). The Act's 'set of social and cultural controls' were 'the most comprehensive and authoritarian since 1945' (Osgerby 1998: 216). However, this Act was rarely used, the police preferring generic public order legislation (Collin 1998; Home Office 1998; Osgerby 1998). Most of the thousand people arrested under it in 1995 were road protesters.

Leah Betts and after, 1995

If 1994 was the high point of the legal narrative of rave, its most powerful symbol came in 1995. On 11 November, Leah Betts collapsed in her home at her eighteenth birthday party after taking an ecstasy tablet and subsequently went into a coma, dying on 16 November. Leah's parents, one a community nurse, the other a former policeman, were clearly respectable, their daughter taking A levels prior to university. The parents publicized their grief, holding a press conference, drafting an open letter to teenagers on the dangers of drugs, and releasing photographs of Leah, including one of her on a life support machine. For the media, her death was 'a potent image of innocence corrupted by a dangerous and malevolent subculture' (Osgerby 1998: 183).

In almost all papers this was front-page news, prompting feature articles on ecstasy and meriting an editorial. The *Mirror*'s 14 November headline 'I sold E at girl's club' was accompanied by an editorial 'Stop the poison pushers'. The 'one million' ecstasy consumers a week only 'want fun' but 'end up like Leah, on a life support machine'. The pushers 'dealing in death' cannot be allowed to 'continue destroying young lives'. The answer is an 'even tougher crackdown' by the police. By contrast, *The Guardian* was more measured, with its headline 'Hopes fade for teenage girl who took ecstasy'. An editorial – 'The hard lessons of Leah Betts: the war against drugs can't easily be won but it can be contained' – castigated the government for failing to heed the pragmatic advice of chief constables and advisory committees. Elsewhere in the paper Suzanne Moore's column identified 'two cultures in Britain which cannot find a way of talking to each other'. For the press 'drugs appear as something deviant that happens to other people and other people's children', while 'for the rest of us drugs are a part of life and have always been around'. Even in the conservative *Times*, feature articles revealed the normality of ecstasy consumption. 'It was as if they had stumbled on an alien universe that had somehow existed for years, unknown and unseen, within their own society' (Collin 1998: 300). In several upmarket papers, columnists attacked media and politicians' hypocrisy about drugs, compared with the enlightened approach of the Dutch. The inquest on 23 November, though adjourned, clearly implied that Leah Betts died not from ecstasy but from water intoxication swelling her brain.

Confusion over ecstasy extended to government policy. Within a week of Leah Betts' death, it launched a national strategy 'Tackling Drugs Together', balancing law and order with harm reduction strategies. It had previously taken the same moralistic line on ecstasy ('the effects can't last for ever/you can only come down') in 1990 as it had earlier taken on heroin ('heroin screws you up', 1985–86) and cocaine ('smack isn't worth it', 1987). Now advice on safe use was made available from the Health Education Authority. However, legal suppression was never far away. Just before the 1997 general election a Public Entertainments (Drug Misuse) Act, passed without opposition, permitted local authorities to revoke licences if police suspected that drug taking or dealing were occurring on the premises. The gap between legal definitions and cultural practice was wider than ever. Club owners tacitly condoned drug consumption, as the police well knew (Saunders 1995: 64). That situation prevailed into the next decade.

Applying the models

Moral panic terminology has been applied haphazardly to rave/ecstasy. Redhead (1991) uses it as self-evidently appropriate. Merchant and McDonald (1994) refer to ravers as folk devils and Henderson (1997) notes that rave supplied all the 'raw material' – drugs, sex and pleasure – for a moral panic. Collin draws loosely on the moral panic concept, perceiving three waves of panic around early raves, the safe dancing campaigns and Leah Betts' death. The first set the tone of 'the ritualised sequence of moral panic – exaggerated press reports, misleading headlines, self appointed moral spokesmen demanding action and weekend on weekend of police raids' (Collin 1998: 90). Osgerby (1998: 182) specifies connections to earlier panics about deviant youth: distorted media coverage, exaggeration of harm and the use of rave as a 'barometer' of social decline. Yet it may not have been that straightforward.

Three narratives

Here we must take note of a complexity. There are not only two analytically separable issues of raves and ecstasy, but also a third, so far ignored: the issue of New Age Travellers. The three issues intertwined but at crucial points, especially the nature of control measures, the narratives diverge.

First narrative: New Age Travellers
The reaction to New Age Travellers is the most clear-cut case. 'Prior to the summer solstice of 1985 and 1986 Britain was in the grip of a moral panic. Travellers to Stonehenge were folk devils, and stories about the threatening lifestyle of the "hippies" abounded in the press and in Parliament' (National Council for Civil Liberties (NCCL) 1986: 37). The 1960s counter-culture had been fitfully kept alive by the squatting movement,

communes and burgeoning interest in eastern religions. New Age Travellers proliferated in the mid-1970s. Their dress, insignia and values connoted a distinct subculture which connected with mainstream youth culture at festivals, peace campaigns (Greenham Common from 1981 onwards), poll tax demonstrations (1990), road protests (Twyford Down 1992) and animal exports (1995). Symbolically important was a network of free annual music festivals at Glastonbury, Windsor and especially Stonehenge (Hetherington 1992). The police sporadically raided these throughout the 1970s, though as late as 1984 the biggest ever Stonehenge festival was tolerated by the police, despite some damage and crime (Earle et al. 1994). But the next one, in June 1985, produced the 'Battle of the Beanfield'. Concerned by damage, owners English Heritage obtained an injunction against the festival. The police established an exclusion zone around the site. One convoy was forced into a field by police who then forcibly removed them, confiscating and destroying their vehicles and property. Though film of the incident mysteriously disappeared from *Independent Television News*, the travellers later successfully sued the police for wrongful arrest and damage to property.

By this time, 'the travellers had become fully-fledged folk devils' (Collin 1998: 187), vilified by Home Secretary Douglas Hurd and Prime Minister Margaret Thatcher. The Public Order Act 1986 specifically prohibited the massing of convoys. In 1991 the Glastonbury festival took place at nearby Longstock, whence emerged Spiral Tribe who toured festivals for the rest of summer, with their insistence on no compromise techno music and free parties. 'Within twelve months, Spiral Tribe had helped transform ecstasy culture into an entirely new entity' (Collin 1998: 210). Police action became more vigorous, deploying riot squads against free festivals. Prime Minister John Major declared at the 1992 Conservative Party Conference: 'New Age travellers. Not in this age. Not in any age.' Police set up Operation Snapshot to document and harass travellers, estimated to number 40,000 in 1993. By 1995 'it appeared that the government had finally defeated the travellers' (Collin 1998: 235).

New Age Travellers were easy meat. A tiny minority, they were politically disorganized, individually and collectively vulnerable, with few experts or legitimized pressure groups to speak up for them. A combination of changes in social security legislation and police harassment weakened them well before the Criminal Justice Act targeted their lifestyle. A contemporary report 'marvelled at the level of intolerance shown to a small group of people who have adopted an alternative lifestyle' (NCCL 1986: 1). This was a classic moral panic, fulfilling every aspect of the processual and attributional models. This was less true of the other two issues.

Second narrative: raves
Even without recreational drugs, raves would have been objectionable. Improvised gatherings of large numbers of young people, out for noisy enjoyment, are always perceived as a threat to public order. On the face of it, raves were outlawed, specifically by the Criminal Justice Act 1994, but the solution had come much earlier, with the realization – especially by the police – that the obviously extensive market for raves would have to be redirected. It was no accident that, starting in London, arcane restrictions on nightclub licensing hours were lifted just when the rave problem peaked. The rave was made manageable: located in predictable venues, with identifiable proprietors, subject to clear legal requirements and with its own internal mechanisms for maintaining order. Raves had been 'integrated into the infrastructure of the entertainment establishment' both 'contained and commodified' (Collin 1998: 120). Pragmatic social control had resolved the problem. Outright suppression would have produced continuous conflict and consumed inordinate police resources. Rave was not put down; it was encouraged to relocate itself. Ecstasy was simply sidelined as 'core concerns – stemming the spread of drug culture and preventing organized criminals from consolidating their power base – went unresolved' (Collin 1998: 121).

Third narrative: ecstasy
Initially following the same trajectory as rave, bifurcation comes when measures are introduced. If raves were officially outlawed and unofficially relocated, a comparable solution was not available for ecstasy. Based on past experience (Young 1971), measures might have included increased police surveillance, changes in the law, spiralling sentencing and the parade of some exemplary cases. Little of this happened. Ecstasy was simply encompassed within legal enforcement procedures and drug education programmes for Class A drugs. Suppressing ecstasy would have required a massive mobilization of the state against a substantial minority of youth. Recreational drug taking had become an intrinsic part of youth culture – its music, magazines and marketing – assuming as normal a status as that occupied by alcohol and tobacco in the adult culture. In effect, New Age Travellers were suppressed, raves institutionalized and ecstasy reviled in principle but condoned in practice. Application of the models has to take account of this complexity.

Processual model

One: emergence: form, novelty, threat. Rave culture, a genuinely new leisure form was initially seen as harmless hedonism but then connected to a drug problem threatening ordinary young people. The public order problem important to the police was less of a general threat.

Two: media inventory: stylization and stereotyping; exaggeration, distortion, prediction and symbolization; sensitization; folk devil. Raves were initially stereotyped as dangerous and the participants as vulnerable. The dangers were exaggerated and distorted. Prediction and symbolization are not evident. The media were sensitized to anything relating to ecstasy. The folk devils were not participants or organizers but the drug dealers.

Three: moral entrepreneurs: significant actors; relationship to media; orientations, images and causal explanations. Moral entrepreneurs were not very evident outside the media. No new or existing groups campaigned about the problem. The police, active in making claims about raves, appeared more reticent about ecstasy.

Four: experts: who; grounds for claims; media accreditation. Experts were thin on the ground. Those closest to young people's pleasures and drug consumption took the pragmatic view of harm minimization, condemned by the popular press, supported by some broadsheets. Medical opinion about the drug's harm was ambiguous.

Five: coping and resolution: proposed solutions, measures adopted; procedural/legal; effective/symbolic. Legal response was of increasing severity, with Acts passed in 1990, 1994 and 1997, giving the police extraordinary powers. Grudging concessions were made to drug education. New Age Travellers were suppressed. The efficacy of the legal measures is doubtful, since the actual solution was to institutionalize raves and incorporate ecstasy into existing policies on recreational drugs.

Six: fade away: timing, recurrence, subsequent status. As raves moved into clubs, media attention faded, occasional deaths reported as isolated instances. No new episodes occurred. Consumption of ecstasy may have declined from its peak.

Seven: legacy: long-term effects; relationship to other issues. The whole issue became routinized as part of the recreational drugs problem. The laws appear to have been little used. In 2002, when police and government contemplated moving cannabis from a Class B to a Class C drug, it was speculated that ecstasy might move from A to B.

Attributional model

One: concern: among whom; how widespread; forms of expression. The police and the media expressed concern but politicians were slow to react. Local opinion may have been more measured (McDermott et al. 1993) but the level of general public concern remains unknown.

Two: hostility; enemy, threat, folk devil. Participants were seen as victims, the perpetrators not entrepreneurs but the mythical figure of the drug dealer.

Three: consensus: clarity, among whom, organized opposition. The police, politicians and of the popular press tried hard to suppress ambiguity. Health and drug educators pursued a different view, youth media dissented and clubbers persisted in their behaviour (Kohn 1997). The consensus was limited and fragile, especially attenuating in the late 1990s.

Four: disproportionality: dimensions and implications; claims versus reality. By any statistical measure, neither rave nor ecstasy posed an immediate health risk. Ecstasy is not physically addictive and more likely to cause psychological than physical harm, such as panic attacks. Some of the 42 deaths associated with ecstasy up to 1995 had other causes. Most were caused when inadequate intake of fluids produced excessive body temperatures. Compared with other risks to young people or other drugs, including tobacco and alcohol, ecstasy did not warrant such a reaction (Saunders 1995).

Five: volatility: length; speed of emergence and decline. Each episode expanded and contracted rapidly but the issue as a whole persisted for nearly ten years, suggesting a serial panic, with volatile outbreaks within a longer period.

(Six): claims makers: principal claims and counter claims makers; motives and strategies; degree of success. The principal claims makers were the police, some parts of the press and politicians. Counter claims came from drug educationalists and youth culture itself. The contest was uneven when it came to passing laws but the obduracy of participants forced considerable concessions.

Rave/ecstasy fits the two models only at some points. There was evidence of stereotyping of young people, moral condemnation by opinion leaders and new laws. On the other hand, there was resistance, even press opinion was divided and the attraction of raves was eventually acknowledged. New Age Travellers apart, the actual resolutions had little to do with the law. It was never wholly clear what the source of the threat was. In Cohen's formulation, it may have been less a 'person' or 'group' who were the object of attention than a 'condition' or 'episode': the rave itself. A folk devil was constructed but already known: the drug dealer, an indistinct figure from the underworld.

The usefulness of the moral panic approach to the analysis of rave /ecstasy is disputed by Thornton (1995). The development of a local reservation into a wholesale critique will be dealt with in Chapter 10. Here we are concerned with her arguments about the case of rave/ecstasy. She sees the model as misrepresenting the complexity of modern mass media, their strategic role in youth culture and their resistance to moral panics. Modern youth culture generates media aimed at and responsive to youthful audiences. Micro media (flyers and listings) and niche media (music and youth magazines) helped to construct the rave phenomenon and to deconstruct its representation by the mainstream mass media. Youth media almost welcome the moral panic as confirmation of their own deviance: ' "moral panics" can be seen as a culmination and fulfilment of youth cultural agendas in so far as negative newspaper and broadcast coverage baptise transgression' (Thornton 1995: 129). A moral panic can be deliberately invited as a marketing strategy. Negative media coverage strengthens rather than weakens the dissemination and popularization of specific youth subcultures. Any moral panic model 'fails to acknowledge competing media, let alone their reception by youthful audiences' and 'overlooks the youthful ethics of abandon' (Thornton 1995: 136).

The argument is trenchant but overstated. Crudely used, the models may concentrate excessively on mainstream media and thus underestimate the subversive role of alternative media. Yet the greater ambiguity and multiplicity of media provide only a potential resource in the contestation over meanings; it all depends on the balance of power. When the police, the tabloid press and the governing party launch a concerted campaign, alternative media are powerless. There is always the potential for an emergent moral panic to be opposed, sometimes effectively; but rave/ecstasy was not such a case. Mooted was a massive mobilization of the state against raves, if necessary by the powers invested in the Criminal Justice and Public Order Act 1994. The pragmatic and compromised nature of the ultimate solution – incorporation of the rave into clubbing – owed less to the vociferousness of the opposition than the intractability and popularity of raving itself. Moral panic models are useful but not adequate. They do not highlight or indicate the beliefs and ideas mobilized in the debate about rave/ecstasy, centred on the problem of recreational drug taking.

Beyond moral panics

Drugs have been associated with most new musical forms in the twentieth century (Lyttle and Montagne 1992: 1169). In modern times the Mods provided the clearest example. Their use of new drug, amphetamines, produced an old reaction, a prohibitive law. In the 1990s the context changed, as recreational drugs have become fundamental to contemporary youth leisure (Measham et al. 1994). Parker et al.'s (1998) surveys amongst schoolchildren aged 14 to 16 in north-west England found three-quarters to have had access to drugs, one-half to have used them and one-fifth to be current users. Though others have questioned the generalizability of their data and con- clusions (Shiner and Newburn 1999), national surveys (McC Miller and Plant 1996) confirmed an inexorable rise: 'What has happened since the late 1980s is a significant broadening of the drug-using constituency encom- passing a much wider range of substances taken by ever-larger groups of young people' (Shapiro 1999: 17).

Researchers agree the most popular drug to be alcohol, followed by cannabis, with tobacco or ecstasy in third place. Parker et al. (1998) describe this process as the 'normalization' of drug use, with six dimensions: drugs are readily available; they are widely tried, regardless of sex or class; drug use is an integral part of youth culture; even those who do not use them know about them; drug use increases with age, well into the 20s; it is con- fined to recreational time and places (Parker et al. 1998: 153–7). Ecstasy was an important moment in this development, 'the watershed whereby drugs moved from subculture status to become part of the mainstream youth cul- ture' (Parker et al. 1995: 24). Ecstasy use has been defined as deviant, despite most people using similar substances (Plant and Plant 1992).

Intervention is justified by defining deviant activity as putting those involved at risk:

> imputation of risk . . . may be used as a means of social coercion and maintaining the moral and social order . . . certain classes of people are singled out as likely victims of hazards, as being 'at risk' and therefore requiring control to bring them back to conforming to moral values.
>
> (Lupton 1999: 49)

However, conventional views of risk are contested by those seeking 'sensual embodiment and the visceral and emotional flights produced by encounters with danger' (Lupton 1999: 149). One form is the individual's struggle to achieve mastery of danger elements, as in extreme sports or even bungee jumping; another is a collective reach for another kind of reality in which 'participants may lose a sense of their autonomous selves, becoming, at least for a brief time, part of a mass of bodies / selves with a common, shared pur- pose' (Lupton 1999: 153). Such activities express 'the pleasures of the "grotesque" or "uncivilised" body' (Lupton 1999: 171).

Rave/ecstasy attracted hostility because the participants doubly trans- gress. They ignore the exhortation to discipline the body to avoid risk and explore the body's potential to forsake discipline for abandonment. Rave/ecstasy subverted the ordered, restrained, chemically pure and self- contained body. Such 'attempts to control the way people display, alter and affect their bodies' are 'connected to deep-seated moral convictions about

MORAL PANICS AND THE MEDIA

order' (Mugford 1992: 201). The basic issue is 'our inability to think hard about the issues of pleasure and consciousness change', unable to forsake the idea 'that it is inherently wrong to seek to alter one's consciousness through artificial means' (McDermott et al. 1993: 242). Such discipline of mind and body is countered by sensual pleasure seeking, in which mind is suspended and bodily sensation explored. 'Common agreement on "the place of drugs in everyday life" still eludes politicians and pundits, researchers and commentators, "ordinary voters" as well as professionals involved in drug services, clinical treatment and law enforcement' (South 1999a: 5). The rave/ecstasy issue pointed up debates about the regulatory system of the body and of pleasure. For its opponents, it involved unnecessary risks; its proponents placed pleasure before risk. Rave/ecstasy generated contested discourses about risk and pleasure which are essentially moral. The next section considers whether that was the basis of social reaction elsewhere.

International comparisons

The comparison made here is restricted to ecstasy as one of the 'dance' or 'designer' drugs. We therefore exclude the work on the 'crack' cocaine panic in the USA (Reinarman and Levine 1989; Orcutt and Turner 1993), including one of the best ever studies of a moral panic, though it barely mentions the term (Reeves and Campbell 1994). There are obvious parallels with previous reactions to cannabis (Goode 1969; Young 1971) some 30 years earlier but on ecstasy little has been published. Detailed accounts of drugs policies and debates are generally restricted to the Anglophone countries and some western European countries (MacGregor 1999). The ecstasy sample is even smaller and would scarcely exist without Jenkins (1999). As Jenkins emphasizes and will be further discussed in Chapter 8, the institutional context for any moral panic in the USA is a federal governmental structure, with a largely regionalized media. Consequently social reaction is often localized. Yet the main moral entrepreneur on drugs is a federal agency with a high media profile, the Drug Enforcement Administration (DEA), formed in 1973. 'News reporting of drug issues over the last quarter century has largely consisted of reprinting or paraphrasing DEA press releases' (Jenkins 1999: 21). Drug debates are distinctively racial in tone. The category of 'designer drugs' (synthetically produced) has framed each new drug appearing. All these factors were evident in scares over ecstasy.

Ecstasy became an issue in two distinct periods, 1985–86 and 1992–95. In the spring of 1985 evidence of ecstasy consumption in California, Texas and gay clubs in New York and Chicago prompted the DEA to declare ecstasy a Schedule I drug. Exaggerated Congressional hearings led to a new law. Within the Anti-Drug Abuse Act 1986 was the Controlled Analogue Enforcement Act, known as the 'Designer Drug Act'. It made illegal any substance analogous to those already prohibited. Two years later, the Chemical Diversion and Trafficking Act strictly regulated legal possession of chemicals used to manufacture synthetic drugs. By 1986 the ecstasy issue faded, as consumers switched to other drugs and the media discovered crack cocaine. Ecstasy reappeared in the early 1990s, imported from the UK in rave culture, but 'never acquired the same enormous vogue in the United States as it did in Manchester or Amsterdam' (Jenkins 1999: 165). It was nevertheless portrayed as posing a particular threat to otherwise respectable young whites. In 1996 the USA found its equivalent of Leah Betts in middle-class Hillary Janean Faries, who died after drinking some 'spiked' Sprite, though the drug alleged to be involved was not ecstasy but GHB (gamma-hydroxyl-butyrate). Though attention subsequently switched to 'date rape' drugs, city councils debated action to suppress raves.

Ecstasy in the USA was part of a serial panic about designer drugs. Legal action against ecstasy was typical of the more or less permanent 'war' on drugs in the USA. The DEA overtly directed the focus and intensity of concern, aided by a compliant media. The irony is that a decentralized government and media system produced a single definition and prescription for the issue, while the UK's more centralized system generated a greater plurality of viewpoints. Jenkins uses moral terminology loosely, offering 'a typical model of the panic cycle in operation' (Jenkins 1999: 183) without reference to existing models. The features are familiar: the authoritativeness of the claims makers, metaphors of threat (epidemics, addictiveness, violence), the dramas of ruined lives and tragic fatalities. Its enduring and serial nature is not explained in broader terms though the result is made clear, continuous repressive measures despite the ubiquity of drug experimentation:

> The battle to suppress ecstasy in all its forms has always been an unequal one, but now the balance of forces has shifted dramatically to the side of experimentation, which can only be suppressed by increasingly rigid laws and ever more intrusive police supported by a wilfully obscurantist media.
>
> (Jenkins 1999: 197)

Hier (2002) studied social reaction to rave in Toronto, Canada during the spring and summer of 2000. An attempt to create a moral panic about rave/ecstasy and to introduce new measures to prohibit them failed because of a counter-campaign. Raves had grown in the city throughout the 1990s, with 20,000 regular attendees by 2000. In 1999 for the first time there were three deaths at raves. The rave community responded by forming the Toronto Dance Safety Committee, supporting the city council passing a 'Protocol for the Operation of Safe Dance Events/Raving'. Health and safety requirements were so strict that future raves could be held only on council property. However, the local mayor, police chief and deputy coroner became convinced that raves were drug dens. With the provincial parliament considering an Act to regulate raves, the local media paraded ecstasy at raves as 'embodying danger and necessitating spatial regulation' (Hier 2002: 42). The mayor persuaded the city council to introduce a temporary ban on 'any event advertised or called a rave'. Following the highly publicized ecstasy-related death of a student, the police formulated an Entertainment Gathering Protocol, codifying powers to regulate raves. The requirement that promoters should pay for a police presence effectively made the costs prohibitive. Raves were being outlawed.

Its supporters embarked on a counter-campaign, triggered by the inquest jury's unexpected recommendation that raves should be held only on city premises. Four initiatives were undertaken: a live and highly critical TV segment on Canada's all-music station; a local hip-hop group released a compact disc (CD) with clips of misleading statements by the mayor; the PartyPeopleProject circulated a reasoned 36-page report to city councillors opposing the protocol; thousands attended a pro-rave rally outside City Hall. The mayor caved in, recommending the reconvened city council to adopt the jury's recommendation. Three months after banning all raves, the council would now become their hosts. Hier (2002) argues that this case supports the McRobbie and Thornton (1995) thesis, since the folk devils organized and fought back, though their success owed much to their status as white and middle class and to funding from commercial interests. Additionally, both the debate and the significant actors operated on a local city rather than a national scale. This made it easier to construct an opposition, be heard in the media and target the people with power.

However, not all local debates about rave had this outcome. In February 2001 the city council of Charlotte, North Carolina unanimously approved an ordinance which prohibited 'dance hall businesses' and 'raves' from staying open beyond licensing hours, in order to prevent illegal drug dealing, sexual predation and violence (Mitchell 2001). Passing such an ordinance was a precondition for the receipt of federal grants to combat club drugs under the recent Ecstasy Prevention Act. An effective adult entertainment curfew was enforced on the basis of suspicion and exaggeration amongst local opinion leaders. There was no organized opposition. Like Ontario, this was a local debate but with a different result. Lack of effective opposition is a precondition for a moral panic; when it arises, the panic will become contested and may well founder. The degree of contestation – partly contested in the UK, successfully contested in Ontario and uncontested in Charlotte – directly affects attempts to legislate or take other forms of action.

Overview

The expansion of rave culture and its association with ecstasy occurred more speedily and profoundly in Britain than elsewhere. The solution was threefold: suppression of New Age Travellers, institutionalization of raves in club culture and routinization of ecstasy as a recreational drug. The original problem was resolved by such varied approaches rather than a single legal stratagem. Proposals from 2002 onwards to downgrade ecstasy's status as a dangerous drug are consistent with this overall drift.

This disparity between the appearance of a moral panic and the reality of a more pragmatic approach indicates a complex model of social control. Ecstasy consumption could not be prevented; the only viable objective was to control the timing, place and conditions of its use. Those profoundly disapproving of it in principle found themselves in practice advocating harm minimization. The persistent attraction for youth culture of the experience of ecstasy required such concessions from adult society.

Further reading

Collin, M. with Godfrey, J. (1998) *Altered State: The Story of Ecstasy Culture and Acid House*, 2nd edn. London: Serpent's Tail.

Jenkins, P. (1999) *Synthetic Panic: The Symbolic Politics of Designer Drugs*. New York: New York University Press.

Osgerby, B. (1998) *Youth in Britain since 1945*. Oxford: Blackwell.

South, N. (ed.) (1999) *Drugs: Culture, Controls and Everyday Life*. London: Sage.

Thornton, S. (1995) *Club Cultures: Music, Media and Subcultural Capital*. Cambridge: Polity.

5

A ROCKY HORROR SHOW: VIDEO NASTIES

Introduction

In the UK the issue of video nasties produced, uniquely, two separate episodes in 1982–84 and 1992–94, almost exactly ten years apart. These two episodes are so strikingly similar that they can be treated as a 'double' panic. We therefore present the two narratives first, then apply the models to both, before reviewing the themes which emerge beyond moral panic analysis and making international comparisons

The first video nasties narrative, 1982–84

The issue emerges, May 1982

The background to the first episode was the rapid take-up of the video cassette recorder (VCR) in the early 1980s. By 1982 one-third of households owned or rented a VCR. About 6000 tapes could be rented from 20,000 locally owned video shops. Coincidentally, Hollywood produced a crop of gruesome horror films. Their irresponsible marketing – on covers, posters and magazines – prompted complaints which the Advertising Standards Authority largely upheld in 1981 (Petley 1984). Video magazine editors agreed new standards for adverts. The press was alerted. Articles in the *Daily Mail* and *Sunday Times* in late May 1982 stressed the extreme violence of such films, including sadism, mutilation and cannibalism. The precise origins of the term 'video nasty' are unclear but it was reappropriated by the *Sunday Times* (Martin 1993). The Metropolitan Police Obscene

Publications Squad seized a copy of *SS Experiment Camp* and referred it to the Director of Public Prosecutions. The **British Board of Film Classification** (BBFC) set up a joint working party with the British Videogram Association ((BVA) representing distributors) to devise a mandatory classification scheme. The **National Viewers' and Listeners' Association** (NVLA), formed in the 1960s to campaign against sex and violence on television, opposed any voluntary code, advocating stricter controls than for cinema. Government answers to parliamentary questions in June 1982 still supported a voluntary code.

Prosecutions, June–September 1982

The distributors of five videos (*Death Trap*, *Cannibal Holocaust*, *SS Experiment Camp*, *I Spit on Your Grave* and *Driller Killer*) were charged under the Obscene Publications Act. The police used Section 3 of the Act, for which the penalty was only forfeiture of cassettes, rather than Section 2, punishable by fines or imprisonment. Prosecutions were successful in July and September, the distributors forfeiting all copies. The police indicated that future prosecutions would be under Section 2. By August 1982 'the video nasty moral panic was well established' (Petley 1984: 70). The **National Society for the Prevention of Cruelty to Children** (NSPCC) issued a press release supporting the campaign (Marsh et al. 1986). The industry now reluctantly recognized the need to clarify the law. Only a few voices were raised in protest, such as Alexander Walker, film critic of the *Evening Standard* (Walker 1996).

Intensified campaigning, October 1982 to March 1983

On 15 December 1982 Labour MP Gareth Wardell proposed a law to prohibit renting of 18-certificated films to children, apparently a crucial moment in priming Parliament (Hill 1985a). Wardell emphasized the vulnerability of the 'emotionally unstable child' and the 'socially or emotionally insecure' adolescent. The motion was passed but the government declined to back it. The opponents of video nasties were not to be fobbed off. In February 1983 the *Daily Mail* launched its 'Ban the Sadist Videos' campaign. In a letter to NVLA leader Mary Whitehouse, Prime Minister Margaret Thatcher indicated her concern. Whitehouse then 'came up with her master stroke' (Petley 1984: 70), planning a screening for MPs of selected extracts from the nastiest videos. The British Videogram Association anticipated a new law.

Government responsive, April–June 1983

In April 1983, the government called a general election for June. Whitehouse claimed that 150 MPs supported legislation. The Conservative Party's election manifesto highlighted 'offences against public decency'. 'We propose to introduce measures to deal with the most serious of these problems, such as the spread of dangerous and obscene video cassettes' (Barker 1984b: 10). Barker offers three reasons for this apparent volte face: its attractiveness as a law and order issue, hostility to the media following the Falklands War and the moral force of the arguments about children. This popular measure would only cost the government parliamentary time. On 14 April, the British Videogram Association launched its voluntary code, requiring stricter certification than for cinema, but it was summarily dismissed by a government representative. The industry regarded legislation as inevitable. Throughout June and July the press discovered court cases where violent offenders blamed videos for their behaviour. Wild stories were published about 6-year-olds exposed to video nasties and sinister gangsters implicated in their distribution. A *Daily Mail* editorial of 30 June was typical. 'The failure of our politicians to turn back this tide of degenerate filth and to prevent it fouling the minds of children and adolescents is nothing short of a national scandal' (Barker 1984a: 6). Films on general release were often drawn into the video nasties net. 'By this time the term "video nasty" had unmistakably become synonymous simply with "horror film" ' (Petley 1984: 73).

Legislation, July–November 1983

After the Conservative election victory the government indicated its intention to proceed via a Private Member's Bill. This ploy had advantages: it was cheaper, the industry need not be consulted and political embarrassment would be avoided if the bill floundered (Barker 1984b; Petley 1984). Graham Bright resigned a minor Home Office post to introduce the Bill, details of which were released on 14 July 1983. It sought to outlaw the sale or hire of any video without a certificate from an authority and the sale or hire of adult-certificated videos to children, with maximum penalties of a £1000 fine and two years in prison. The NVLA pressed for the prohibition of named acts being portrayed on screen. The Bill passed its first reading the same month, its second in November 1983. In between the NVLA held its screening for MPs.

David Mellor, under-secretary at the Home Office, effectively took charge of the Bill. In November he declared that 'No one has the right to be upset at a brutal sex crime or a sadistic attack on or mindless thuggery on a pensioner if he is not prepared to drive sadistic videos out of our high streets' (Barker 1984b: 29). The Bill was subsequently amended. The British Board of Film Classification would be 'aided' by guidelines from the Director of Public Prosecutions and should pay 'due regard' to the fact that videos were likely to be seen in the home. The maximum fine was increased to £20,000. The Bill became law as the Video Recordings Act 1984.

The second video nasties narrative, 1993–94

The Bulger murder and trial, February–November 1993

On 12 February 1993 2-year-old James Bulger was abducted from the Strand shopping centre in Bootle, taken to a nearby canal and then two and a half miles to a railway track, where he was brutally beaten to death, his body left on the rails to be cut in half by a passing train. Shock at this horrific murder was compounded when two 10-year-old boys were charged with the crime. Immediately, the Prime Minister and the Home Secretary made speeches, the NVLA issued a report and the BBFC hurriedly commissioned research – all on the effects of media violence.

The boys, Jon Venables and Robert Thompson, were tried for 17 days in November 1993, found guilty of murder and sentenced to be 'detained at Her Majesty's Pleasure'. The trial judge, unusually, made a statement in open court after the boys had been taken away. He observed that 'it is not for me to pass judgement on their upbringing but I suspect violent video films may in part be an explanation'. He singled out *Child's Play 3* which 'had some striking similarities to the manner of the attack on James Bulger'. Sky TV, which had already shown it twice, cancelled its broadcast due the next day. The police officer in charge of the case told *The Guardian* that he 'had no evidence to suggest that the boys had access to any videos worse than might be found in many households'. No matter, a scapegoat had been found. This was the starting point for the second major moral panic about 'video nasties'.

Press reaction, November 1993

Analysing immediate press coverage, Franklin and Petley (1996: 134) argue that 'Even by the skewed standards of the British press, the "normal" requirements of reporting were abandoned in favour of undiluted, vitriolic editorialising'. In the two days following the verdict, coverage was 'phenomenal'. There was an 'unrelentingly retributivist and punitive' attitude towards the boy murderers. Two significant emphases were the state of childhood and the complicity of video nasties. The childhood theme was evident in a 25 November *Times* editorial:

> children should not be presumed to be innately good. In the lexicon of crime there is metaphysical evil, the imperfection of all mankind; there is physical evil, the suffering that humans cause each other; and there is moral evil, the choice of vice over virtue. Children are separated by the necessity of age from none of these.
>
> (cited in Franklin and Petley 1996: 139)

The press wanted to lay the blame for moral decline on liberal permissiveness, the collapse of family life and the failings of schools.

But the real culprit was obvious: 'the Bulger case came to be dominated by arguments about the effects of the media' (Buckingham 1996: 21). 'Every single paper focused in detail on the alleged (although utterly unsubstantiated) influence of "video nasties" such as *Child's Play 3*' (Franklin and Petley 1996: 137). The Bulger case was related to other examples of media-induced violence, such as the 1987 Hungerford massacre, the ongoing trial for the murder of Suzanne Capper and the recent controversy over the film *Reservoir Dogs*. Liberal MP David Alton asked in the *Express* (26 November 1993): 'Doesn't this demonstrate that levels of violence on video and television have reached unsurpassed levels?' An editorial in the same paper declared: 'More and more children are growing up in a moral vacuum, which for so many is being filled with fetid junk from the lower depths of our popular culture – video nasties, crude comics and violent television.' In the broadsheet press, *The Times* and *Daily Telegraph* accepted the diagnosis, though sceptical about a legislative cure; only *The Guardian* and *Independent* expressed any dissent. Logical argument was not necessary elsewhere. The front page of the *Sun* the day after the trial simply declaimed 'for the sake of our kids BURN YOUR VIDEO NASTY'. Liberal MP David Alton was quoted at length on the culpability of videos.

Newson report, April 1994

The campaign for action against video nasties gained momentum following the trial of Venables and Thompson. Opinions changed. For example the *Telegraph* had initially (26 November 1993) said that the solution lay with parents but by 12 April 1994 it was concluding that 'some parents are so feckless and irresponsible that the law has to intervene for the sake of the others' (Buckingham 1996: 27). Crucial to such shifts was the Newson report. On 1 April 1994 Professor Elizabeth Newson sent a letter and a research paper signed by 33 childcare experts to Home Secretary Michael Howard. They had revised their previous opinions; 'we were naive in our failure to predict the extent of damaging material and its all too free availability to children'. This report was not unsolicited, since Newson had produced it at Alton's request. The *Mirror* called the experts 'vidiots'. The *Mail* welcomed their agreement that 'video nasties are a poison in society'.

Barker (1997) and Buckingham (1996) have discredited the report. Its authors were not experts on the media. They had no new evidence to offer. Most of the paper was a highly emotive account of the Bulger case. There was no substance to the claim that the allegedly rising level of child violence was attributable to violent videos. In the media, however, the authors' expertise was not questioned. More typical of academic research was the BBFC-commissioned report from the Policy Studies Institute (PSI), published in April immediately before a parliamentary debate (Hagell and Newburn 1994). This showed few differences between the viewing habits of delinquents and non-delinquents. The media questioned the research more rigorously than the Newson report. An open letter by 23 leading academics in media studies attacking Newson was completely ignored.

The Alton amendment, April 1994

Much of the campaign had been orchestrated by a fundamentalist religious organization, the Movement for Christian Democracy (MCD). In January 1994, they drafted an amendment to the Criminal Justice Bill about to go through Parliament, calling for the banning on video of all films 'likely to cause psychological harm to children'. David Alton, a Catholic and Liberal MP who spearheaded the campaign, claimed the support of over 200 MPs from all parties. The campaign was now irresistible (Buckingham 1996). Nevertheless, Home Secretary Michael Howard rejected the amendment as unworkable, effectively banning many films already granted a cinema certificate. He offered instead tighter guidance to the BBFC. Its director, James Ferman, argued that the amendment would lead to the banning of mainstream films such as *Schindler's List*, *Dances with Wolves* and *Jewel in the Crown*: 'in 1985 we began classifying 12,000 videos. Within 12 months, all the video nasties which had regularly been found depraving and corrupting by the courts had been banned' (*Guardian*, 11 April 1994). *Texas Chainsaw Massacre* and *Driller Killer* were no longer available. *Straw Dogs*, *The Exorcist* and *Death Wish* had been denied video certificates and *Reservoir Dogs* was on hold.

But, as Parliament returned after the Easter break, it became clear that Howard would lose the vote. In eleventh-hour negotiations with Alton and

Labour leader Tony Blair, Howard agreed to change the legislation. Penalties for supplying unlicensed videos or adult videos to children would be increased and the BBFC would have to pay regard to videos which 'present an inappropriate model for children or are likely to cause psychological harm to a child'. The *Daily Mail*'s leader (13 April 1994) was ecstatic about a measure which would 'distinguish between video images of man's inhumanity to man (which may be cathartic for mature citizens to contemplate) and vicious trash (for which there should be no place in any decent home on the land)'. It signalled 'nothing less than a return to responsible censorship by popular demand.' This remains the current law in the UK on video certification.

Applying the models

Academic commentators suggest that the first episode was a 'moral panic . . . whipped up by the National Viewers' and Listeners' Association, the tabloid press, teachers, churchmen and others' (Petley 1984: 68). Others have concurred that 'a major piece of legislation has been discussed amidst an atmosphere of moral panic' (Brown 1984: 87) and that 'a gigantic campaign to create a moral panic' was 'carefully orchestrated, given unquestioning publicity by the media' (Barker 1984a: 4). The validity of these judgements can be examined by applying the two models to both episodes together.

Processual model

One: emergence: form, novelty, threat. The problem in the first episode was that the VCR enabled anyone to watch at home films which were not shown in cinemas at all or only to restricted audiences. This coincided with a rash of 'slasher' films. The clearest definition of video nasties was 'films that contain scenes of such violence and sadism . . . that they would not be granted a certificate by the British Board of Film Censors' (Barlow and Hill 1985: 171). Such films did exist, could be obtained and just possibly might be seen by children. In the second episode the focus was on horror films which already had certificates and were, like *Child's Play 3*, even being shown on satellite television. In the first episode the newness of the technology and films were stressed; in the second, the Bulger trial renewed and redefined the issue.

Two: media inventory: stylization and stereotyping; exaggeration, distortion, prediction and symbolization; sensitization; folk devil. Barker

(1984a: 6) identifies 'an hysterical press campaign [which] got going through 1982 and climaxed in 1983'. The key newspapers were the *Daily Mail* and *Sunday Times*. The films were stereotyped, ironic and parodic elements being read literally. Sensitization was apparent in the spurious links between crimes and videos. Those who might have been cast as folk devils – makers, distributors and retailers – were not. A new media technology, the VCR, and a new cultural product, graphic horror films, became the objects of campaigning. In the second episode, some parents and children, especially among the 'underclass', were briefly stereotyped but not developed into folk devils.

Three: moral entrepreneurs: significant actors; relationship to media; orientations, images and causal explanations. The pace was clearly set by Christian-based organizations, the NVLA led by Mary Whitehouse in the first episode, the MCD led by David Alton in the second. They had established allies in the mid- and downmarket press, which relished the prospect of a moralistic campaign. Upmarket papers, led by the *Sunday Times*, followed suit. This mixture of newspaper and pressure campaigning exerted pressure on government, largely through backbench MPs. The image of childhood corrupted by viewing video nasties was generalized in the first episode and vividly symbolized in the Bulger murder in the second.

Four: experts: who; grounds for claims; media accreditation. The nature of the issue was regarded as so clear-cut that little expert opinion was required. Barker (1984b) notes the prominence in the first episode of psychiatrists and teachers. In the second, the penitent experts of the Newson report were derisively welcomed by the press, whereas the PSI research was greeted sceptically and expert academics ignored. On this issue, no group of experts could effectively claim ownership so that claims makers went largely unchallenged.

Five: coping and resolution: proposed solutions, measures adopted; procedural/legal; effective/symbolic. In neither episode did the government respond enthusiastically. In the first episode, legislation became politically expedient. In the second, the government resisted until the very last moment. Both measures changed in the law affecting the BBFC's video certification procedures. The 1984 Act outlawed uncertificated videos already illegal under the Obscene Publications Act (Harris 1984). The 1994 amendment introduced a different system of classification for videos from cinema with little long-term effect. Many so-called video nasties were eventually certificated for video release, albeit some years later and with some cuts. The measures were more symbolic than effective. Existing laws and procedures could deal with what problem there was.

Six: fade away: timing, recurrence; subsequent status. In both episodes, the issue faded fast once a law had been passed. The 1993–94 episode might not have happened but for the judge's remarks. It has not recurred since, despite widespread viewing by children of films they are not supposed to see.

Seven: legacy: long-term effects; relationship to other issues. Video nasties condensed three longstanding issues of concern: violence in the media, violent crime and the status of childhood. The legacy was less on the availability of videos than on the symbolization of these issues, especially by the Bulger murder.

Attributional model

One: concern: among whom; how widespread; forms of expression. How far concern about video nasties in 1983–84 spread beyond the elites of church, parliament and press is unclear. In Parliament, Graham Bright cited 'the wide public concern' and 'rising tide of public anxiety' but aside from newspapers, public opinion appeared as 'a large number of letters to MPs which . . . seemed to come mostly from the followers of Mrs Mary Whitehouse' (Harris 1984). Campaigners against video nasties and their supporters in the media believed public opinion was on their side but had no proof. Barker (1984b) cites a September 1983 poll for the BVA showing public approval of video censorship but not of films they had seen. Public opinion was less consulted than constructed, since 'it never was a *real* general public that was appealed to in the debates. It was a specially defined group of people with certain qualities who could make up a "proper" general public' (Barker 1984b: 26, original emphasis). Buckingham (1997: 39) is sceptical that 'campaigns to increase the censorship of media violence necessarily represent the views of the population at large, however much appeal they may have for their elected representatives'. Later research showed continuing confusion among the public, agreement that there is too much violence on television but giving other reasons for violence in society. Even the Bulger case had not cemented the video fiction/real violence connection in the public mind. It was, however, enough for elites to be convinced.

Two: hostility; enemy, threat, folk devil. There was no folk devil. The enemy was taken to be, and hostility directed against, an object not a person or group.

Three: consensus: clarity, among whom, organized opposition. Elites arrived at a consensus, first Christian groups, then sections and eventually the whole of the press, finally and crucially MPs. Opposition to 'the media hysteria and the ill-conceived legislation' was 'almost non-existent' (Petley 1984: 74). As a Private Member's Bill, the 1984 measure needed only minimal parliamentary opposition to be wrecked (Marsh et al. 1986). Unlike the

Obscene Publications Act of the following year (Marsh et al. 1987), none was forthcoming.

Four: disproportionality: dimensions and implications; claims versus reality. If the basic problem in 1983–84 was the numbers of children who ever saw the 30 or so videos defined as 'video nasties', the evidence was very slight. 'At every stage of its journey into law, this campaign has misrepresented the threat and enlarged the restrictive nature of the proposed "remedy" ' (Walker 1984: 5). In the later episode, there was slightly more evidence. Britain's VCR ownership at 70 per cent was the highest in Europe. Since 1981, the video rental market had increased tenfold to £528 million and sales to £643 million, though there was increasing competition from satellite film channels. Horror films constituted only 3 per cent of the overall market but some children did see on video films they could not see in the cinema. Buckingham (1997: 41) confirmed that 'substantial numbers of under-age children have seen the kind of material which it is officially illegal for them to watch'. Exposure does not, however, guarantee effect. Children understood films as fiction. *Child's Play 3* provided no model for violent imitation. It had been given a 15 certificate in the cinema and an 18 on video. The film is clearly an ironic fantasy in which the villain, Chucky, is defeated. Buckingham found children to be more disturbed by television news coverage of the Bulger case than by any horror film. In both episodes, disproportionality was clearly evident. The remedies were largely spurious since 'the imposition of centralized regulation is becoming an ever more difficult struggle' (Buckingham 1997: 41).

Five: volatility: length; speed of emergence and decline. Episode one lasted two years, with February to July 1983 as its climax. The second was more condensed, with just six months between the trial verdict and the Alton amendment. In both cases, the issue declined very fast.

(Six): claims makers: principal claims and counter claims makers; motives and strategies; degree of success. The principal claims maker in 1983–84 was the NVLA whose 'lobbying on the issue of video nasties is an object lesson in How To Do It' (Petley 1984: 70). Their obsession with 'obscenity' in the media discovered an issue which was novel, newsworthy and brooked no opposition. They exploited Christian networks in powerful institutions, notably the churches and Parliament, to diffuse their concerns. The MCD consolidated such contacts in 1993–94, focusing on Parliament. Opposition was fragmented and unorganized.

The models are sound frameworks for understanding the video nasties double panic, with one exception and some qualifications. The exception is the absence of an identifiable folk devil. One qualification, more of the attributional than the processual model, is that concern and consensus appear to be necessary only among elites who represent, rather than react to, concern among the public. On the other hand, the attributional model more than the processual model draws attention to the motives and methods of claims makers. The video nasties issue cannot properly be understood without attention to the strategic role of fundamentalist Christian organizations, one of several features taking us beyond moral panics.

Beyond moral panics

Three special characteristics of the 'debate' about video nasties the models only partially incorporate: its promotion by fundamentalist Christians, the childhood theme and the dangers of the violent underclass.

Religion

Outside the press, the chief actors in the double moral panic were fundamentalist religious groups, first the NVLA and then the MCD. Barker traces their theological basis to Manicheism, 'the heresy that the world is the scene for a permanent struggle between a coeval God and Satan. Whoever is not of the good is a representative of evil' (Barker 1984b: 8). Some insight into the mind set and strategies of such organizations is evident from the documented activity of the Parliamentary Video Group (PVG) (Brown 1984; Barlow and Hill 1985). The PVG was 'a private organization funded and run by a body called the Organization of Christian Unity, which is also active in campaigning to tighten up abortion and divorce law' (Harris 1984: 141). Its leading light was Clifford Hill, once a lecturer in religious studies, then a police adviser networked with probation officers and the NSPCC. His allies were Lady Watherston of the Order of Christian Unity and Raymond Johnston, research director of the Christian Action Research and Education (CARE), an evangelical organization. A meeting was convened at the House of Lords in June 1983 to discuss how to provide hard evidence to back up their claim that children had access to violent and obscene videos. Money was made available for a six-month research project, starting in September to be carried out at Oxford Polytechnic by Brian Brown.

Almost immediately, in July, the Bright Bill was announced. Conflict ensued between Hill and Brown about the conduct of the research. Brown heavily criticized Hill's draft interim report as failing to substantiate its assertions, conclusions and recommendations. The unchanged report was published on 23 November. 'It was sold to an expectant Fleet Street as:

(a) an official churches' report, (b) bearing parliamentary authority, (c) the work of an academic working party' (Brown 1984: 85).

On 25 November, while Brown was away from Oxford, Hill removed all the data and related correspondence from his office. In December 1983 Oxford Polytechnic disowned the report. In February 1984 Methodist and Catholic representatives withdrew from the PVG. Part Two of Hill's report was issued in March 1984. Some conclusions had been toned down but its findings still lacked scientific validity. Subsequent publication of a book revealed Christian objectives. Its conclusion (Hill 1985b) makes four specific objections to video nasties: they are viewed unregulated in the home, offer realistic and sadistic portrayals of violence, are devoid of moral messages and invite emotional identification with the perpetrator. Moreover, they appear at a time when society is undergoing disturbing social and moral change, with violence of all kinds on the increase. Video nasties symbolize moral degeneration. The evil is popular culture, undermining public (and implicitly Christian) morality.

If the PVG was symptomatic but marginal in 1983–84, the MCD was crucial in 1993–94. It too had a specific theological stance (Murray and McClure 1996). Its newsletter revealed that £13,000 had been raised to support the campaign, a parliamentary draughtsman employed to draft the amendment and a petition circulated with 100,000 signatories (Petley 1994). Even the upmarket press made no sustained attempt to reveal the religious agendas of the NVLA or the MCD. They established themselves as expert authorities, a remarkable feat of claims making. Thompson (1990) concluded from his analysis of the Child Protection Act 1978 targeting pornography that the role of fundamentalist organizations in fuelling moral panics has been underestimated. The case of video nasties bears this out.

Childhood

Christian concern latched onto child protection as an incontrovertible agenda. 'The fact that it is the health and safety of *children* which is at stake suggests the possibility of public and government support for a new initiative if clear evidence *compels* attention' (Barker 1984b: 14, original emphases). Petley (1984: 71) noted how 'the spectre of children watching horror videos seems to have upset a certain traditional ideology of "childhood" '. This ultra-conservative ideology implicitly targets working-class children as being at risk. The assumption is made that such children will copy whatever they are shown. It rests on a 'sentimental, picture-postcard image' of children as threatened by 'sadists and molesters, profiteers and perverts' (Barker 1984b: 38).

The Bulger murder intensified the perceived crisis in childhood. In the press 'the "innocent angels" of an earlier social construction of childhood were replaced by "little demons"' (Franklin and Petley 1996: 134). Adult categories – of good and evil, innocence and guilt – were applied to Venables and Thompson, who represented the abandoned state of childhood. Barker and Petley rightly insist that 'this whole discourse is not about real, live children but about a *conception of childhood*' (1997: 5, original emphasis). Buckingham (1996) argues that simply labelling video nasties as a moral panic will not reveal 'much more fundamental anxieties', buried in 'a highly contradictory notion of childhood'. The 'Romantic view', of children as 'innocent and vulnerable', is pitted against 'an even older Christian view' defining them as 'potential monsters' with 'anti-social tendencies', 'liable to be triggered at any moment'; in short, 'guilty of original sin' (Buckingham 1996: 33). This childhood theme will be picked up again in Chapter 11 as it is evident in several case studies. For the moment, we move on to one of the sins children may commit: violence.

Violence and the underclass

Coupling of video nasties with violence in 1983–84 also had wider connections with 'a much larger range of issues and behaviours (rape and sexual violence, AIDS, the censorship of videotape, gay rights, and street violence, the behaviour of children in schools, drug abuse, etc.)' (Taylor 1987: 109).' Ten years on, 'a potent strain of class dislike and fear' (Petley 1997: 85) emerged early in the debates about the Bulger case, especially about the convicted boys' parents. Here is columnist Lynda Lee Potter in the *Daily Mail* (13 April 1994).

> There are thousands of children in this country with fathers they never see and mothers who are lazy sluts. They are allowed to do what they want, when they want. They sniff glue on building sites, scavenge for food and, until now, they were free to watch increasingly horrific videos. By 16, they are disturbed and dangerous.

This class emphasis was 'much more pronounced, unashamed and naked in 1993/4 than in 1983/4' (Petley 1997: 100). Not as obvious as the childhood theme, this fear of the 'dangerous classes' created a folk devil at one remove.

International comparisons

Sweden, 1982–83

Britain was not the last country to experience a moral panic over video nasties. Nor was it the first, which appears to have been Sweden. 'By international comparison video came early to Sweden' (Roe 1985: 13). Sales expanded rapidly as early as 1980. The ensuing debate began in 1981, peaked during 1982–83 and waned in 1984, just as it was climaxing in the UK. The coincidence of growing VCR ownership and retail outlets with slasher films occurred as in Britain, though Swedish censorship of both television and cinema was even stricter. Roe (1985) applies Cohen's (1973) model very precisely, especially the inventory phase involving sensitization, symbolization, exaggeration and distortion. In the Swedish press, video embodied 'the negative aspects and consequences of new media technology and the threat posed by it to traditional culture' (Roe 1985: 15). Sensitization was apparent, with youth deviance – truancy, drug taking, sexual activity and alcohol consumption – associated with video watching. The rhetoric of childhood innocence was evoked. He cites a February 1983 newspaper article, which referred to 'children's and adolescents' needs' being paramount, since 'they have the right to be protected from the damaging effect of video violence'.

Roe (1985) suggests that the teaching profession, parent–teacher associations and education ministers were the principal claims makers. The ultimate measures involved a tax on all VCR and tape purchase and legal changes to enable prosecution of retailers selling very violent films. It was mooted but not then instigated that videos should be certificated in the same manner as films. Roe (1985: 17) argues that the episode 'fulfilled very accurately many of the conditions identified by Cohen', with the video as folk devil. The evidence to justify the concern was negligible, since only a minority of Swedish children had seen videos and very few violent ones. Though he does not emphasize it, Roe's account indicates a problem framed around state responsibilites with the disciplinarians, primarily teachers, seeing video as threatening socialization processes. Neither religious groups nor an underclass appear in Roe's account. The actors and themes are distinctively Swedish but in most other ways the dynamics and outcomes are very similar to those in the UK. Neither served as a model for the other. In the later case of New Zealand, the British debate was an explicit reference point.

New Zealand, 1986

Shuker (1986) analysed the controversy over video nasties in 1986, culminating in legislation. He refers to the moral panic model but does not apply it, his main interest being in the underlying issues. Nevertheless, there are striking similarities with the UK case. The spread of VCRs coincided with the crop of horror movies. Existing laws were thought inadequate to deal with the problem. Prominent groups, such as Women Against Pornography and the Society for the Protection of Community Standards, sought to prioritize the issue, taken up by some sections of the press. The nature of the films was stereotyped and their potential harm to children emphasized. Eventually, a new law was passed, the Video Recordings Act 1986. There were also some differences. It occurred after the 1983–84 UK episode, which became a reference point. The sexualized nature of video violence was more prominent, especially for feminist critics. The underlying issue 'beyond moral panics' in New Zealand Shuker (1986) takes to be the 'social construction of sexuality'. We should need more of narrative to explore the comparison further. The debate was wider and more considered than in the UK. The outcome, however, was very similar, even though New Zealand set up a separate Video Recordings Authority. Not an exact replication, the New Zealand case overall bore a striking resemblance to the British panic of 1983–84.

Australia, 1996

In 1984 some Australian states changed definitions of film classifications in response to video nasties, though apparently without a specific panic (Dwyer and Stockbridge 1999). This came 12 years later. In April 1996 at Port Arthur in Tasmania, Martin Bryant shot dead 35 people. Following a media outcry, the newly elected Liberal government instigated two measures. Additional restrictions were placed on the ownership of automatic weapons. Film certification and regulations governing the timing of violent films broadcast on television were tightened. Stockwell (1997) has analysed this as a moral panic. The sensitizing context comprised the **Dunblane murders** in Scotland a few weeks before, an ongoing debate about gun laws and racist parties campaigning in a recent general election. Legislation on gun ownership Stockwell (1997: 57) sees as justified and commensurate, hence not a moral panic: 'is it possible to have a moral panic when the devil is real?' By contrast, the connections made with film violence and videos in particular were spurious, enabling 'a moral panic to develop about violent TV and videos' (Stockwell 1997: 57). After the massacre, the press concentrated on allegations that Bryant had an extensive collection of violent videos. *Child's Play 2* was claimed to have provided a model for his crime. Explicit references were made to two British murders supposedly implicating videos, Suzanne Capper in 1992 and James Bulger in 1993. The head of the Film Classification Board vainly pointed out that the 2000 videos found in Bryant's home were all owned by the previous female occupant and were largely musicals and classics. A government inquiry produced predictable recommendations: 'the result of the moral panic over video violence has been government action to produce more stringent classification of movies, further limiting of time slots in which adult material might be broadcast on television and requiring all new TVs to contain a V-chip that allows parents to limit their children's viewing' (Stockwell 1997: 58). Two years later, however, only the changes to classification had been introduced (Dwyer and Stockbridge 1999).

Stockwell identifies two issues for moral panic theory. The first is the absence of a folk devil: 'guns and videos, though perhaps most feared in the hands of "deviant' lower class males, are nevertheless objects, not people' (Stockwell 1997: 60). The second is the narrowness of debate: 'its real entrepreneurs were the government and the media themselves' (Stockwell 1997: 59). A more precise comparison would be with the 1987 Hungerford massacre in the UK when Michael Ryan randomly shot and killed 16 people and then himself. Videos of *Rambo* films were implicated on specious grounds (Webster 1989). There are still clear parallels with the Bulger case – violent crime, media campaign, government action – but pressure group activity is absent and politicians more immediately receptive. Religious and child-related themes are absent though there is an implicit theme of a violent underclass. However, the complicity of fictional video violence in producing actual violence is posited, yet again, without any evidence at all.

Overview

In some other countries, as well as Britain, video nasties provoked episodes of moral panic, albeit without a folk devil. The underlying problem was a new media technology, located in the home where viewing could not be regulated, with supposedly dangerous implications for the moral integrity of children and young people. The precise form of the British panic was shaped by historical contingencies, the coincidence of a rash of 'slasher' films with VCR expansion and the idle speculation of the Bulger trial judge. Australia had the Port Arthur massacre, yet Sweden and New Zealand illustrated how panics could unfold even without such triggers.

Video as a technology, as much as horror films themselves, symbolized moral degeneration and justified renewed moral regulation. The vulnerability of children justified increased censorship but in the long run new laws could not prevent children viewing at home films they could not see in the cinema. Both debates and legislation were largely symbolic, a ritualistic response to change in media technology. 'Every new panic develops as if it were the first time such issues were debated in public, and yet the debates are strikingly similar' (Drotner 1992: 52).

Further reading

Barker, M. (ed.) (1984) *The Video Nasties*. London: Pluto.

Barker, M. and Petley, J. (eds) (1997) *Ill Effects: The Media/Violence Debate*. London: Routledge.

Barlow, G. and Hill, A. (eds) (1985) *Video Violence and Children*. Sevenoaks: Hodder and Stoughton.

Buckingham, D. (1996) *Moving Images: Understanding Children's Emotional Responses to Television*. Manchester: Manchester University Press.

6

SUFFER THE LITTLE CHILDREN: CHILD ABUSE IN FAMILIES

Introduction

In Britain, what would eventually be termed child abuse has three overlapping phases. The earliest involves the dangers of physical abuse to children in the family, starting with the 1973 death of Maria Colwell, with many similar cases in the next 30 years. The other phases are more self-contained. The 'Cleveland affair' of 1987 hinges on possible sexual abuse in the family. The third phase concerns claims in 1990–91 about ritualistic or satanic sexual abuse of children in or around the family. The narrative is constructed and the models applied for each phase separately, before considering issues beyond moral panics and making international comparisons for child abuse as a whole.

The physical abuse narrative

The 'battered baby' syndrome

Following Pfohl (1977), Parton (1985) traces the genesis of the physical abuse problem. The 'battered baby syndrome' was identified in an influential American article by Thomas Kempe and colleagues (1962). In 1963 the first article on the topic appeared in the *British Medical Journal*. The issue attracted paediatricians but public awareness required its adoption by a campaigning organization, which became the National Society for the Prevention of Cruelty to Children. Its tradition of intensive casework was jeopardized by the creation in the early 1970s of new social services departments specializing in child welfare. Child battering provided a new campaigning focus and an area of specialist expertise for the NSPCC, which formed a new specialist unit in 1969. Central government was rapidly sensitized to the issue. Department of Health and Social Security (DHSS) circulars of 1970 and 1972 encouraged local authorities to develop early warning systems and at-risk registers.

However, interest remained confined to specialists until the inquiry into the death of Maria Colwell. Aged 7, Maria Colwell was battered to death in January 1973 by her stepfather, eventually sentenced to eight years for manslaughter. She had been returned to the family after five years in the foster care of her aunt. The trial received very little media coverage. The catalyst was the decision by Sir Keith Joseph, then Minister for Social Security, to hold a public inquiry. Joseph favoured the 'cycle of deprivation' theory, that inadequate parents produced inadequate children in a self-perpetuating cycle. He had been influenced by the Tunbridge Wells Study Group, an ad-hoc grouping of paediatricians, social services directors and academics. Joseph and senior civil servants attended their May 1973 conference on 'Non-Accidental Injury'. Thus was created an alliance of authoritative opinion that action was needed about physical abuse of children.

The inquiry and after

The Colwell inquiry's 1974 report criticized the social work system, sparking media interest. Press coverage managed 'to publicise the problem of "battered babies", criticize social workers and suggest certain people should not be parents, all in one go' (Parton 1985: 93). Stricter supervision of social workers and their families was advocated, the press moving beyond reporting into an 'active, campaigning, crusading role' (Parton 1979: 441). Interest was sustained during 1973–76 and then subsided until further cases and inquiries, such as those of Jasmine Beckford, Tyra Henry and Kimberley Carlile in 1985–87. Altogether there were 30 such cases by 1990 (Hill 1990).

Childcare practice was reformed. Area committees and at-risk registers were strongly recommended in a 1974 DHSS circular on 'non-accidental injury'. Detailed procedures were prescribed, with social workers as key personnel. The Children Act 1975 required decisive social work action to protect children. In the early 1990s further cases – Stephanie Fox, Tracy Wilkinson, Sudio Rouse – received only transient media interest. The political impetus to exploit such cases to attack a 'soft' welfare state had abated; social work's 'significance as a political symbol and metonym has diminished' (Aldridge 1999: 100). But cases still occur. In February 2000

8-year-old Victoria Climbié died, after having been repeatedly tortured by her great-aunt and boyfriend, who were imprisoned for life in January 2001. The family and the social worker were black. In April 2001 a judge was appointed to conduct a public inquiry. Nearly 30 years after Maria Colwell, the cycle was being repeated.

Physical abuse as moral panic

Parton is quite clear that 'reaction to the case and the events that followed . . . took on the proportions of a moral panic' (Parton 1985: 70). He reveals the strategic roles of campaigners and experts, with poor families and their hapless social workers as folk devils. The panic was politically motivated. The inability of social workers to guarantee children's physical safety became a pretext for attacking the principles of the welfare state. Social anxiety among a middle class about moral decline, especially in the family, was activated. Evaluating the processual model, Parton finds Cohen's (1973) too ahistorical, unable to explain why specific issues arise at particular moments; while that of Hall et al. (1978) is too deterministic to recognize strategic intervention. These criticisms will be picked up again in Chapter 10. For the moment, we shall consider whether his basic argument that this was a moral panic is justified.

Processual model

One: emergence: form, novelty, threat. The 'new' problem was the physical abuse of children, initially termed baby battering then non-accidental injury, validated by the inquiry into the Colwell case.

Two: media inventory: stylization and stereotyping; exaggeration, distortion, prediction and symbolization; sensitization; folk devil. Parents were presented as brutal and social workers as hapless but not as folk devils posing a generalized threat to society. Better training and supervision, not punishment, was advocated. Parents made more convincing folk devils but could be identified only in retrospect (Aldridge 1994).

Three: moral entrepreneurs: significant actors; relationship to media; orientations, images and causal explanations. The press demanded reform to remedy the incompetence of social workers but wider ramifications did not attract moral reformers.

Four: experts: who; grounds for claims; media accreditation. Experts influenced the formulation and dissemination of the problem before it attracted media attention but did not encourage vilification of social workers.

Five: coping and resolution: proposed solutions, measures adopted; procedural/legal; effective/symbolic. The legal context of social work was reformed but social workers' powers and parents' rights were largely unaffected.

Six: fade away: timing, recurrence; subsequent status. The Colwell case did fade but others periodically replaced it. In this serial moral panic, inquiries became a ritualistic response.

Seven: legacy: long-term effects; relationship to other issues. The Colwell case had an immediate effect upon childcare law and practice reaching far into the following decades (Hutchinson 1986). Physical abuse was progressively sidelined by sexual abuse.

Attributional model

One: concern: among whom; how widespread; forms of expression. Though intense, this was limited in scope and influence.

Two: hostility; enemy, threat, folk devil. Neither violent parents nor their social workers threatened the moral order of society.

Three: consensus: clarity, among whom, organized opposition. The press and the inquiry found social workers to blame. The profession did not effectively defend itself.

Four: disproportionality: dimensions and implications; claims versus reality. The problem was less disproportionality, since the problem of physical abuse was now being recognized, than distortion. The varying degrees of physical abuse, its causes and the complexities of social work practice were simplified.

Five: volatility: length; speed of emergence and decline. The Colwell issue was short-lived but the general theme of physical abuse was not.

(Six): claims makers: principal claims and counter claims makers; motives and strategies; degree of success. Claims making was not performed in public but within restricted semi-private networks. Nobody tried to estimate its prevalence. The NSPCC emerged as the key pressure group.

The moral panic model does not stand or fall by the existence of folk devils alone but there has to be a clear target for a campaign. This does not appear to be the case with physical abuse.

The sexual abuse narrative: Cleveland

Public recognition of sexual abuse in families scarcely existed until the events in Cleveland in the spring and summer of 1987 (La Fontaine 1990; Kitzinger 1996).

Events at Middlesbrough hospital

The basic facts about Cleveland are contested, though the official inquiry (Butler-Sloss 1988) outlined the main events. Local inter-agency conflict had failed to develop a clear strategy for dealing with child abuse cases in Teesside in the mid-1980s. In June 1986, Sue Richardson was appointed as child abuse consultant to Cleveland County Council Social Services Department. In January 1987 Dr Marietta Higgs was appointed as consultant paediatrician at Middlesbrough General Hospital, joining Dr Geoffrey Wyatt. Both the women felt that child sexual abuse was going unrecognized and expressed their views to Social Services Director Mike Bishop. Higgs had become interested in the reflex anal dilation (RAD) test, an examination of a child's anus purporting to reveal whether sexual penetration had taken place.

From February to June at Middlesbrough Hospital, three 'waves' (Butler-Sloss 1988) of children were diagnosed as having been sexually abused. The first wave lasted from February until early May. The police expressed concern over the use of RAD, the failure to involve the police surgeon and the use of police photographers to gather evidence. Social services lacked the resources to complete follow-up interviews. The second wave of admissions occurred over the second Bank Holiday in late May. The police expressed increasing hostility to Higgs and Richardson. Meetings of a Joint Abuse Working Party broke up in acrimony. The third wave came in June, with alleged abuse of children from a special school and some while in hospital.

On 18 June angry parents besieged the hospital. They formed an action group, aided by local MP Stuart Bell; 202 children were alleged to have been taken into care. The regional health authority set up a panel to investigate the diagnoses. Local police surgeons publicly criticized Higgs and Wyatt. Bell instigated debates in Parliament where he attacked the two doctors. On 7 July he submitted a dossier of evidence to the Minister for Social Services. The government announced that Lord Justice Butler-Sloss would chair an official inquiry.

The Butler-Sloss report

Butler-Sloss delivered her report in July 1988. Confined to issues of management, it clarified some matters of fact. In five months 121 cases of sexual abuse had been diagnosed. Many had been referred on suspicion of child abuse but others had not, including some siblings of the original child patient. Most of the 121 had been separated from their parents, 70 per cent by place of safety orders. However, 98 of the 121 had been returned home by the time of the report. Butler-Sloss was even-handed in her criticism. The doctors were found to have been 'overconfident' in their views, social services to have failed to review procedures and the police to have personalized the issue. Her severest criticisms were reserved for the obduracy of Stuart Bell and some sections of the press. 'The report concluded, in essence, that everyone was to blame' (Jenkins 1992: 141) but did appear to accept that child sexual abuse was a major problem.

The report eschewed consideration of the three specific accusations made against the doctors. The first was that use of the reflex anal dilation test was indiscriminate and uncorroborated; the second that children admitted for other reasons were routinely examined for sexual abuse; and the third that some diagnoses implied children to have been abused while in hospital. These allegations remain contested. In the aftermath, there was a substantial defence of the doctors' actions (Illsley 1989; La Fontaine 1990). Most of the children were originally referred because others suspected abuse. In only 18 of the 121 cases was RAD the only physical symptom and in no case was it the sole source of diagnosis. The regional health authority's panel supported three-quarters of the original diagnoses, in any case only a fraction of the 2700 children were examined by the doctors in five months. Some children involved were subsequently referred back to social services. 'It seems likely that many of them were correctly diagnosed, although adequate proof of the diagnosis was lacking' (La Fontaine 1990: 215–16). This was not the immediate verdict of the media.

Media coverage of Cleveland

The *Daily Mail* broke the story on 23 June under the headline 'Hand Over Your Children, Council Orders Parents of 200 Youngsters'. Other media immediately picked up the story. Coverage lasted a year and was 'extensive and without precedent' (Franklin and Parton 1991: 19). The press portrayed the doctors and social work personnel as part of a 'conspiracy of dogmatic radicals anxious to overthrow society, regardless of the human cost' (Jenkins 1992: 143–4). The essential basis of the statistical claims about child sexual abuse, a survey commissioned by Channel 4 Television (Wilson and Duncan 1985), was derided. Media coverage has been heavily criticized (Illsley 1989; La Fontaine 1990; Franklin and Parton 1991) for its implication that most diagnoses were based on RAD alone; suppression of important points of detail; continuous insistence on using the inaccurate figure of 202 children taken into care; and partisanship in siding with the parents against the doctors. Press coverage was 'sensational, sometimes trivial, both pro and anti parent by disposition, simplistic, often factually inaccurate and eager to scapegoat' (Franklin and Parton 1991: 28–9). Higgs was presented as peculiar: Australian, with a househusband, probably a feminist. The inquiry's findings were systematically misrepresented in the press (Franklin and Parton 1991; Donaldson and O'Brien 1995).

Cleveland as moral panic

Nava (1988: 104) has argued that 'In certain important respects the Cleveland affair can be defined as a moral panic . . . though it may not fit this definition in a predictable way'. Press coverage sided with the traditionalists, overwhelmingly male, who defended the families, as against the radicals, overwhelmingly female, who claimed that a real problem of sexual abuse had been identified. The personal vilification of Dr Higgs ensured that 'the spectre of feminism becomes the folk devil' (Nava 1988: 105). However, the thesis is offered only in general terms. Illsley (1989: 34–5) also selects one aspect, public anxiety, which all sections of the press elicited and expressed. Application of the models may clarify matters.

Processual model

One: emergence: form, novelty, threat. The media-defined problem was doctors and social workers taking children into care on the flimsiest of pretexts in one city. Particular to a time and place, it was not generalizable across society.

Two: media inventory: stylization and stereotyping; exaggeration, distortion, prediction and symbolization; sensitization; folk devil. Individuals were stereotyped but not as folk devils. Details were exaggerated but there was no effort to generalize the problem.

Three: moral entrepreneurs: significant actors; relationship to media; orientations, images and causal explanations. The press led the way but few others followed. Those who might have done, such as the police or the NSPCC, were already implicated.

Four: experts: who; grounds for claims; media accreditation. No experts denounced doctors, social workers or feminists. Medical authority supported most of the consultants' actions. Despite the press bias, Cleveland was a contested issue. Those supporting the doctors (Campbell 1987) were as active as those sympathizing with the parents (Bell 1988). The expert inquiry was inconclusive.

Five: coping and resolution: proposed solutions, measures adopted; procedural/legal; effective/symbolic. The sanctions applied to those involved were professionally serious. Both doctors were moved from paediatrics and social work personnel left but there were no formal disciplinary or legal proceedings.

Six: fade away: timing, recurrence; subsequent status. Cleveland has never been resolved but became a touchstone for subsequent issues. It proved to be the peak of press interest in sexual abuse (Kitzinger and Skidmore 1995).

Seven: legacy: long-term effects; relationship to other issues. Cleveland demonstrated the difficulty of sustaining claims about child sexual abuse within families.

Attributional model

One: concern: among whom; how widespread; forms of expression. Parents and their sympathizers had their concerns endorsed by the press but it remained a local scandal.

Two: hostility; enemy, threat, folk devil. Those culpable were individuals. No wider group could realistically be portrayed as a threat to society.

Three: consensus: clarity, among whom, organized opposition. Cleveland was continuously contested. Press consensus was achieved only by suppressing alternative perspectives.

Four: disproportionality: dimensions and implications; claims versus reality. This does not apply since there was no implication that these professional practices were widespread.

Five: volatility: length; speed of emergence and decline. The original controversy and inquiry report were the two focal points, a year apart. To a case rather than an issue, volatility does not seem to apply.

(Six): claims makers: principal claims and counter claims makers; motives and strategies; degree of success. Claims made by aggrieved parents and their allies forced the inquiry but it was inconclusive.

The Cleveland campaign never realized important conditions of a moral panic, such as generalizable folk devils, intervention by moral entrepreneurs, supportive expert opinion, new punitive measures, consensus of opinion or successful claims making. The implications remained ambiguous. Cleveland appeared to set back recognition of child sexual abuse in the family but in the world of medicine and social work, it continued to gain ground. Unfortunately, it was about to become sidetracked by extreme claims about ritual and satanic abuse.

The ritual abuse narrative

The cases

Towards the end of the 1980s, a new item appeared on the social work agenda: ritualized sexual abuse in families, sometimes with satanic elements. This idea was developed in the social work press and at a series of regional conferences (Clapton 1993). The NSPCC, ChildLine and the Social Services Inspectorate were apparently convinced of its existence (Jenkins 1992). In 1989 a group of adults in an extended family from Nottingham received extensive prison sentences for child abuse. In the next two years, allegations of ritual abuse became rife. In February 1991 in the Scottish Orkney Isles nine children were taken into care in dawn raids. It was alleged that ritual abuse led by a retired church minister had taken place at an abandoned quarry. Parents organized an action committee but social services refused all access to the children. In April the cases came before a Scottish sheriff who dismissed all the claims out of hand, criticizing interviews conducted with the children (Jenkins 1992), though his ruling was eventually overturned in a higher court. The subsequent official inquiry (Clyde 1992) replicated that into Cleveland.

From March to September 1991, 20 children were made wards of court by Rochdale Social Services in northern England on suspicion of ritual sexual abuse. Media coverage began in September when a ban on reports was lifted. The police announced that there would be no criminal charges. Rochdale Council requested a report from the government's Social Services Inspectorate, delivered in October. In March 1993, at the end of a legal hearing, a High Court judge made severe criticisms of Rochdale Social Services, whose director resigned (Aldridge 1994: 72). The Chief Inspector of Constabulary remarked that 'Police have no evidence of rituals or satanic abuse inflicted on children anywhere in England and Wales. A lot of well-intentioned hype has got out of control' (Jenkins 1992: 187).

Media reaction

The press viewed this as another Cleveland, with innocent parents the victims of social workers obsessed with a mythical evil (Aldridge 1990, 1994). This precipitated a new attack on social workers and the NSPCC. Familiar images were recycled of family heartbreak, children damaged in care, dawn raids and social workers susceptible to fundamentalism. The NSPCC switched emphasis from ritual to 'organized' abuse. Social work journals also changed tack. Feminist journalist Beatrix Campbell, almost alone, persisted in the belief (Jenkins 1992). The government commissioned an inquiry by Professor Jean La Fontaine into evidence of ritual abuse.

La Fontaine's inquiry

La Fontaine's review was published in 1994. She defined ritual abuse as 'sexual abuse where there have been allegations of ritual associated with the abuse, whether or not these allegations have been taken any further or tested in the courts' and satanic abuse to imply 'a ritual directed to worship of the devil' (La Fontaine 1994: 3). She examined the evidence in 84 cases. Her conclusions were devastating. No evidence of satanic abuse could be found. In only three cases was there any evidence of ritualistic abuse and then 'only as strategies to achieve the sexual abuse' (La Fontaine 1994: 25). Allegations had been elicited from children by adults using dubious interview techniques. The issue had been defined by Christian fundamentalists and self-appointed experts. La Fontaine deplored an 'obsessional desire' (1994: 31) to root out evil, which not only affected interviewing techniques but also distorted general understanding of sexual abuse.

Ritual abuse as moral panic

Ritual abuse had no basis in reality: 'a panic had been manipulated into existence out of literally nothing' (Jenkins 1992: 187). Jenkins assumes that the 'panic' was generated by social workers and their allies but they later became the focus of attack. Aldridge (1994) suggests that, while physical abuse had not demonized social workers, ritual abuse did. Social workers' 'victimization' of families made them appear more sinister.

> Social workers now more nearly fitted the 'folk devil' description. Among the 'inventory' of their characteristics were dogmatic feminism; gullibility; impetuousness; pathological secretiveness, lack of factual knowledge and of basic techniques, for example conducting an evidentially reliable interview; and a tendency to useless dramatic gestures like dawn raids.
>
> (Aldridge 1994: 212)

However, these are professional and ideological failings, not manifestations of evil. Hence application of the models to ritual abuse produces an argument parallel to that of Cleveland, so closely that we shall review the models only briefly.

Processual model

One: emergence: form, novelty, threat. The defined problem is social workers abusing their powers when seduced by a mythical idea.

Two: media inventory: stylization and stereotyping; exaggeration, distortion, prediction and symbolization; sensitization; folk devil. Social workers were stereotyped as gullible and heavy-handed but not folk devils threatening the social order.

Three: moral entrepreneurs: significant actors; relationship to media; orientations, images and causal explanations. The campaign was limited to the parents and the press.

Four: experts: who; grounds for claims; media accreditation. The main experts were those conducting inquiries about management issues.

Five: coping and resolution: proposed solutions, measures adopted; procedural/legal; effective/symbolic. There was chastisement for individuals, some of whom resigned, but none was formally disciplined nor were any new measures introduced.

Six: fade away: timing, recurrence; subsequent status. Ritual abuse was a one-off although some of its adherents subtly changed their target to 'organized' abuse (Bibby 1996).

Seven: legacy: long-term effects; relationship to other issues. Combined with Cleveland, the long-term effect was to delegitimize all claims about child sexual abuse in families.

Attributional model

One: concern: among whom; how widespread; forms of expression. This was restricted to the press and those involved in official inquiries.

Two: hostility; enemy, threat, folk devil. Social workers could not adequately be made to fit this role.

Three: consensus: clarity, among whom, organized opposition. There was no effective contestation of the inappropriateness of the social work interventions.

Four: disproportionality: dimensions and implications; claims versus reality. No claim was made that these were anything but isolated instances.

Five: volatility: length; speed of emergence and decline. The whole affair lasted 21 months and has not re-emerged since.

(Six): claims makers: principal claims and counter claims makers; motives and strategies; degree of success. The claims were made by the press but not sustained.

Unlike Cleveland, ritual abuse cases were not contested. Even so, the vital ingredients of a moral panic were missing: folk devils, moral entrepreneurs, experts, punitive measures, consensus of opinion and successful claims making. If there is one single reason why neither physical nor sexual abuse of children in families became a moral panic, it is the lack of an appropriate target. Social workers, much less the police and the NSPCC, did not lend themselves to being portrayed as folk devils. They did not undermine the moral order. Franklin and Parton (1991) suggest that the use of moral panic models to analyse child abuse founders on their inability to explain how social workers rather than abusers became the folk devils or how a panic can be based on the proposition that the problem does not exist. The models do indeed fail but, as in the case of AIDS, this is because the events themselves did not approximate to a moral panic. Jenkins' (1992) continuous and loose usage of the term does not seem to be justified.

Beyond moral panics

There are many potential issues beyond moral panics in child abuse, including the enduring effects on childcare law and social work practice, the functions of public inquiries, the rhetoric about childhood and family life and debates about control and supervision of professionals. Most striking is the political construction and interpretation of child abuse, conducted outside the arenas of party politics or public opinion in the organizations of civil society. In moral panic literature, these would all be called claims makers or moral entrepreneurs. These blanket terms seem too simplistic. Provisionally we can divide them into three groups: the advocates of child abuse, their significant audiences and ideologists interpreting child abuse as a political issue.

Advocates

There are three kinds of advocates: professional experts, pressure groups and, for ritual abuse, fundamentalist Christians. There was a progressive decline in the expert validation of child abuse. Physical abuse was endorsed by medical and social work professionals, though inquiries were conducted by lawyers (Dingwall 1986; Parton 1996). Sexual abuse in families was in Cleveland identified by local doctors and social workers, with guarded support from fellow professionals. Ritual abuse was supported by some social workers and self-appointed expert consultants. Their claims were finally discredited by a government nominated anthropological expert. The perceived credibility of the claims made was in direct proportion to the status of the experts supporting them.

The most influential pressure group in the whole child abuse issue was the NSPCC. Despite being implicated in ritual abuse cases in Rochdale, and its Scottish equivalent in the Orkneys, and tenuously arguing that it had only ever alleged 'organized' abuse, it continued its campaigning unabashed. A stream of press releases, reports and campaigns powerfully dramatized child abuse, making the NSPCC 'very involved in developing the vocabulary of "dangerousness" with all its connotations of the identifiable and contain-able (probably working-class) and unchallenged majority (mostly white middle class)' (Aldridge 1994: 157). Other less prominent pressure groups were also active, such as ChildLine, a telephone help service set up in 1986 following a television documentary on child abuse.

The third set of advocates were highly influential in defining the ritual abuse issue, mostly behind the scenes. The British Evangelical Alliance pros-elytized American fundamentalist assertions about the dangers of Satanism. Experts invited to Britain transpired to be religious fundamentalists. Both Jenkins (1992) and La Fontaine (1994) identify such religious groundings to the ritual abuse issue, and admit social workers' susceptibility to religious ideas, yet then deny that this was the root of the problem.

> The study of cases in detail showed that the Evangelical Christian cam-paign against new religious movements has been a powerful influence encouraging the identification of satanic abuse. Despite this, it would be too simple to explain such cases as entirely its product.
>
> (La Fontaine 1994: 31)

This seems excessively generous. The myth of ritual abuse was manu-factured almost entirely by religious fundamentalists. The bizarre nature of their beliefs is obvious; less clear is why anybody endorsed them.

Audiences

Advocates of child abuse directed their arguments less towards the general public than specialist audiences. Politicians responded only fitfully. A much more important audience were influential policy-makers, ministers and civil servants within the DHSS. Their sensitivity to expert and pressure group opinion was evident in the Children Acts of 1975 and 1989, framed by Colwell and Cleveland respectively (Hill 1990). DHSS circulars to local authorities rapidly endorsed each new label: battered children, 'non-accidental injury' and 'child abuse' in the 1970s, then emotional and sexual abuse. Claims making penetrated the inner circles of policy-makers. The other significant audience was the social work profession as a whole. Social services directors actively disseminated information about physical child abuse. The established professional network of conferences, training seminars and articles in the social work press, *Community Care* and *Social Work Today* (Clapton 1993), publicized claims about sexual and ritual abuse. Events in Cleveland were preceded by a 'stunning' symposium on child abuse held at Teesside Polytechnic in 1984 (Dunn 1994). The profession as a whole seemed highly susceptible to new definitions of dangers to children and remarkably unwilling to question the evidence on which they were based. Those resisting or expressing scepticism were termed 'in denial'.

Ideologists

In the public realm child abuse was politicized by conservatives and radicals. For right-wing newspapers like the *Daily Mail*, the issue of child abuse provided an opportunity to perform as 'a consistent advocate of conventional values, notably the patriarchal family and the strong state' (Aldridge 1999: 96). The main targets of its hostility were social workers. Portrayed as alternately ineffective (in physical abuse cases) and authoritarian (in sexual abuse cases), social workers became symbols of a soft welfare state. Often the abuser became a 'marginal figure in media accounts' (Franklin and Parton 1991: 17); the real enemy was social work and what it represented. The press tended to 'focus reporting not on the death of the child, or the criminal trial of the abuser, but overwhelmingly on the proceedings of the committee of enquiry and the publication of the report' (Franklin and Parton 1991: 18).

   This conservative view was countered by feminism, especially over sexual abuse. For feminists, sexual abuse within the family exemplified the extremes of patriarchal exploitation (Smart 1989). A whole edition of the academic journal *Feminist Review* was devoted to child sexual abuse in 1988. Such ideas were disseminated in the social work press and upmarket newspapers, especially by Beatrix Campbell. Jenkins (1992: 199) argues that the result was a 'de facto coalition of feminists and religious fundamentalists' but Atmore (1996: 344) has disputed this attempt to put feminists on a par with the Christian Right. At key moments, notably Cleveland, child abuse became embroiled in this dispute about the politics of the family. It was this, as much as the details of individual cases, which led to contestation over child abuse. But none of this was peculiar to Britain, since child abuse emerged as an issue in other countries as well.

International comparisons

The USA

This chapter has actually been written backwards, since events in the USA prefigured those in the UK. Physical abuse was directly comparable but sexual abuse was located outside the family.

Physical abuse

The pioneering work of Kempe was exploited by the Child Department of the American Humane Association to influence policy-makers (Johnson 1985). By 1967, five years after Kempe et al.'s (1962) article, all 50 states had laws mandating doctors to report all suspicious child abuse. The 1974 Child Protection and Prevention Act provided further incentives for local state laws mandating social workers, educators and the police. Annual allegations of abuse expanded to 1 million in the early 1980s (Nelson 1984; Best 1990) and 2.5 million by 1989 (McDevitt 1996). The 1974 Act was updated by the Child Abuse Prevention and Treatment Act 1988 (Costin et al. 1996). However, President Reagan's dismantling of welfare produced a system unable to deliver minimal protection to children.

Missing children

Murders of young children between 1979 and 1981 provoked massive coverage across the US media. The parents of one child victim, Adam Walsh, were especially active (Fritz and Altheide 1987). It was alleged that 1.5 million children went missing each year, 50,000 abducted by strangers. Following Congressional hearings during 1981–82, two new federal laws were passed unanimously. The Missing Children's Act 1982 extended the role of the Federal Bureau of Investigation (FBI) in tracing missing children. The Missing Children's Assistance Act 1983 established a National Center for Missing and Exploited Children. Pictures of missing children appeared on television, in the press, at gas stations, in shopping malls and on milk cartons. A 1984 nationally networked docudrama, 'Adam', heightened awareness. However, from 1985 onwards claims were challenged in the print media. New Congressional hearings revealed statistical claims as dubious. Revised annual estimates now suggested that between 50 and 100 children, mainly teenagers, were murdered by abductors (Putnam 1996).

Satanic/ritual abuse

In 1983 a 2-year-old child at the McMartin Preschool in Manhattan Beach, California made a statement which social workers interpreted as an allegation of satanic sexual abuse by carers; 369 current and past children at the centre had allegedly been victims. Despite naming politicians and television stars as abusers and providing bizarre accounts of rituals, children were believed. Extensive local and then national press coverage provoked further allegations elsewhere. All told, over 100 day care centres were investigated nationally between 1983 and 1991. The trials which followed were lengthy, with most initial convictions overturned on appeal. Alleged abusers contested the allegations in the media and the courts. As in the case of missing children, opinion slowly turned against the claims makers and no allegations were made after 1991.

Moral panic analysis
All these phases have been exhaustively analysed within the constructionist position outlined in Chapter 2. Best (1990) argues that claims about physical abuse were successful because the reforms were institutionalized and generalized; missing children claims were temporarily successful but could not be sustained; and satanic abuse, initially successful, eventually foundered under legal and public challenges. The latter two appeared to be moral panics, eventually discredited but not before significant legal reforms. Missing children claims succeeded because of skilled claims makers enlisting the help of the media (Fritz and Altheide 1987), the emotional appeal of the issue and the lack of opposition (Gentry 1988). For Jenkins and Maier-Katkin (1992: 62) the satanic scare consisted of a 'tissue of improbable charges' from 'unreliable witnesses' creating a 'classic moral panic'. Religious fundamentalist claims were endorsed by social work and mental health professionals, psychotherapists, lawyers and police officers (Bromley 1991; Richardson et al. 1991a; deYoung 1998). Claims continued at conferences of feminists and childcare workers, despite lack of evidence (Putnam 1996). DeYoung (1998) suggests that, though the moral panic model fits in broad terms, it cannot account for folk devils fighting back, divided public opinion and ambiguous resolution.

Though the themes of child abuse were similar in the USA compared with Britain, the events were not. There were no dramatic cases of children forcibly removed from their families, no immediate disputes among expert authorities, no official inquiries. American claims makers had more organization, skills and credibility. The whole cultural climate seemed more susceptible to the acceptance of outrageous claims. Child abuse issues could therefore more easily assume the form of moral panics.

Other countries

Physical abuse

Two cases of physical child abuse have been documented in Australia, following the US and UK examples (O'Donnell and Craney 1982). Carment (1987: 7) has detailed a three-month 'tide of outraged concern' over physical abuse in Sydney, New South Wales in late 1986. Police called to a house fire found grossly neglected children. The parents were arrested and charged with grievous bodily harm. Double-page spreads in the local evening tabloid press wildly exaggerated estimates of abuse and mythologized the 'monster' parents, though the press rapidly lost interest. In 1990, in Melbourne, Victoria, 2-year-old Daniel Valerio died after repeated beatings by his stepfather (Goddard and Liddell 1995). The media focused on continual failures by child protection services, the police and doctors to respond to repeated referrals. Initial interest was low but expanded over three years with an inquiry, two trials and an inquest. In 1993 the *Herald Sun* newspaper successfully campaigned for a state mandatory reporting law.

Sexual abuse

The Cleveland case had an almost exact parallel in the Netherlands in the same year: a female paediatrician using controversial diagnostic techniques, especially the anatomical doll, to identify increasing numbers of sexually abused children; a parents' organization resisting the claims and attracting media attention; an official inquiry confined to matters of management; vilification of the doctor as a moral zealot (Edwards and Soetenhorst-de Savornin Lohman 1994). Atmore (1991, 1996) studied two New Zealand controversies about child abuse in 1998–99. The first concerned claims made in a Telethon promotion that one in four girls and one in ten boys were victims of sexual abuse. Newspapers attacked the source, the Mental Health Foundation, as dominated by 'feminist theories of child sexual abuse, and "militant" feminist child protection advocates' (Atmore 1996: 338), with lesbian officials. The second story concerned the Spence family. Christchurch hospital diagnosed a young girl as having been sexually abused by her father. For the media this was a clear case of an innocent family victimized by state professionals with their own distorted agendas. In 1992 Australia had its own ritual abuse case when dawn raids in Victoria and New South Wales removed children from a religious group The Children of God. The children were quickly returned and no further action taken (Scott 1995). Canada was fertile ground for the accusations of satanic abuse cases in the late 1980s (Lippert 1990).

Overview

Three observations may be made about the child abuse issue. First, it is extraordinarily difficult to gain acceptance for the idea that the family is the primary site of child abuse. Any such assertion is immediately contested. Policy interventions provoke opposition. Allegedly unjustified interventions by social workers in families provoke the press into an emotive defence of innocent parents against political targets, agents of the state or feminist ideas. The problem of abuse is overwhelmed by discourses about the sanctity of family life.

Second, there is the term 'child abuse' itself. Like drug abuse (Goode 1969), child abuse now defies definition, incorporating as it does physical, emotional and sexual maltreatment of children. The prevalence and causes of each particular form, physical abuse being associated with social deprivation while sexual abuse is not, is suppressed by a blanket term which 'obscures important nuances of psycho-social reality' (Carment 1987: 34). Its cluster of connotations about threats to children obscures recognition of the most frequent forms, perpetrators and places of 'abuse'.

The third aspect is the politically motivated selection of targets for media campaigns. Abusers, adults in family households, are not excoriated. Their deviance is taken for granted, while critical attention is focused on health, social work and police personnel who have failed to prevent abuse. Such campaigns cannot easily convert into moral panics because such professional groupings are not easily portrayed as threats to the moral order. They also have the resources to contest such definitions. For all these reasons, it is inherently more believable for the source of abuse to be outside the family. That is why the 'ideal' abuser is the predatory stranger. All the complexities around abuse in families would ultimately be resolved by concentrating on the paedophile, the subject of the next chapter.

Further reading

Aldridge, M. (1994) *Making Social Work News*. London: Routledge.
Franklin, B. and Parton, N. (eds) (1991) *Social Work, the Media and Public Relations*. London: Routledge.
Jenkins, P. (1992) *Intimate Enemies: Moral Panics in Contemporary Great Britain*. New York: Aldine de Gruyter.
Parton, N. (1985) *The Politics of Child Abuse*. London: Macmillan.

7

MONSTROUS IDEAS: PAEDOPHILIA

Introduction

Presenting and analysing paedophilia as a public issue in the UK in the 1990s pose special problems. Since there are few secondary sources for the UK, a narrative has to be constructed from primary sources. The basis for this chapter is a CD-ROM search of *The Times* from 1990 to 2001 and the *Daily Mail* from 1993 to 2001 for all articles containing the word 'paedophile'. Its appearance is a matter of editorial discretion, used rarely until the 1990s and then inconsistently.

Terms and images used earlier are indicated by Soothill and Walby (1991). They studied sex crime coverage in the British press, especially during 1985. Four findings are relevant here. First, the press used a restricted set of labels to describe offenders, with sex 'monster', 'beast' or 'fiend' the most common. Second, attempts to situate physical and sexual abuse of children in the family were discounted, the press concentrating on dangers posed by predators. 'Indeed, in the best of all possible worlds, all rapes and sexual assaults would be committed by just a few sexual maniacs and the press could then help to orchestrate the national search against these declared aliens in our midst' (Soothill and Walby 1991: 37). Third, serial murders of children were increasingly important. Fourth, there was discussion of a register of sex offenders, following a sexually motivated murder in 1984. Considered in March 1985, the Home Office eventually rejected in July as unnecessary, since the police would vet those working with children by using a new computer database. The word 'paedophile' does not appear in this study but its related themes do: the extremity of language, the concentration on predators, the newsworthiness of child murders and the debate over a register. All established parts of the press discourse about sexual abuse of children by the mid-1980s, they would be condensed into the figure of the paedophile.

The paedophilia narrative

Jenkins (1992: 71) outlines how 'from the late 1970s on, the image of the rather pathetic child molester would be fundamentally altered into a new and far more threatening stereotype: the sophisticated and well-organized paedophile'. He identifies two early phases in the emergence of the paedophile issue up to 1990. Figure 7.1 shows the quarterly figures of paedophile-related stories in *The Times*, *Sunday Times*, *Daily Mail* and the *Mail on Sunday* from 1990 to 2001. Its peaks and troughs indicate four further phases emerge to supplement Jenkins' two. The narrative is structured around these six phases.

Phase 1: the 'paedophile' emerges, 1976–82

In this phase, the term paedophile is introduced and linked to child pornography, organization into rings and conspiracies among social elites. 'Paedophile' is not in standard dictionaries before 1973 or in the *Times* index before 1977. 'The emergence of the term and its image can be precisely dated to debates that occurred in 1977 and 1978' (Jenkins 1992: 73). Three events were important. First, the foundation of the Paedophile Information

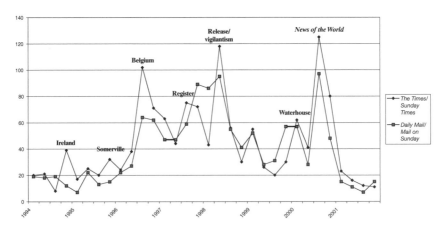

Figure 7.1 Paedophile-related stories by quarter, 1994–2001

Exchange in 1974 to proclaim the 'rights' of paedophiles both disseminated the word and associated it with organized activity. Second, a campaign against pornography, led by the NVLA, secured the Protection of Children Act 1978, making it a criminal offence to produce, import or sell child pornography. Third, a series of high-profile court cases established 'the image of upper-class perverts who were concealed by their colleagues' (Jenkins 1992: 78).

Phase 2: rings and murders, 1983–89

In these years, paedophiles are associated with the organized abduction and murder of children. In 1986 the police launched a national investigation 'Operation Stranger' into 14 children murdered or missing between 1978 and 1986, reinforced by a police operation against child sex rings in London 1987. Under the Criminal Justice Act 1988, possession of child pornography became a criminal offence, to enforce which the Metropolitan Police formed a Child Pornography Squad. In 1989 four men, including Sidney Cooke and Robert Oliver, were given lengthy sentences for the manslaughter of Jason Swift, a teenage male prostitute killed during a 'homosexual orgy'. By the end of the decade the paedophile threat was well established.

> The danger was no longer confined to London and the cities: it could strike at any time, in any village or suburb, and no amount of street-proofing could safeguard children from abduction, assault or murder. The figure of the paedophile had become one of the most terrifying folk-devils imagined in recent British history.
>
> (Jenkins 1992: 99)

Phase 3: a dormant issue, early 1990 to late 1994

The use of 'paedophile' terminology in news stories from 1990 to 1993, barely once a week, was much rarer than it would later become (Table 7.1). In retrospect, this is extraordinary for there were two major instances of paedophile crimes. The first was the case of Robert Black (Wyre and Tate 1995). In August 1990 he was sentenced to life imprisonment for kidnapping and sexually assaulting a 6-year-old girl near Edinburgh. In March 1992 he was charged with four other abductions and murders of young girls in the 1980s. Tried and found guilty in May 1994, he received ten life sentences, with a minimum of 35 years in prison. Black, who had been committing offences for over 30 years since the age of 16, was a serial paedophile killer. The trials were reported but there was no media

Table 7.1   Paedophile-related stories in *The Times/Sunday Times* and *Daily Mail/Mail on Sunday*, 1990 to mid-1994

	The Times/Sunday Times	*Daily Mail/Mail on Sunday*
1990		
January–June	32	n/a
July–December	15	n/a
1991		
January–June	12	n/a
July–December	16	n/a
1992		
January–June	16	n/a
July–December	11	n/a
1993		
January–June	29	11
July–December	15	18
1994		
January–June	41	37

campaign or policy debate, despite glaring failures by the court, probation and police services.

The second case was that of Frank Beck (Aldridge 1995). In November 1991 he was convicted of 17 charges of rape, buggery and sexual assault against both girls and boys and some staff in Leicestershire local authority homes where he had worked for 13 years. Despite numerous complaints, the council and police took years to compile adequate evidence. The press showed little interest, even in the outcomes of three separate inquiries. Aldridge (1999: 101) argues that this was because 'he raised too many questions about the solidity of the social and institutional order'. Cases from other nations would not be so neglected.

Phase 4: Ireland and Belgium, mid-1994 to mid-1997

The first peak in the use of the 'paedophile' label, mainly in the upmarket press, arose from events in Ireland (Table 7.2). The ruling coalition fell apart in November 1994 when Taoiseach Albert Reynolds persisted in attempts to appoint Harry Whelehan as Attorney-General. Whelehan had failed to

Table 7.2   Paedophile-related stories in *The Times/Sunday Times* and *Daily Mail/Mail on Sunday*, mid-1994 to mid-1997

	The Times/Sunday Times	Daily Mail/Mail on Sunday
1994		
July–December	47	31
1995		
January–June	42	29
July–December	52	28
1996		
January–June	62	49
July–December	173	126
1997		
January–June	107	94

extradite to Northern Ireland a Catholic priest, Brendan Smyth, wanted for sexual offences against children. The implications for Irish politics and the Roman Catholic Church were explored for several months. A brief renewal of interest occurred with the arrest of television newscaster Julia Somerville in November 1995. Photographs of her naked daughter in the bath were passed by the film processors to the police, who eventually exonerated her.

A second and much bigger surge in coverage arose from events in Belgium in the autumn of 1996. A released paedophile, Marc Dutroux, was arrested and charged with a series of brutal child murders. High-ranking politicians and civil servants were implicated in covering up the case and paedophile networks. The case became symbolic. In a *Times* editorial (22 August 1996), the Dutroux case, linked to sexual killers Rosemary and Fred West and the recent Dunblane massacre, becomes evidence of 'the unfolding horror' of 'behaviour lower than beasts'. Definition of the issue is not complex. 'Paedophilia is of a different order from most other crime, not just in its capacity to shock but in the pathology of its perpetrators'. Compared with other criminals, 'paedophiles follow a different pattern, closer to that of other addicts and little moved by social pressure or moral restraint'. Paedophiles are 'obsessive and compulsive'; psychological treatment is ineffective. A scheme of compulsory registration is justified but public attitudes must be reviewed. 'The nation's values insufficiently safeguard the nation's innocents'. By mid-1996 the unique threat posed by 'paedophiles' is well established.

Subsequent events are fitted into this framework. In September 1996 the government announced an inquiry into abuse in North Wales children's homes in the 1970s and 1980s. In October, licensing of handguns was debated following the Dunblane massacre. The government then announced its intention to take over a Private Member's Bill to inaugurate a register of convicted sex offenders in a Sex Offenders Act, interpreted as political opportunism. Receiving all party support, the Bill was published in February 1997. Local newspapers naming paedophiles in their area provoked community protests. The Home Office calculated that, of 230,000 past sex offenders, 110,000 would have qualified for the new register. Father Brendan Smyth, the priest at the centre of the Irish scandal, was sentenced to 12 years for sexual offences against children.

Phase 5: legal and illegal reactions, mid-1997 to mid-2000

This phase is dominated by legal change and 'vigilantism' (Table 7.3). The Sex Offenders Act, passed in March 1997, came into force on 1 September, shortly after the election of a Labour government. The efficacy of the sex offenders register dominated coverage. Access was restricted to the police and professionals. Convicted paedophile Robert Oliver was released in November. Protests when he was housed in Swindon forced him to take refuge in Brighton police station.

Table 7.3 Paedophile-related stories in *The Times/Sunday Times* and *Daily Mail/Mail on Sunday*, mid-1997 to mid-2000

	The Times/Sunday Times	Daily Mail/Mail on Sunday
1997		
July–December	147	148
1998		
January–June	161	181
July–December	86	96
1999		
January–June	81	80
July–December	50	88
2000		
January–June	103	85

Table 7.4   Daily Mail/Mail on Sunday article headlines, March 1998

---

1   Call to house the child abusers
2   Protest as sex killer is moved
3   Suspended
4   Police chief tells of ordeal as cub scout
5   Beyond reform or redemption*
6   How can they call this justice? He was Lavinia Tildesley's baby, her youngest child. 'My Mark' she called him. Next month, the paedophile who killed him will walk free
7   For our children's sake, keep these men in prison: Six dangerous paedophiles prepare for freedom
8   Six evil predators bound for freedom: Commentary; The *Daily Mail* has long campaigned against the release of violent paedophiles. Now people's worst fears are coming true
9   For the sake of the children*
10 Paedophiles move with cunning stealth. They share addresses, share networks, share their victims. No family should feel safe, however respectable
11 How The Web Was Won: Where's the most lawless place on earth? Answer: cyberspace
12 Electronic tags for up to 30,000 offenders
13 Right to know*
14 Nowhere to hide for paedophiles as judges back police
15 Tarnished gold muddle
16 Sick 'research' leads to probation internet ban on student of porn traced by FBI
17 Keep this man in prison: Campaign grows to ensure that child killer is never released
18 Vigilante warning as parents wait for paedophile's return
19 2,000 letters herald return of paedophile
20 Pervert wants to live next door to little girl he raped
21 Gross betrayal of the public interest*
22 Lolita film release fury: Shocking movie will encourage child abuse, say critics
23 This soft-porn travesty
24 Police watch will leave child sex killer with no place to hide
25 Four more danger men flock to last resort for perverts

Note: *editorials (four)

At the height of this phase, the *Daily Mail* is less reporting paedophile news than creating it. Its tenor can be gauged from the headlines of the 25 main articles on paedophilia in March 1998 (Table 7.4).

The *Daily Mail*'s paedophile vocabulary is limited and repetitive. A few adjectives – 'dangerous', 'perverted', 'degraded', 'lacking remorse' and 'cunning' – and even fewer nouns – sex offenders and child sex killer – are enough. Extending its long-standing campaign against the release of paedophiles, a *Mail* editorial (13 March 1998) asks 'What kind of law is it that plays Russian roulette with the lives of our children?' The only solution is to ensure that paedophiles are locked up for life. A *Mail* story on 4 April 1998 is indicative: 'Beyond belief . . . Within 48 hours this vile paedophile and killer will be walking the streets again – all because of a huge legal blunder'. Sidney Cooke cannot hide since the 'hatred and loathing of an entire nation will fall on him as mercilessly as he once fell on the defenceless bodies of a series of children.' Though disavowing vigilantism, the *Mail* informed its public on 18 April that Cooke 'will spend the weekend in the Yeovil area before being transferred to Bristol on Monday'. Consequent local protests were condemned as thuggery, undermining the cause of 'decent, law-abiding people' who are 'genuinely fearful'.

With the coverage of the register and the vigilante action against Oliver and Cooke paedophile coverage seemed to have peaked, briefly revived by a few events: the enforced resignation of the Chief Constable of the Grampian police after the bungle of a paedophile murder case, paedophile activity in Ashworth Special Hospital and, most intensely, publication of the Waterhouse report into organized abuse in North Wales children's homes. But as 2000 wore on, paedophilia was slowly declining as an issue, only to erupt yet again in the summer.

Phase 6: the News of the World *campaign, mid-2000 to end 2001*

In 2000 paedophile coverage reached unprecedented heights, following the sexual murder of a child (Table 7.5). A detailed analysis is available elsewhere (Critcher 2002; Silverman and Wilson 2002). On Monday 17 July 2000 the naked body was discovered of 8-year-old Sarah Payne, who had been missing for two weeks. Staying with her grandparents, she had gone to

Table 7.5 Paedophile-related stories in *The Times/Sunday Times* and *Daily Mail/ Mail on Sunday*, mid-2000 to end 2001

	The Times/Sunday Times	*Daily Mail/Mail on Sunday*
2000		
July–December	205	145
2001		
January–June	39	26
July–December	23	22

play in a field with her older brothers. Setting off alone to return to her grandparents' home, she was never seen alive again. Scraps of her clothing were found and the police appealed for information. Suspects were interviewed, one several times, but no immediate arrest was made. This was front-page news, defined unequivocally in the press as a paedophile murder.

On 23 July, six days after the body's discovery, the *News of the World* (*NOTW*) published an edition which would provoke weeks of controversy. *NOTW* had obtained the files of the Scouts Association containing information about convicted sex offenders and declared its intention to name and shame 100,000 known paedophiles. The photographs, offences and the current location of 49 largely male paedophiles were detailed. The main demand was that paedophiles sentenced to life should never be released. Daily papers were initially hostile or indifferent to the *NOTW* campaign. They cited authoritative sources – the Association of Chief Police Officers (ACPO), the National Association for the Care and Resettlement of Offenders (NACRO) and Shadow Home Secretary Anne Widdecombe – as opposing the *NOTW* campaign which would increase public anxiety, vigilantism and paedophile evasion of the register. The same week (27 July) the government published a consultation document on reform of sexual offence laws, which proposed new offences of persistent child abuse, voyeurism, trafficking for the purposes of sexual exploitation and familial sexual abuse, to carry much heavier sentences. Briefly noted in the press, the report was largely ignored in the ongoing debate.

The second *NOTW* campaigning edition (30 July) advocated 'every parent's right to know if there is a convicted paedophile living in their neighbourhood' as well as 'real' life sentences. A law requiring community notification already existed in the USA, known as Megan's Law after a child victim. As its equivalent, the paper now demanded a 'Sarah's Law' in the UK. Another set of offenders were named and shamed. A meeting was scheduled between *NOTW* and ACPO, NACRO, the Association of Chief Officers of Probation (ACOP) and the NSPCC, though without government representatives. The meeting produced a compromise. *NOTW*'s demands were subtly reworded and qualified. Access would be restricted to 'responsible' members of the public, with stiff penalties for misuse. Indeterminate detention was one sentencing option. In return for all parties signing up to 'Sarah's Charter', *NOTW* agreed to abandon its naming and shaming campaign. However, from 4 August crowds gathered nightly on the Paulsgrove council estate in Portsmouth. Initially targeting the house of Victor Burnett, named by *NOTW*, they moved on to picket residences of other alleged paedophiles. Cars were set alight and slogans daubed on houses. The press predictably condemned the 'mob violence' of vigilantism (Lawler 2002).

The government still refused public access to the register. The Paulsgrove protest was called off after a week of night marches. In early September, Sarah Payne's parents met Home Office Minister Paul Boateng, handing him the *NOTW*'s petition for Sarah's Law, with 700,000 signatures. Next day Home Secretary Jack Straw announced a package of measures, conceding most of the demands in Sarah's Charter but rejecting 'controlled access' to the register. The *NOTW* expressed its disappointment on 17 September and resolved to continue the campaign but its momentum had temporarily been lost. The whole episode produced the highest ever figures for 'paedophile' stories in both *The Times* and the *Daily Mail*.

On 12 December 2001, 14 months later, after a 19-day trial, Roy Whiting was convicted of the kidnap and murder of Sarah Payne and sentenced to life imprisonment without parole. Virtually every daily newspaper made this the front-page lead, with extensive inside feature articles and masses of photographs of the perpetrator, the victim and her family. Whiting had been convicted five years previously of abducting and sexually assaulting a 9-year-old girl. Sentenced to four years, he had served two and a half. The press expressed outrage. Three other issues were debated. Few papers advocated Sarah's Law but all now supported 'real' life sentences. On whether previous offences should be disclosed in court, press opinion was mixed.

The *News of the World* of 16 December was triumphalist. It also had a new scoop: the Metropolitan Police had asked it to publish the photographs of four convicted paedophiles missing from the Sexual Offender Register. A double-page spread reviewed the outcome of the campaign. Of the 14 measures advocated in Sarah's Charter only one – controlled access to the register – had not been achieved, confirmed in a signed article by Home Secretary David Blunkett. In the following week, Deputy Prime Minister John Prescott controversially praised the *NOTW* campaign. In a radio interview, the judge at Whiting's original trial defended his sentence. In a further radio interview broadcast on 26 December 2001, Lord Chief Justice Woolf, Britain's senior law officer, supported imprisoning suspected paedophiles. By the beginning of 2002, the issue had finally abated. In mid-January, the *Guardian* reported government intentions to implement the recommendations of the Sex Offences Review.

Overview

This narrative has stressed the importance to constructing paedophilia of the **key events** providing the peaks on Figure 7.1: Ireland, Somerville, Belgium, the register, paedophile releases, the Waterhouse inquiry and the *News of the World* campaign. The narrative progressively produces its own events, as

Table 7.6   Main paedophile stories in *The Times/Sunday Times*, 15 key months 1994–98

Criminal cases	58
Sex Offenders Act	51
Media representations	46
Prison releases	39
Belgium	38
Ireland	33
Sex tourism	15
Somerville	7
Catholic priests	2
Total	289

media and public reactions themselves become news. Other themes embedded in the narrative, not immediately obvious, are revealed by a content analysis of the main stories in *The Times* in fifteen crucial months in the five years from 1994 to 1998 (Table 7.6).

The Times was sensitized to paedophile crimes: arrests, trials, suicides, escapes. The other prominent topic embedded in the narrative was controversy over media representations with paedophiliac themes: films, novels, fashion models and the Internet. Two topics – sex tourism and Catholic priests – appeared rarely. We now consider how far the main narrative and subsidiary themes constituted a moral panic.

Applying the models

Moral panic analysis has seldom been applied to paedophilia. Webster (1998) claims that there was a moral panic over 'organized' abuse in children's homes, with residential workers as the folk devil. Collier (2001) has argued that paedophilia fits many elements of moral panic theory, though paedophiles were not classic folk devils because they were not 'vulnerable' or 'unfairly maligned'. Kitzinger (1999) argues that moral panic analysis is unhelpful because it is media centric, implies that the panic is unjustified and assumes it is supported by the state. The immediate problem is the prolonged nature of the panic. Its origins are in the 1970s, with high points throughout the 1990s and beyond. It should be a conclusion but has to be a starting point that paedophilia should be tested as a serial moral panic. The models will be applied to the 'panic' as a whole.

Processual model

One: emergence: form, novelty, threat. As a new name for an old crime, 'paedophile' condensed a wide range of connotations. Obessive, dangerous, incurable and predatory, paedophiles threatened any child anywhere at any time.

Two: media inventory: stylization and stereotyping; exaggeration, distortion, prediction and symbolization; sensitization; folk devil. The paedophile is an unequivocal folk devil: inherently evil and incapable of reform; cunning and devious; operating on secret networks; posing a constant threat to all children. Estimates of past offenders enable the degree of threat to be exaggerated. Newspaper sensitization is evident in the attention paid to routine crime and controversies over media representations.

Three: moral entrepreneurs: significant actors; relationship to media; orientations, images and causal explanations. Child pressure groups are important early on and the police throughout but the press reaction proceeds with little reference to other claims makers. The Sex Offenders Act 1997 is interpreted as political opportunism. The roll call of groups responding to the *NOTW* campaign (ACOP, ACPO, NACRO, NSPCC) may indicate who most influenced government policy. All shared the same image of the paedophile.

Four: experts: who; grounds for claims; media accreditation. There is no clear hierarchy of expertise on this issue. Claims makers on child abuse, such as the NSPCC, assume the mantle of expertise. Experts are sought by upmarket papers like *The Times* from authoritative sources, psychologists or lawyers who have chaired inquiries, or psychiatrists and specialist therapists. The *Daily Mail* ignores all expertise since it already knows what the problem is.

Five: coping and resolution: proposed solutions, measures adopted; procedural/legal; effective/symbolic. The Sex Offenders Act 1997 was an unprecedented piece of legislation, justified by the exceptional nature of the crime. How far the register actually increased supervision of offenders within the community remains controversial. Soothill and Francis (1998: 292) see it as 'a political gesture which is probably misleading, potentially mischievous and almost certainly mistaken'. Concessions made to the *NOTW* campaign anticipated radical changes in sentencing policy.

Six: fade away: timing, recurrence; subsequent status. Paedophilia is a recurrent, serial panic. A permanent focus of news and policy-making, it is likely to be reactivated at any time.

Seven: legacy: long-term effects; relationship to other issues. Paedophilia may have long-term effects on penal policy, as the government contemplates indefinite attention for prisoners with a 'severe personality disorder'. 'It remains to be seen whether policies designed for a small number of sex offenders may have a much wider impact on polices directed toward other criminals, juvenile delinquents, and the mentally ill' (Jenkins 1998: 236).

Attributional model

One: concern: among whom; how widespread; forms of expression. Vigilantism and the *NOTW* petition indicated an unusual degree of concern among the general public, provoked by claims making and media coverage. No other issue considered in this book provoked such intensive and extensive concern.

Two: hostility; enemy, threat, folk devil. The paedophile is constructed as a known and universal enemy, a threat to all children. The paedophile is personified in the pictures and criminal records of figures like Sidney Cooke and those named and shamed in the local and national press. Sub-humans, paedophiles should be permanently removed from society.

Three: consensus: clarity, among whom, organized opposition. There is a clear consensus about who paedophiles are, what they represent and what action should be taken about them. There is no significant opposition.

Four: disproportionality: dimensions and implications; claims versus reality. Disproportionality is a matter of perspective. Sexual abuse or murder of children is most prevalent in and around the family. The 'paedophile' figure actively misrepresents the dimensions and sources of threats to children. Yet any murder of a child by a known sex offender is a legitimate justification for exceptional preventive measures. Marshall (1998) estimated that by 1993, 100,000 men had committed offences which would have required registration under the Sex Offenders Act 1997. It is the distortion of the nature of the issue, rather than its disproportionality, which is important.

Five: volatility: length; speed of emergence and decline. Individual episodes are volatile but the issue a permanent focus.

(Six): claims makers: principal claims and counter claims makers; motives and strategies; degree of success. Early claims making by pressure groups and the police had little immediate effect, despite serious and serial sexual crimes. Only after Dutroux and Dunblane did the issue achieve prominence, intensifying because of legislation and vigilantism, then the Sarah Payne case. Pressure groups, local and national newspapers, politicians and policymakers reinforced each other's concerns with no dissenting voices.

Overview

Paedophilia meets virtually all the criteria in both models. It resolved ambiguities apparent around sexual abuse in the home. In the paedophile was finally found the figure who was indisputably guilty, evidence of whose crimes was incontrovertible, the nature of whose distorted personality was self-evident. Yet even this transparent issue is not wholly caught by the models. In the processual model of moral panics, the problem emerges, is stereotyped and moralized about, experts are cited, new laws passed and the problem fades away. Paedophilia does not follow this precise sequence. The label of 'paedophile' emerges well before the panic crystallizes: it is already available for mobilization. The main key event, the murder of Sarah Payne, happens towards the end rather than at the beginning of the panic. The political origins of the Sex Offenders Act 1997 appear to lie in the policy community, including the police. It appears alongside, rather than as a result of, the panic. Its alleged inadequacy then becomes the source of new campaigning, eventually placated by changes to legal procedures and promises of new legislation. This serial moral panic feeds upon itself, with the media implicated in provoking the vigilante action then used to justify media concern. Moral panic models may indicate the general processes at work, but cannot account for the precise chronology, the events which take on symbolic power or the cumulative development of the definition of the issue. There are also inevitably issues beyond moral panic analysis.

Beyond moral panics

Lest there be any mistake, it has not been the argument of this chapter that paedophilia is a fabrication. Before the 1990s the legal system had failed to acknowledge the special nature of sexual offences against children. Men whose sexual attraction to children makes them dangerous may need to be removed from the community or strictly supervised within it. The problem with the construction of paedophilia is that it misrecognizes the nature of demonstrably real threats to children's safety. Children are more likely to be harmed by accidents than adult violence (McNeish and Roberts 1995). Most sexual abuse and murder of children occurs in or around the family (La Fontaine 1990; Grubin 1998; Pritchard and Bagley 2001). Stranger danger appears to be the single biggest worry for parents (McNeish and Roberts 1995) but such fear is not necessarily accurate or appropriate. Constructing a single homogeneous category of the 'paedophile' prevents understanding the variable nature of sexual offenders and the dangers they pose

(Wyre and Tate 1995; Soothill et al. 1998, 2000; Hood et al. 2002). Male sexual offenders with a previous record of violent offences as well as abuse – 'multi-criminal child abusers' – appear to be particularly dangerous (Pritchard and Bagley 2001). A more precise definition of paedophilia would be confined to those attracted to children lacking secondary sexual characteristics (Ames and Huston 1990). Actual threats to children and the nature of sexual offenders are obscured, not clarified, by blanket use of the term 'paedophilia'.

Moral panic analysis does help to understand how and why such distortions happen; the case of a paedophilia fits both models more closely than any other example inside or outside this book. Yet, though a necessary starting point, it is never a sufficient explanation. Two issues arise beyond moral panics: first, how the paedophile discourse was constructed in the national public arena, and second, the specific role played by local publics and media in expressing and activating hostility towards paedophiles.

The paedophile discourse

The effects of the discourse about paedophilia have been clearly specified. Kitzinger (1999: 207) argues that it 'locates dangerousness in a few aberrant individuals who can be metaphorically (if not literally) excluded from society', obscuring the family as a site of sexual violence. The term diverts attention away from 'the recognition of abusers as ordinary men' towards 'a small minority who are fundamentally different from most men' (Kelly 1996: 45). Redfern (1997) notes that parents cannot by definition be paedophiles, so confirming the threat as located outside the family. There have been fewer attempts to explore precisely how this discourse was constructed. A remarkable attempt appeared inside the press by Matthew Parris. Writing in *The Times* in April 1998 he deconstructed the word which 'lends the patina of science to a category so wide as to be meaningless'. It is a 'scary name', 'with a medical ring, but with just a hint of suppressed hysteria'. The 'characteristic' becomes 'the name of the person who exhibits it' who is 'depersonalized, robbed of the ability to be more than his condition' or to cast it off. 'A few people, completely, are psychopaths; the rest, completely, are not'.

An academic deconstruction has been undertaken by Collier (2001), who suggests that the paedophile embodies a particular conception of dangerousness, unnerving because, while the danger he represents is known, exactly who he might be is not. Relating this fear to the psychology of risk society (further discussed in Chapter 12) and shifting expectations of masculinity, Collier sees the paedophilia discourse as an index of uncertainty about the meaning of society and the place of men within it. A more straight-forward explanation may be available. The paedophile discourse is primarily a discourse of evil. In a reflective piece in the *Sunday Times* in May 1998, Brian Appleyard discovered the roots of the paedophile hysteria in 'a need for evil'. In place of political or racial enemies, we light upon one which attacks innocence. 'Child abuse becomes, therefore, the only absolute evil.' The status as evil is more than simple deviance. The language of the paedophile discourse is replete with images of evil: monsters, sex maniacs, beasts, perverts, twisted, weirdo, depraved. If paedophiles are less than human, then complexity can be denied. 'If paedophiles are literally "evil personified", then such evil can be exorcised by the exclusion of these individuals from society' (Kitzinger 1999: 218). This is not an inevitable construction. Men committing sexual offences could be regarded as sick but this option is rejected because 'hostile sentiments towards sick people are not legitimate. The sick person is not responsible for his acts' (Gusfield 1967: 180). No expert ever dared to say that paedophiles might be mentally ill, so pervasive and established was the discourse of evil.

Local media and local publics

Kitzinger (1999) has emphasized how many campaigns against paedophiles were rooted in local communities. In 1997–98 community protests were supported by local newspapers in Aberdeen, Leicester, Torquay and Belfast. Released paedophile Robert Oliver was named and shamed by the *Brighton Evening Argus* in October 1997. The *NOTW* campaign was preceded by one in the *Scottish Daily Record*, publishing in February 1997 the photographs and offences of 38 paedophiles. Vigilantism was unpredictable and indiscriminate but Kitzinger suggests that local communities had legitimate grievances. The workings of the Sex Offenders Act 1997 meant that offenders appeared to have more rights than the public. They had the right to council housing but only a few professionals had the right to know that they were there. Local newspapers gave voice to these grievances and sought to defend their communities. Policy-makers sought to resist and condemn such expressions of outrage but could not stem the tide which 'led to the policy makers and "the professionals" losing control of the agenda' (Kitzinger 1999: 212). Bell (2002) argues that the protests represented a challenge to the legitimacy of government, resolved only when the *NOTW* campaign was incorporated into normal processes of policy-making.

More is implied here than a contrast between rational, incremental and dispassionate policy-making and emotive, urgent and committed popular feeling (Critcher 2002). Collier (2001: 235) argues that 'the position of law has become increasingly contested by popular knowledge'. At times of perceived crisis 'popular knowledge', voiced on the one hand by the press and on the other by community activism, becomes the more significant political force. Unlike most panics, paedophilia touched the everyday anxieties of parents. The discourse was grounded.

International comparisons

As with physical and sexual abuse, the USA had previously constructed paedophilia. Though some details differed, the essentials – from the word itself to the legal remedy – provided a model, as did key assumptions about child sexual abuse: its pervasiveness, the monstrous nature of its perpetrators, its likely escalation into violence and even murder, and its grave consequences for the victims. Jenkins argues that 'The discovery of the *physical* abuse of children was the essential prerequisite for popularising the concept of child abuse' (Jenkins 1998: 120, original emphasis). Sexual abuse was related to pornography, child prostitution and homosexuality. Feminists allied with moral conservatives, aided by the emerging 'child abuse profession'. The formation in 1978 of a paedophile grouping, the North American Man–Boy Love Association, confirmed claims makers' fears. By 1984 'child sexual abuse was one of the leading social issues reported in the mass media' (Jenkins 1998: 140) and remained so. The 1980s panics over missing children and then satanic abuse, while eventually discredited, established sexual abuse as occurring outside the family: 'it achieved its greatest power when it was framed in terms of molesters and paedophiles who attacked from outside the home and family, of what now came to be known as sexual predators' (Jenkins 1998: 188).

Early in the 1990s individual states such as Washington introduced laws requiring compulsory community notification and exceptional powers to reimprison 'dangerous' offenders due for release. The national catalyst occurred in 1994 when 7-year-old Megan Kanka was raped and murdered by a released sex offender. The state of New Jersey immediately passed 'Megan's Law' based on the Washington model. In 1996 this became federal law.

For Jenkins paedophilia was a construction of those interest groups already established by earlier phases of child abuse: 'the same professional groups and ideological strands can be identified in each successive campaign' (Jenkins 1998: 215). Significant were social workers, child pressure groups, psychiatrists and therapists, law enforcement agencies, religious or moralistic groups and feminists. The media took up their cause and politicians were obliged to respond.

The USA's definition of and reaction to paedophilia were exported. The issue has been globalized: 'most advanced countries have demonstrated a sensitivity to child-protection issues quite akin to what was occurring in the United States, and they have often done so under American influence' (Jenkins 1998: 230). Australia, Belgium, Canada and Japan, as well as Britain, all followed the same trajectory. Canada immediately reproduced American concerns about paedophilia though there it was subsumed into a wider campaign about child pornography (Doyle and Lacombe 2000). In Australia, Redfern (1997) points to the importance of the 1985 Woods Royal Commission on sexual offences and a subsequent law criminalizing sexual abuse overseas. He argues that 'the recent articulations of the New South Wales media and the legal apparatus position paedophilia firmly as a contemporary moral panic' (Redfern 1997: 47). His interest in applying the work of Foucault on discourse prevents him from pursuing the point. Wilczynski and Sinclair (1999) suggest that paedophilia as an issue was endorsed by a New South Wales inquiry into the police service in 1997. The extent to which Australia followed the American model and whether this was before or after Britain cannot be judged.

It does appear that, like physical abuse and to a lesser extent sexual abuse in the family, the basic definition of paedophilia, its connotations and the fears it engendered were first established in the USA. This 'diffusion' of social problem definitions is the focus of the next chapter.

Overview

Paedophilia fulfilled virtually every criterion in the ideal type of a moral panic: a newly discovered problem of identifiable folk devils threatening moral order, with consensus among media, pressure groups and politicians about its prevalence and increasingly severe legal sanctions. It has evoked such emotional intensity that any dispassionate discussion is liable to be interpreted as defending paedophiles. It must nevertheless be insisted that the construction of the paedophile distorts our understanding of both sexual attacks on children and those who perpetrate them.

A Home Office commissioned study concluded that 'while sexual abuse by a stranger' concerns media and public opinion, 'it is actually abuse within the family, or by an adult who has a relationship of trust with the child, that is not only more common, but also on the whole more damaging' (Grubin 1998: 13).

Since paedophiles cannot by definition be family members, the threat is externalized. Paedophiles are otherwise found in all forms and guises, as predators, priests or pornographers. Suppressed are crucial distinctions between fantasy and action, persuasion and coercion or fixation and opportunism. Ironically, the one characteristic they nearly all share, masculinity, is hardly discussed. Nor does treatment appear on the moral panic agenda. Society is remarkably uninterested in what might be done about paedophiles, other than locking them up for life.

Sexual abuse of children is a reality, though its magnitude remains unclear. The 'paedophile' label contributes nothing, indeed actively prevents, investigation of its frequency and nature, the different groups of men who perpetrate it and how it might be prevented and detected. A narrow focus on a small group of predatory strangers pre-empts a broader perspective on a wider spectrum of men exploiting children who know and trust them. In vilifying, pursuing and incarcerating 'known' paedophiles, we maintain an illusion of effective action. Moral panics distort our capacity for understanding, even when they appear to recognize a genuine problem.

Further reading

Critcher, C. (2002) Media, government and moral panic: the politics of paedophilia in Britain 2000–1, *Journalism Studies*, 3(4): 520–34.

Jenkins, P. (1998) *Moral Panic: Changing Concepts of the Child Molester in Modern America*. New Haven, CT: Yale University Press.

Kitzinger, J. (1999) The ultimate neighbour from hell? The media representation of paedophilia, in B. Franklin (ed) *Social Policy, the Media and Misrepresentation*. London: Routledge.

Soothill, K. and Walby, S. (1991) *Sex Crime in the News*. London: Routledge.

Part III
THE IMPLICATIONS

The question remains of how we know whether a theory is right or wrong (the crucial epistemological question). The simple answer is that we don't, but we can make judgements between more or less adequate explanations offered by a theory. Such judgements are not simple, they must involve a number of aspects that are different for different types of theory; but we must always remember that we are living in a world in which there are no final answers. As the world changes and becomes a different place, so the theory by means of which we understand it will change.

(Craib 1992: 23)

8

UNIVERSAL PICTURES:
INTERNATIONAL COMPARISONS

Introduction

For each case study in Part II, we included analyses from other countries. Apart from AIDS, the material available in English was meagre, largely confined to Anglophone countries or those of north-west Europe. For other parts of Europe, the whole of Asia, Africa and South America, there is no documentation in English of moral panics. This handicaps realizing the 'urgent necessity' (Jenkins 1992: 230) for international comparison. The potential dimensions of such comparisons are daunting. As outlined by Atmore (1996) for child abuse, they include

> differences in legal, welfare and medical-psychiatric systems; religious versus secular pressures; size of the country and geographical location; governance; media structures; histories of class, ethnicity, racism, colonialism; and changes wrought by local social movements like feminism and child protection.
>
> (Atmore 1996: 343)

That is quite a list, one well beyond the competence of this author. We shall rely on the testimony of those who, in the course of moral panic analysis, have made explicit comparisons or at least indicated how they might be made.

Jenkins' (1992) comparison of the USA and Britain remains especially helpful. Five possible dimensions emerge:

- the widest context of political, economic and social changes and the cultural climate they produce

- the nature of key institutions in society, especially but not exclusively, their degree of centralization
- how specific issues are symbolically interpreted in different national contexts
- the role of the USA in diffusing its definitions of social problems to the rest of the democratic industrialized world
- (most tentatively) some suggested connections between moral panics and modernity.

Political, economic and social change

Broad trends in the nature of western societies are thought to affect the appearance and course of debates about social problems as 'common responses to underlying social and economic trends, which have affected the entire Western world to different degrees' (Jenkins 1992: 226). Politically, the decline of class alignments and ideologies provides opportunities for contests over moral questions. Interest groups assume more importance in defining issues for political action. With politics becoming more dependent on media presentation, governments are more sensitive to perceived public opinion. Globalized competition between nations produces economic instability and a generalized sense of insecurity, especially during times of recession. This may predispose audiences to scapegoat moral deviants for problems which are economic and political, as Jenkins (1992) suggests happened in Britain under Mrs Thatcher. Uncertainty increased with massive cultural changes, beginning in the 1960s and affecting legal and moral values, especially around family life and sexuality. Increasingly, lifestyle issues have been individualized into matters of personal preference rather than legal or moral prescription. The case studies in Part II registered these changes: questions of sexuality were raised by AIDS, censorship issues by video nasties, drug consumption by ecstasy and the inviolability of the family by child abuse.

For conservatives, such changes are symptomatic of a fundamental breakdown in the moral and social order. One key example, often cited in accounts of significant change, is the family. All western nations have experienced rises in abortion and divorce rates, as well as single parenting. Women have entered the workforce in increasing numbers and housewives become a minority. Such changes allegedly provoke anxiety, as the previous cornerstone of social life, the nuclear family with clearly demarcated sexual roles, appears to disintegrate. Destabilization of the moral order may predispose the general public to seek out the moral certainty which derives from identifying a common enemy.

Such factors suggest a convergence in the political, economic and cultural experiences of western nations so that we might expect greater commonality in their responses to real or assumed social problems. However, there are significant differences in the cultural climates of different nations, even those apparently similar. A specific example is what looks initially like the influence of religion. In the British case, religious groups were influential in the panics over video nasties and ritual child abuse, though not elsewhere. Jenkins makes religion one of the deepest contrasts between the USA and Britain. 'We are, after all, comparing the most religious society in the advanced world with one of the least' (Jenkins 1992: 225). Religious adherents are numerically small in Britain but exert an undue influence on social issues, with fundamentalist and evangelical strains prominent. But, unlike the USA, there is not a religiously inspired New Right political movement. Reviewing the policies of Thatcherism at its height in the late 1980s, Durham (1989: 65) argued there to be 'no sign of American-style campaigning by a New Right using sexual anxieties as the focus of its appeal'.

On a wider scale, the degree and nature of religiosity of a nation may help explain the prevalence and targets of moral panics. The Protestant/Catholic religious divide cannot be applied simplistically. In the case of AIDS in Germany, for example, the Protestant view of AIDS was generous while the Catholic Church took a punitive view (Frankenberg 1992). The Protestant Netherlands has a history of accommodating deviant lifestyles, though that has more to do with its political than religious culture. However, this may be less a matter of theology than whether there is a predisposition to perceive the presence of 'evil', in religious or secular form.

Secular evil may have been evident in Sweden. Moerkerk and Aggleton (1990) have emphasized the ambiguity of Sweden's policy response to AIDS. It was incorporated into the pre-existing comprehensive programme of public health care and there was a concerted attempt to avoid stigmatizing homosexuals. Yet other aspects were highly controlling, with compulsory testing of possible victims. This stemmed from the general view that 'the state should regulate and set clear boundaries on social behaviour', raising questions about 'the extent to which anti-gay sentiment is enhanced by an approach which seeks to use punitive measures to control sexual expression and behaviour' (Moerkerk and Aggleton 1990: 186). Henriksson and Ytterberg (1992) have explored why an otherwise tolerant nation took such a punitive attitude towards those infected with HIV. The controlling response to AIDS, like Sweden's highly restrictive drugs policy, is not rooted in the moral right but the moral left's 'profound commitment to the well-ordered life' (Henriksson and Ytterberg 1992: 335). Those failing to achieve this goal are subject to corrective control. Gould (1994) found exactly the same tendencies in Swedish resistance to needle-exchange schemes in 1988–89. Though not a theme of his analysis, Roe's (1985) discussion of the video nasties scare in Sweden indicates that concern came from those wanting to restore moral order through the state: government ministers, local councils, teachers and youth workers.

A quite different example can be found in the attitudes to child abuse in France. Strikingly absent are high-profile cases, judicial inquiries or attacks on social workers (Cooper 1995). Victor (1998) noted that claims of satanic abuse did not occur in France or indeed any other European Catholic country. It may be that Catholic countries have more stable family structures or that they simply deny the existence of child abuse. But there also seems to be less of a disposition to perceive the devil to be in our midst. Some cultures seem more religiously or politically puritanical than others and hence more likely to see deviant behaviour as evidence of social or religious evil. As with all the suggestions in this chapter, only more systematic comparison between countries across a range of issues can test its validity.

Key institutions

In contrasting American and British panics, Jenkins stresses divergences in political and legal institutions: 'in every detail, the British system is structured in fundamentally different ways' (Jenkins 1992: 227). Somewhat simplified, a centralized system in Britain contrasts with a decentralized one in the USA. The most obvious example is government itself. Considerable state autonomy in the USA compares with the virtual absence of local governance on significant issues in Britain. The same applies to political parties. In the USA these are alliances of often quite disparate groupings, whereas in Britain party discipline is strictly enforced. A similar pattern emerges in the media with American local newspapers, television and radio stations much more important than in Britain, where the media systems are largely national in scope.

Legal institutions are also more centralized in Britain than in the USA. Though formally organized into regional forces, Britain's police are effectively controlled by a government minister. In the USA local forces are much more fragmented and autonomous. The whole law enforcement system in the USA is highly politicized with police chiefs, district attorneys and judges directly elected or political nominees. In Britain, chief constables and judges are professional careerists expected to suppress political views or ambitions. Centralization is also important in the activities of claims makers or pressure groups. In the USA these often begin and operate locally, though aspire to national exposure, while in Britain they are much more firmly directed to and from the political centre.

Consequently, American panics are more likely to begin locally and spread nationally. The whole system seems to be more leaky, liable to produce situations where a few strategically placed individuals, who believe in or wish to exploit a scare, have few constraints on their conduct, whereas in Britain they would rapidly be held accountable to national bodies. What applies to individuals, also applies to whole groups. Jenkins stresses that professional groups like lawyers, psychologists and psychiatrists are most numerous and influential in the USA. Psychiatrists and therapists are more likely to be called as expert witnesses in trials and their testimony is more readily accepted than would be the case elsewhere, especially in Britain.

This comparison of two nations cannot simply be used as a model for others. Much of it is potentially generalizable. Federal systems, to which Britain is an exception, often allocate significant legislative powers to local levels over such issues as health, drugs, childcare and even media censorship. The dynamics of such panics are likely to be quite different from centralized systems in which a campaign has to be mounted at the national level where legislative power resides. The degree of **federalism** also affects the potential power of local or regional media, police, judiciary and public opinion. The overall effect may be more on the location of panics than their frequency, with federal systems more likely to produce successful local panics but perhaps posing more problems in achieving goals at the national level.

There are other areas of comparison to supplement federalism. In some countries, for example the Netherlands, tabloid newspapers and their sensationalist brand of journalism are virtually unknown. The determinants for panics in the larger nations remain the best explored. Altman (1986), for example, roots the peculiarities of the American response to AIDS in its political culture.

> The openness, localism and the communal basis of the American system all help explain the particular way in which Americans respond to political and social crises. In some ways they tend to defuse passions, despite the strong apocalyptic tendencies in American political life and the fondness for seeing things in terms of black and white. It may well be that the panic over AIDS is more easily restrained than would be the case in countries with a more centralized media and state system and where there is both greater expectation of government response and less willingness to criticize what governments do.
>
> (Altman 1986: 182)

Lupton (1994) sees the Australian responses to AIDS as different from both the USA and Britain as a result of 'the greater liberalism of the Federal Labour government which held power in Australia from 1983 onwards, the inclusion of gay men in policy-making bodies, the tradition of state-provided health care and the lack of a strong political presence of radical religious conservatives' (Lupton 1994: 117). There was not the same ideological emphasis on family values nor such a dramatic split between the conservative and liberal press compared with the UK, or the neglect of the issue by government and media so apparent in the USA. Other countries need not all be positioned with reference to the USA and the UK but in many cases this will serve as a useful starting point.

Specificity of issues

The specificity of issues refers to whether in a particular national context a given issue appears at all, the form in which it appears and the themes to which it is related. The most obvious universal issue was AIDS but even this apparently common problem was perceived differentially.

> A single viral threat had imposed itself on nations at very different levels of economic development; with very different political systems, cultural backgrounds and attitudes towards sexuality, drug use, and privacy; and with very different conceptions of the role of the state in protecting the public health . . . all these would have profound effect on how AIDS and those with HIV infection would be treated.
>
> (Bayer and Kirp 1992a: 1)

Not only the responses but also the definition of the issue varied across countries. Misztal and Moss (1990b) have identified seven factors affecting the development and outcome of AIDS policies:

- the competition between international and distinctively national definitions and responses
- the major groups actually contracting the disease
- the perceived deviance of those affected and toleration of their difference
- the degree of organization of affected groups especially the gay community
- the established balance between voluntary and state agencies
- the degree of politicization of the issue
- the organization and resourcing of the health system.

As just one example, in Canada there was no moralistic condemnation of gay lifestyles as found in the USA and Britain (Rayside and Lindquist 1992).

This demonstrates 'how widely the understanding and management of an infectious disease can vary in societies too frequently considered as a homogeneous cultural and institutional bloc' (Moss and Misztal 1990: 20).

Our other case studies either did not appear elsewhere or did so in distinctive forms. Ecstasy and rave never achieved the same popularity in the USA, where the whole issue was subsumed in the permanent 'War on Drugs'. Action against the rave as a leisure form was in federal systems, like the USA or Canada, a matter for local council or state rather than national legislation. Video nasties as an issue did not appear in the USA, where campaigns over media content are more muted because of the politics of the constitution and the economics of Hollywood. In Sweden (Roe 1985) they were frowned upon by state officials rather than moral entrepreneurs, while in New Zealand (Shuker 1986) video nasties were interpreted in terms of sexual violence, a theme absent from the British context. Nevertheless, in western European countries undergoing the VCR expansion in the early 1980s, 'the arguments brought forwards in the debates, the professions of the contestants, and the very course of the reactions are strikingly similar across the map' (Drotner 1992: 43).

While physical abuse in families has assumed similar forms in most Anglophone countries, differences in welfare systems produce quite distinct demands for action. Where sexual abuse in families has been raised as an issue there has been a common tendency to associate it with the extremes of feminism but its precise form has varied. Only perhaps the paedophile emerges as a genuinely universal folk devil, with perceptions and remedies much more uniform than in any other issue. Otherwise, even where nominally the same issue emerges, it will take the forms and bear the themes which are specific to the cultural context in which it appears. This remains so, even when the USA is the common source of the social problem definition.

Diffusion

Jenkins (1992: 219) wants 'to rebut the simple view that problems are a direct imitation of American concerns, disseminated by way of US cultural and political hegemony'. He explores both receptivity and resistance to such hegemony. Britain is receptive because American ideas are diffused along low and high channels. Low channels are the media and popular culture: films, television, popular music, even slang. High channels are those open to elites. Academics and policy-makers are highly sensitive to American developments. 'American experience frequently comes to be regarded as normative' (Jenkins 1992: 222). Journals, conferences and exchange visits reinforce this view. British police are influenced by American police views of new forms of crime and their prevention. Political or social movements of quite different kinds share this susceptibility. Both evangelical Christianity and the feminist movement in Britain have taken cues from their American counterparts.

However, this diffusion from the USA to Britain encounters obstacles, especially anti-Americanism. For all its attractiveness, the American way of life can be seen as a negative example. There is a specific objection to irrational elements in American public life. Religious fervour is especially regarded with suspicion. To be accepted, American ideas have to have receptive audiences in Britain but this is not always the case. Specific attempts to offer the USA as a model are sometimes rejected. The USA has not successfully exported its war on drugs, except possibly to Canada (Fischer 1998). Predictions by the US Drug Enforcement Administration that Europe would suffer its own crack epidemic were specifically rejected by the British police (Bean 1993). American definitions of child abuse have been more influential, though locally inflected. On physical abuse and paedophilia American definitions held sway. Though sexual abuse in the family owed much to American feminist ideas, it has not been publicly recognized there.

The clearest example of the USA exporting a ready-made panic was satanic abuse. Victor (1998) and Henningsen (1996) note that allegations about satanic abuse spread from the USA to the UK, Canada, the Netherlands and Germany in the late 1980s and to Australia, New Zealand, Sweden, Norway and Denmark in the 1990s. But there were important differences in such allegations.

> In the USA they are mainly found in middle-class environments, and the charges are not brought by the public authorities, but as a result of 'moral campaigns' amongst parents against alleged sex offenders. In Europe the accused normally belong to the underclass and cases are started by public bodies.
>
> (Henningsen 1996: 584)

Victor (1998) has suggested why satanic abuse accusations spread with such speed and to these precise locations. Among the crucial factors were a common language, similar structures of strategic occupations – medical and mental health professionals, clergy, police, journalists – and feminist movements which foreground issues of sexuality. Two influences stand out. The absence of Catholic countries from the list indicates the importance of a Protestant religious culture with fundamentalist strands. The second influence is the open channels and extant networks of professional communication. Medical, mental health and social work personnel are habituated to looking to the USA for the latest ideas in the field. American 'experts' are invited to address national and international conferences. Satanic abuse claims were exported from the USA along established routes of cultural trade.

Victor (1998) suggests that France shared none of these characteristics; resistant to linguistic domination, a Catholic country where belief in the devil is minimal, with a feminism which is economic rather than cultural, and excluded from North American communication channels and professional networks. Nevertheless, Satanism has been cited as the paradigm case of diffusion from the USA:

> The development of a virulent antisatanist movement in the US has, as one of its consequences, led directly to the spread of concern to other countries receptive to ideas from the US and culturally attuned to American society. This represents a form of cultural diffusion of an American derived moral panic and hysteria.
>
> (Richardson 1997: 77)

Atmore objects that this diffusion model underestimates cultural differences. 'Societies like Australia do have important similarities to the United States, but also require study in their own terms – the influence of the Christian Right being just one important difference' (Atmore 1997: 12). The challenge for comparative analysis is to recognize the potential hegemony of the USA over social problem definition, how this is accepted or resisted on specific issues and the channels of communication through which it operates.

Moral panics and modernity

Trends common to moral panics in western societies have been identified in two analyses of panics about popular culture and the media. According to Drotner (1992: 45), modernity refers to how industrialization, urbanization and secularization produce 'the constant transformation of traditions and relations'. In such a context, popular culture is often regarded as undermining the moral order, especially if appealing to the young. Panics attempt to restore certainty and continuity, two conditions modernity persistently undermines. Boethius (1994: 53) has argued that as a result of modernity, 'Moral panics seem less easy to achieve now than they were at the beginning of the century'. The proliferation of mass media and popular culture, increasing tolerance of diversity of taste and the collapse of high and low culture distinctions make the media an infertile terrain for moral panics. More generally, the heterogeneous and anonymous relations of large cities militate against moral certainty, while the lessening of class antagonisms offers less opportunity to politicize moral issues. Hence his conclusion that

> moral panics nowadays are most easily inflamed in religious societies where economic, social and cultural development has still not progressed as far as it has in the rich countries in the west, whereas panics are more and more rare in the secularized and pluralistic mass media societies of the west.
>
> (Boethius 1994: 56)

No evidence is presented for this wide-sweeping claim. The general thesis that panics are more difficult to mount may have some validity for panics about media forms in what are, strictly speaking, conditions of late modernity or even postmodernity. Internet child pornography may prove a test case (Jenkins 2001). It does seem that in postindustrial societies some sites offer more potential for the construction of moral panics than those where boundaries between normality and deviance, good and evil, have become blurred. In a context of consumerism as a whole way of life, attempts to regulate drug taking or media exposure are resisted, less by organized opposition than the sheer scale of their availability and the obduracy of their adherents. For this reason, childhood becomes the securest terrain for a panic, since moral boundaries are more easily secured. Comparative study might seek to establish that trend, rather than tendentious statements about moral panics, media and modernity.

Further reading

Jenkins, P. (1992) *Intimate Enemies: Moral Panics in Contemporary Great Britain.* New York: Aldine de Gruyter.

Kirp, D.L. and Bayer, R. (eds) (1992) *AIDS in the Industrialized Democracies: Passions, Politics and Policies.* Montreal: McGill-Queen's University Press.

9

NO NEWS IS GOOD NEWS: THE ROLE OF THE MEDIA

Introduction

Modern moral panics are unthinkable without the media, though medieval witch trials managed without them. As we saw in Chapter 1, Cohen (1973) established the centrality of the media, later elaborated by Hall et al. (1978). The social constructionists reviewed in Chapter 2 have been criticized because 'they often treat the mass media as mere channels through which passes information about deviance or about labels that others have assigned' producing 'little recognition that the mass media may themselves transform information and affect the deviance of people or groups' (Shoemaker et al. 1987: 353). Generally there is agreement that 'news organizations are active in constituting what are social problems and what should be done about them' (Ericson et al. 1987: 70); the question is how precisely they do this.

Before exploring that, we need to make four qualifications. The first is the difficulty of separating out the media from other agencies involved in the construction of moral panics, illustrating 'the *limitations* of viewing the media as a discrete topic and the *importance* of examining how the media are fundamentally enmeshed in the societies in which they operate' (Kitzinger and Miller 1998: 223, original emphases). Hence Schlesinger and Tumber (1994: 272) view the media as a 'constitutive and constituent part' of social problem definition and policy-making. The second qualification is the danger of generalizing about the media as a monolithic whole, 'the question of whether all news media are relatively similar in their practices of knowledge production' (Ericson et al. 1987: 75). It is important not to elide distinctions between different types of institutions (broadcasting and the press); newspapers (upmarket, mid-market and downmarket); constituencies (local and national); and genre (hard news and background exploration or commentary).

Third, there is the possible significance of media which are not 'mass' in the traditional sense. Both old media, such as magazines, and new media, such as the Internet, articulate the interests of small but specialist groups, from social workers to clubbers. Yet their influence on public debate is negligible, unless becoming organized movements. 'The media have changed; the visualization of crime, deviance, and control for public drama and political instruction have not' (Ericson et al. 1987: 59). The fourth qualification is that the term moral panic has itself passed into some areas of journalistic discourse (Hunt 1997). Appearing first in left-wing weeklies, used by sociologists when journalistic sources, its loose and often ironic use has compounded the term's original ambiguities. Mindful of these qualifications, we consider connections between media newsmaking and moral panics around four pairs of issues:

- news values and **inferential structures**
- primary definers and claims makers
- **agenda setting** and public opinion
- **news attention cycle** and narrative closure.

News values and inferential structures

News values

News media report some events and not others. Those they do report have to be interpreted. News values and inferential structures explain these respective processes. News values are journalists' rules of thumb about what does and does not make a good story. Rarely written down, they have to be learned on the job. Galtung and Ruge (1981) provided a list of twelve core news values. Subsequently lists have been produced for crime news (Chibnall 1977), television news (Golding and Elliott 1979) and social problem news (Ericson et al. 1987; Shoemaker et al. 1987). Galtung and Ruge's original list of twelve news values has proved remarkably robust:

- frequency (time span)
- threshold (absolute and relative)
- unambiguity
- meaningfulness, cultural proximity or relevance
- consonance (predictable and demanded)
- unexpectedness, unpredictability or scarcity

- continuity (with other stories)
- composition (of bulletin or edition)
- elite persons
- elite nations
- personification
- negativity.

Galtung and Ruge (1981) saw the first eight as universal, the last four as specific to western media. Alternatively, values can be grouped into organizational requirements, selection filters and presentational devices.

The news values framework is effective within certain boundaries. It can explain why crime is a universal news focus, since it satisfies all the criteria, and why some crimes are more likely to be reported than others. Crime may be such a good fit because it exemplifies an overriding news value, not represented in Galtung and Ruge's (1981) list: 'deviance in a broad sense is the staple, defining feature of newsworthiness' (Reiner 1998: 196). News depends on events of sudden duration, which are unexpected, negative in import, serious in implication, seen as part of a pattern, personified, made meaningful and rendered morally unambiguous, all appropriate for moral panics.

Among the many criticisms of such frameworks (Palmer 1998), the variability of news values is especially relevant to moral panics. The relative weighting of news values is not fixed, since 'the identification of given events as news worthy is time-bound' (Schlesinger and Tumber 1994: 146). Which events are selected as news is crucial to the development of moral panics. So is their interpretation by the news media. Ericson et al. (1987: 143) call this a 'news frame'; the original formulation was the inferential structure.

Inferential structures

The term 'inferential structure', originally coined by Lang and Lang (1955), was developed by Halloran et al. (1970). It refers to a structure or system of inferences or underlying assumptions. The assemblage of 'facts' into a story necessarily involves some kind of explanatory framework. Deviance is perceived to breach patterns of normal behaviour. The deviant–normal axis is easily exaggerated into a contest between good and evil. There is no need to recognize complexity or competing definitions. 'Morality as a process involves the use of evaluative dualisms (e.g. good–evil, brave–timid, free–enslaved) to assess objects' (Ericson et al. 1987: 7). Moral panics are always a struggle to achieve this kind of clarity. An inferential structure can become the driving force behind news construction. Events are selected and presented for their fit with current media preoccupations. A dynamic view of news values (Kitzinger and Reilly 1997) identifies 'what underlying construct ties the indicators together into a meaningful "newsworthiness" package' (Shoemaker et al. 1987: 349). In this process, the news media do not act alone: to interpret, create and discover stories, they continuously interact with the sources who can provide them with the raw material.

Primary definers and claims makers

Primary definers

The debate here, familiar to media scholars, is about how far the media act as mouthpieces for the views of primary definers who set the agenda for social problems. In their original formulation, Hall et al. (1978) argued that some definitions of social problems and issues come to have prominence, establishing the parameters of debate which others have to follow. These they called primary definers whom they saw principally as representatives of the state: government, judiciary and police. The media act as secondary definers whose function is to reproduce the definitions of primary definers and, in the popular press especially, to 'translate' official statements into everyday language.

Crime offers consistent support to the primary definers thesis (Chermak 1994; Welch et al. 1997) but it seems too inflexible for other issues. Schlesinger (1990), for example, argues that identifying one set of primary definers whom the news media automatically legitimize ignores the conflict over definitions frequently involved, especially over novel problems. The model underestimates the capacity of news sources outside the state to gain credence for their definitions, often against the interests of the powerful. The dominance of primary definers should not be assumed. It is 'an achievement rather than a wholly structurally determined outcome' (Schlesinger 1990: 78).

The primary/secondary definers model appears to be a partial version. The media may reproduce primary definitions, which may or may not be contested, depending on the nature of the issue and the balance of opinion. 'Media strategies of official sources or powerful groups do not succeed, and those of the less powerful and activist groups do not necessarily fail' (Skidmore 1995: 86). Some activists are claims makers or moral entrepreneurs.

Claims makers

Schlesinger and Tumber (1994) emphasize the importance of 'investigating the social organization of non-official sources and of assessing their relationships to the state' with 'implications for how we think about the wider functioning of the public sphere' (Schlesinger and Tumber 1994: 24). Ericson et al. (1987) similarly stress 'the interaction between different types of source, official and non-official, and what this tells us about the workings of the wider policy arena' which 'has been ignored by conventional media research, and has therefore been effectively hidden from view' (Ericson et al. 1987: 33). Claims makers have to 'acquire their credibility, legitimacy, and authoritativeness' through 'developed media strategies', aiming to establish an 'aura of expertise' (1987: 41–2).

Schlesinger's (1990) ideal type of the successful source requires a clear message for media outlets primed to receive information, opposition to which has been neutralized. It requires institutionalization, financial support and cultural capital. Constructionists generally pay more attention to the 'rhetoric' of claims making. In his study of the missing children problem in the USA, Best (1990) has identified a 'rhetorical chain'. Primary claims makers 'must first define a social problem to their own satisfaction', then 'present their claims in a fashion likely to draw media attention'. As 'the media transform those primary claims into secondary claims' (Best 1990: 187), policy-makers and public respond. Missing children claims makers were highly successful. 'The combination of big numbers, broad definitions and horrible examples made these claims compelling' (Best 1990: 60).

Our earlier case studies suggest a complex picture of who acted as primary definers and which claims makers were successful. In the case of AIDS, the primary definition was eventually assumed by the health establishment. The primary definers of rave/ecstasy were the police, supported by the popular press. For video nasties, the primary definers were actually the claims makers themselves: fundamentalist Christians aided by mid- and down-market newspapers. Physical abuse of children was primarily defined by professionals – paediatricians and social work managers – with direct connections to government. In Cleveland there was no primary definition, despite newspapers' attempts to construct one. On ritual abuse attempts to make claims and define the issue by quite disparate groups – Christian fundamentalists, social workers, pressure groups for children and some feminists – were summarily dismissed by the press. On paedophilia, a primary definition was common across media, pressure groups, policy-makers and government, despite differences about the appropriate measures.

A few generalizations can be deduced from these complex examples. First, primary definers are less likely to be discrete groups than alliances, such as government and policy community or media and pressure groups. Second, for primary definitions emanating from claims makers to become successful they require endorsement by significant sections of media or political elites, preferably both. Third, on some issues there is no primary definition and on others few claims makers outside sections of the press. Fourth, on some very few issues, primary definition is ceded to authoritative experts from medicine (in the case of AIDS) or law (as in child abuse inquiries).

At one level, every issue or situation is different. At another, the same actors appear to determine the eventual balance of forces. Here the media, more accurately particular kinds of newspapers, are strategic. Sometimes they are the principal claims makers seeking to become primary definers. At other times they take up a cause already espoused by others, becoming secondary definers or claims makers. For either role to be successful, the agenda must be accepted by other media of higher status, first upmarket newspapers, then broadcasting. Only then will the weight of opinion require response from government. A newspaper may conduct whatever campaign it chooses but it will gain momentum only if supported by other claims makers and media. Conversely, claims-making groups make progress only if they can enlist the support of newspapers, their route to government. The idea that there are different arenas in which to establish social problem definitions is the basis of agenda setting models.

Agenda setting and public opinion

Agenda setting

According to Dearing and Rogers (1996: 2), agenda setting attempts to explain 'why information about certain issues, and not other issues, is available to the public in a democracy; how public opinion is shaped; and why certain issues are addressed through policy actions while others are not'. An agenda is a recognized set of issues arranged in order of priority. There is permanent competition for status on the main agendas of the media, the public and policy-makers. A major influence is the 'trigger event' defined as 'a cue-to-action that occurs at a point in time and serves to crystallize attention and action regarding an issue's salience' (Dearing and Rogers 1996: 40). It is comprehensible and emotive for audiences. The public's agenda, their perceptions of pressing issues and the reforms required as measured by opinion polls, reflects that of the media.

The policy agenda is the 'outcome of activity and influence on the media agenda and on the public agenda' (Dearing and Rogers 1996: 72). Policy action seeks mainly to defuse the issue, with a 'function not to solve difficult societal problems but to institutionalize a response to those problems' (Dearing and Rogers 1996: 72). Policy formation does not make good news since it is protracted, technical and largely hidden from view. Nevertheless, policy-makers are highly sensitive to media agendas, as 'government officials and politicians take the amount of media attention given to an issue as an indirect expression of public interest in the issue' (Dearing and Rogers 1996: 77). The media agenda clearly predominates. It determines the public agenda and aims to influence the policy agenda. → *The media 決定 public agenda, aims to influence the policy agenda.*

Dearing and Rogers (1996) provide wide-ranging examples to support their analysis but admit it begs several questions, such as how and why issues rise and fall or governments act on some issues and not others. These are not its only failings. It is unremittingly positivistic in its analysis of media and public agendas and portrays public debate as the competition of ideas in the marketplace, ignoring unequal resources and ideological conflict. Despite these weaknesses, the agenda setting framework has a lot to offer moral panic analysis. First, the concept of an 'agenda', its existence in the three areas of media, public and policy makers and their interrelationships, specify the dynamics of moral panics, the most obvious example being the *News of the World*'s 'naming and shaming' of paedophiles analysed in Chapter 7. Second, agenda setting does ultimately place the media as the most influential agenda which the public follows and politicians must deal with. The case studies provided many examples of the media setting the agenda on a social problem, drawing it to the attention of the public and demanding policy responses, one instance being rave/ecstasy. Third, agenda setting sees issues as socially constructed regardless of actual changes in the incidence of social problems. 'Perceptions, not real-world indicators, count' (Dearing and Rogers 1996: 71). This applied to both episodes of video nasties. Less useful is the model's insistence that public opinion plays a significant role in the construction of social problems.

Public opinion

The moral panic model has been criticized because 'it tends to attribute to the mass media considerable power to manipulate public opinion' (Rocheron and Linné 1989: 417) and 'fails to distinguish between . . . what the papers *say* and what the public *thinks*' (Hunt 1997: 645, original emphasis). The criticisms are justified. The claim is invalid, the distinction unnecessary. The case studies showed little evidence of public concern about issues. They seemed, if anything, confused or indifferent. In practice, it does not matter whether the 'public' do become concerned about the issue. It has been persistently difficult to apply Goode and Ben-Yehuda's (1994) criterion of 'concern' because it is not the amount but the locus of concern which is vital. In moral panics support from the public is a bonus not a necessity. In any case, it can be constructed, largely by the media. 'In the long term media

Public opinion 被 Agenda setting 影響，所 [以]

coverage not only moulds public opinion, to all intents and purposes it *is public opinion*, or at least that visible version of it to which politicians and administrators respond' (Golding and Middleton 1979: 19, original emphasis). The media neither reflect nor create public opinion; they construct it. Astroff and Nyberg (1992) argue that a 'discourse *of* the people is a discourse *about* not *by* the people. Their viewpoint is frequently assumed while they remain absent' (Astroff and Nyberg 1992: 10, original emphases).

In moral panics we have a circuit of communication between the mass media, claims makers and the political elite. If enough of these decide there is an issue and that action is required, a moral panic becomes possible. Conversely, if there are differences of opinion within them, a moral panic is more likely to founder. A study of crime policy revealed its elite basis:

> those with policy expertise have their own way of communicating with themselves. The rest of us may listen in to the passing messages if we are so inclined . . . many do indeed believe that rational political action and debate are important, but for them the rational public that counts, and the media that service it, are actually limited to the circles of the powerful and influential.
>
> (Schlesinger and Tumber 1994: 272–3)

From a broader angle comes the view that the media are an integral part of a 'deviance-defining elite':

> Journalism is concerned primarily with communications among elite authorized knowers. Journalists are oriented to the audience of regular sources-as-reporters who join them in their hermeneutic circle. Everyone else is left to watch, listen to, or read the distant representations that form this symbolic spectacle.
>
> (Ericson et al. 1987: 351)

So the media are linked to the elites on whom they report, decide who can join the ranks of this elite and construct for the elite a version of 'the public' who are addressed and invoked but never actually consulted. This has important implications for moral panic analysis. If the agenda setting model is to be used, it must be reformed. The public agenda is actually irrelevant. The three sets of agendas need to be rethought as elite agendas. To the media and policy agendas we should add not the public but claims makers or pressure groups. Their interaction with the media and policy-makers is crucial. The support of the 'public' is only a means to this end. All involved will encourage public support and if necessary manufacture it by commissioning an opinion poll, setting up petitions or organizing letters to politicians. But ultimately power lies with the media and the politicians whose agendas claims makers must target, 'influencing the elite via the quality press and current affairs radio and television journalism' (Schlesinger and Tumber 1994: 79). For moral panic analysis only, we can abandon attempts to elicit or measure 'public opinion'. In the cycle of moral panics, it needs only to be invoked. The logic of that cycle is independent of 'public opinion'.

News attention cycle and narrative closure

News attention cycle

An unresolved problem in any model of moral panics is how to account for their growth and decline. Cohen's (1973) seminal formulation remains vague. One answer, originally proposed by Downs (1972), lies in the issue attention cycle. Each social problem 'suddenly leaps into prominence, remains there for a short time, and then – though still largely unresolved – gradually fades from the centre of public attention' (Downs 1972: 38). Downs' explanation is the fickleness of media audiences, constantly expecting to be entertained by something new, bored by the recycling of the same issues. The media are driven by the search for novelty. A 'new' social problem will be seized upon, covered until its full news potential has been exploited, then dropped as the next new problem, with its fresh news angles, is discovered. This was also the conclusion of a substantial empirical study of crime. ' "New" crimes become predominant in the news media until the level of saturation reaches a point where future events are deemed to be of no further interest to the public unless they exhibit some unusual characteristics' (Schlesinger and Tumber 1994: 146). Skidmore (1995) found journalists referring to 'child abuse fatigue', as the issue seemed to drag on beyond its novelty value.

This issue or news attention cycle is renewable, if an old issue is given sufficiently fresh impetus (Kitzinger and Reilly 1997). Otherwise it will gradually fade as the news media and possibly their publics tire of it. Goode and Ben-Yehuda (1994) termed this 'volatility' but cases were more complex. Some had concentrated peaks (video nasties), others quite protracted ones (paedophilia). An established issue might decline and then reappear serially in new forms (child abuse). The intensity of moral panics, perhaps a better descriptor than volatility, is sustainable only for short periods because the attention span of the news media is so short. An alternative way of exploring the dynamics of moral panics is through the idea of narrative.

Narrative closure

Moral panics take the form of narratives, with a beginning, a middle and an end. The processual model tells us much about the middle but little about the beginning and the end. Here we address a puzzle for moral panic analysis: when and why do moral panics start? Kepplinger and Habermeier (1995: 372) have suggested that 'waves of new coverage arise' in reaction to key events. Golding and Middleton (1979: 6) also identify 'an initial precipitating event of sufficient dramatic power to focus a number of the themes which become the binding strands of ensuing debate'. Key events change the agendas of the public, the media, pressure groups and policy-makers. They establish a news theme in which new and old events can be located (Murdock 1997). More events are drawn into the net, which Cohen (1973) recognized as 'sensitization'. Pressure groups and policy-makers construct events, such as press conferences, reports or case histories, to sustain media interest. By providing prototypes (Brosius and Eps 1995) or **templates** (Kitzinger 2000), key events provide a frame for subsequent events.

Kepplinger and Habermeier (1995: 73) note that rare, extreme or spectacular happenings are not necessary for a key event to evolve since 'there is only a loose connection between the character of the happenings and their becoming a key event'. The key event – which could be an announcement, a report or a speech, as much as a dramatic crime or death (Molotch and Lestor 1974) – has to be defined as symptomatic of a wider problem, even a crisis.

> The journalist uses the 'crisis' frame to establish the event as newsworthy and to transform it into news discourse. In turn, the elevation of an event into a crisis provides an opportunity to make explicit and intensive confirmations of reality. The crisis formulation quickly establishes the reality of the 'problem' so that particular 'immediate' solutions can be called for and effected. It frequently inhibits the asking of alternative or critical questions. The news formulation takes on the character of reality, and the preferred solution takes on the character of inevitability.
>
> (Ericson et al. 1987: 62)

If the event is to signify a crisis, to be 'resonant' (Gamson and Modigliani 1989), then there must already be in circulation a claim about its nature and dimensions which the event seems to validate. In each case study, we find death of children or young people to be a powerful signifier of crisis. The inquiry into Maria Colwell's death confirmed expert diagnoses of physical abuse. Leah Betts' death confirmed the dangers of drugs and the murder of James Bulger those of video nasties. The murder of Sarah Payne confirmed problems in supervising released paedophiles. Such signification has to be constructed. 'No story is the inevitable product of the event it reports; no event dictates its own narrative form. News occurs at the conjunction of events and texts, and while events create the story, the story also creates the events' (Manoff 1986: 228). In Goode and Ben-Yehuda's terms, the timing and content of a key event are crucial. There is always a pool of moral panics waiting to happen but it needs the right conjunction of circumstances.

The potential beginnings of moral panics are many and complex. Fortunately the ending is more transparent, at least from the evidence of our case studies. Those which most approximated to moral panics (rave, video nasties and paedophilia) all culminated in legislative action. This reflects the real political purchase of moral panics. Yet, paradoxically, much – though not all – of this legislation is symbolic and has in practice been rarely used, at least against the folk devils of the original moral panic. What the law represents, then, is *a symbolic resolution of the moral panic*. Viewed from another perspective it is *form of narrative closure*.

We do not have to apply formal theories of narrative (Toolan 2001) to note that most moral panics tail off when Something Has Been Done – or, more accurately, when Something Has Been Seen To Be Done. If what we have here is a kind of moral fable, in which retribution is exacted upon the perpetrators of evil, then moral panics can be deconstructed as narratives. That news is a form of narrative is not an original observation. Altheide (1997) has argued that the 'problem frame' has as one of its elements a narrative structure involving a beginning (that something is wrong), a middle (the problem is specified and solutions proposed) and an ending where remedial action of some kind is taken. Jacobs (1996: 373) has argued that ' "Narrativity" is the central factor structuring news work'. It shapes the selection, presentation and consumption of the story. Jacobs is discussing individual stories but it could as well be applied to the ongoing narrative of which the individual story is an episode. If we combine this narrative theorization with the news attention cycle, then we may have a convincing explanation for the demise of the moral panic. Its genesis, however, remains elusive.

The *Daily Mail*

This selective review of interconnections between newsmaking and moral panic analysis has consistently emphasized complexity. We can end by reminding ourselves that though the course of moral panics are varied and uncertain, once set in motion, their outcomes are simple. The issue and responses to it are exaggerated, distorted and simplified, much as Cohen (1973) originally claimed. Moreover, at the height of a moral panic, the complexities and variations within and between the news media and their sources are erased. They coalesce around a single dominant definition, an ideological closure of the crisis and its resolution. It is also, at such times, relatively easy to identify the key actors. The case studies in Part II had a single common denominator: the presence and agency of the *Daily Mail*. In Britain during the 1980s and 1990s, no other individual, organization or group has had such a profound effect on the development of moral panics. Occupying the space between the high ground of the upmarket papers and the low ground of downmarket papers, it is an exceedingly powerful institution, whose rationale is to speak for middle England. In moral panics, it was both the primary definer and the chief claims maker about rave/ecstasy, video nasties, child abuse in the family and paedophilia. If there is a need to refine all the issues about newsmaking reviewed in this chapter, there is an equal need to understand how and why the *Daily Mail* has come to exert such an influence. If we resolved that, we should understand a great deal more about the role of the news media in moral panics.

Further reading

Dearing, J.W. and Rogers, E.M. (1996) *Communication Concepts 6: Agenda-Setting*. Thousand Oaks, CA: Sage.

Ericson, R.V., Baranek, P.M. and Chan, J.B.L. (1987) *Visualizing Deviance: A Study of News Organization*. Milton Keynes: Open University Press.

Schlesinger, P. and Tumber, H. (1994) *Reporting Crime: The Politics of Criminal Justice*. Oxford: Clarendon.

10

TIME FOR A MAKE-OVER: THE MODELS REVISITED

Introduction

This chapter considers criticisms of moral panic models. Their terminology has been used indiscriminately for 'anything from single mothers to Ecstasy, and from pornography to the Internet to the dangers of state censorship' (Miller and Kitzinger 1998: 221). This usage is often highly selective. Only the first paragraph of *Folk Devils and Moral Panics* (Cohen 1973) is quoted; or only loose references are made to folk devils, deviancy amplification or primary definers (Kidd-Hewitt 1995: 2). Ironically 'moral panic' has itself become a label, its application used as proof that little more need be said.

Most critiques stem from single case studies. Watney (1988) and Miller and Kitzinger (1998) focus on AIDS; Buckingham (1996) on video nasties; McRobbie and Thornton (1995) mainly on rave; Parton (1981) on physical child abuse and deYoung (1998) on satanic abuse. Most discuss Cohen (1973) rather than Goode and Ben-Yehuda (1994). We initially discuss five kinds of criticism of moral panic models: ambiguities in basic terminology, an inability to specify basic dynamics, an apparently deterministic view of human agency, a speculative notion of social anxiety and an inadequate sense of historical change. Then we consider whether 'it is time to take another look at classic moral panic theory' (deYoung 1998: 277) and if it 'is deeply in need of revisiting and revamping' (McRobbie 1994: 198).

Terminology

The first set of criticisms express unease about the term 'moral panic'. Few wish to dispense with 'moral' though hardly any have attempted to define its boundaries. It is agreed that moral panics are about morality, with the deviant groups or object constructed to enable a simplified dichotomy between good and evil. If the adjective 'moral' is to stand, then they must be consistently differentiated from other problems or panics. One response would be to define three ways in which a panic must embody moral concerns. It must centre on deviance as an inherent condition of a group, condition or activity. It must involve a perceived threat to the moral order as a whole rather than a merely localized problem. It must ultimately cast this threat in the most basic terms of good and evil. Moral panics focus on inherent deviance which embodies evil, so threatening the moral order (Goode 1969; Lauderdale 1976). The distinction between moral and other panics is a fine one. Very similar processes, such as media construction, may be involved but the moral dimension is distinctive.

The term 'panic' causes more disquiet than 'moral'. Boethius (1994), Buckingham (1996) and Miller and Kitzinger (1998) all object to its imputed irrationality. It implies that reason has been forsaken. Objectors may underestimate how moral panics evoke extreme, intense and emotional reactions. Hawdon (2001: 420) distinguishes between rational concern and fearful panic, induced by a sense of threat and crisis. There is resistance to using an everyday word which lacks sociological precision but panic remains the best available descriptor of the emotional force generated by the issue.

Dynamics

The key issues here are whether the moral panic models provide any means for ascertaining the rise and fall of moral panics, their serial nature and likely outcomes. The original model is vague about how moral panics start. Parton (1981: 394) argues that moral panics do not emerge 'arbitrarily' but because some people make them happen for specific reasons in identifiable historical contexts. There are as many triggers for a moral panic as there are sources of news events. Required is a particular constellation of newsworthy events, media campaigns, pressure group activity and political responsiveness. These are identifiable only in retrospect.

The model has also been criticized for its inability to explain why moral panics decline (Miller and Kitzinger 1998). Our case studies showed that the denouement of moral panics is usually a substantial change in the law or the procedures by which it is enforced, even though this resolution may be 'more symbolic than real' (deYoung 1998: 272). Watney (1988) emphasizes that repressive measures are only the most obvious legacy of moral panics. They also serve to establish a discourse in which the problem and others like it will be presented in future, evident in the connotative terms which moral panics establish, such as 'rave', 'video nasty' or 'paedophile'. Where they are able to mobilize a prevailing discourse, such as childhood or sexuality, we have a serial panic. Such thematic links are not recognized if each panic is only considered separately, as 'discrete and unconnected' (Watney 1988: 60) since this 'obscures the "overhead narrative" of such phenomena as one panic gives way to another and different panics overlap and reinforce one another' (Watney 1988: 57).

Determinism

Moral panic models appear to be deterministic; once the process has started, it follows a predictable trajectory. Such a view 'tends to be overdeterministic in its explanations and leaves little room on occasions for the influence of social actors' (Parton 1981: 395). Miller and Kitzinger (1998: 216) also criticize this 'lack of agency'. The problem affects three groups: the folk devils themselves, agents of social reaction, especially the media and the state, and the audience or public. Folk devils are presented as hapless victims, 'already marginalized individuals' with 'neither the credibility nor the resources to counter the claims against them' (deYoung 1998: 268). Some groups can resist the folk devil label by mobilizing support and combating accusers through the media and in the courts. In the case of Cleveland, this defence of putative folk devils – doctors and social workers – occurred almost immediately and forestalled a panic. Folk devils may be defended by 'pressure groups and self-help groups' which 'now play a major role in contesting what they perceive as dangerous stereotypes and popular misconceptions' (McRobbie 1994: 214). White-collar workers and professionals will have the necessary resources and motivations to resist when they themselves, or those they represent, become possible objects of a panic. The folk devil is more likely to be recruited from groups who cannot speak for themselves and have nobody to speak for them.

Moral panic models tend to present 'social reaction' as if it were a single and predictable set of responses: 'the assumption of classic moral panic theory that societal reaction is hegemonic'. This devalues the role of 'counterclaims and counter-narratives' 'in shaping the course of the moral panic' (deYoung 1998: 271). Miller and Kitzinger (1998: 216) agree that the concept of 'control culture' elides 'distinctions between the media and the state, between the media and public belief, and between the state and other social institutions and groups'. State reaction is not automatic; it has to be achieved. Parton (1981) and Watney (1988) object to a simplified notion of the state, bereft of contestation: 'what is at stake is the entire relationship between governments and other uneven and conflicting institutions address-ing a supposedly unified "general public" through the mass media' (Watney 1988: 56). If such criticisms are valid, then we need to rethink how social problems are constructed:

> the old rectangular relationship of positions and processes which held the old moral panic model together (the sociologists on behalf of the deviant; the agencies of social control; the media; the moral guardians and experts) has been replaced by a more diverse and more fluid set of institutions, agencies and practices which sometimes interlock.
>
> (McRobbie 1994: 211)

This seems to be true up to a point. In various case studies we saw how, within and around the state, responses to the perceived crisis were far from uniform. Government itself was often reluctant to act. Established experts sometimes resisted the panic. Groupings within the state, such as the police, reacted according to their perceptions and interests. The politics of moral panics should recognize that the balance of power and interests is never given but depends upon the issue and its context. But the original formu-lation was correct in suggesting that the fully fledged moral panic does eventually produce a uniform social reaction. Paedophilia is the paradigm case.

The model also assumes 'a straightforward relationship between state interests, media content and public opinion, in which the media circulate reactionary social wisdom, the public believe it, and the state is then able to secure consent for its actions' (Miller and Kitzinger 1998: 221). All the case studies indicated the complexity, even inconsistency, of the public's views. Critics advocate viewing the audience as more active (McRobbie and Thorn-ton 1995; Buckingham 1996; deYoung 1998; Miller and Kitzinger 1998). Chapter 9 argued that this is not necessary for moral panics. The public is only tangentially involved. It is invoked rather than mobilized. As the case of paedophilia showed, when public opinion is mobilized, its actions may jeopardize the social order. Overall, the intervention of significant agents does affect the trajectory of any potential panic. The media and the state are not monolithic entities; pressure groups and experts can intervene on behalf of putative folk devils; the public may or may not underwrite the panic. Yet such variations do not undermine the status of the moral panic model as an ideal type. The realization of a fully fledged moral panic depends precisely on the non-existence or elimination of these variations and interventions.

Social anxiety

A central issue for moral panic analysis is why the public apparently exhibits a predisposition to panic. The answer given is social anxiety. Downs, writing in the early 1970s about the USA, detected 'a general rise in personal and social anxiety' attributable to 'increased tensions caused by our rapid rate of technical and social change' and 'the increase in worldwide communication through the media' (Downs 1972: 46). A decade later in Britain, Parton (1981) identified 'certain social changes in the post-war period' which had undermined 'basic values and images of the social order' among 'significant sections of the population'. Their 'social anxiety' produced 'a predisposition to the use of scapegoats onto which disturbing experiences were condensed' (Parton 1981: 399). Ten years further on, back in the USA, Stevens (1991) sees 'prolonged social anxiety' resulting when 'a significant proportion of people' no longer trust 'social or governmental institutions' (Stevens 1991: 23). The problem is that moral panics are presented 'as a consequence of some (hypothetically universal, endlessly cyclical) feature of social life, namely panickyness' (Sparks 1995: 55). Since this has been identified in British, American and other societies for a range of issues over a period of 40 years, social anxiety must be a permanent state in modern societies. However, 'no effort is made to determine whether these subterranean dissatisfactions have existed for periods of time without provoking panics' (Ungar 2001: 278). Such a hypothesis is extraordinarily difficult to prove. The existence of social anxiety is deduced from the success of moral panics without other evidence to support it.

The error is in the location of social anxiety. The anxieties which matter are located less in the general public than among strategically place elites. The media, pressure groups and politicians are permanently oriented to moral issues. Disapproval of deviants and confirmation of moral boundaries remains a staple function of the press. Pressure groups are often motivated by a sense of moral injustice, seeking protection of a defined group from threats to its integrity. Politicians use morality as the justification for their use of power. In modern democracies discourse about morality informs public debate. Instead of attributing a hypothetical social anxiety to whole populations, we should examine the political mobilization of the rhetoric of morality among elite groups. If anybody panics, has a sense of historical decline, harks back to a golden age of moral certainty, calls for the devil to be cast out of our midst, then they do. The affirmation of who 'we' are is achieved by a moral castigation of those who are most obviously 'them'. That in times of permanent change the need for such confirmation increases in intensity is on balance a more enduring hypothesis than speculations about projections of social anxiety.

Change

Social anxiety has failed to situate moral panics historically. An alternative view is that history has overtaken the models. Significant changes in the politics and culture of society have made them outdated. Boethius (1994: 50–2) argues that moral panics, at least over youth and media, have become less easy to sustain because of four specific changes: the explosion in new media and popular culture; greater pluralism and diversity of both moral and cultural values; decline in social and political tensions between classes; and greater heterogeneity in the social composition and lifestyles of the population. McRobbie and Thornton (1995) also emphasize the media as proliferating beyond the control of political or economic interests. It becomes 'impossible to rely on the old models with their stages and cycles, universal media, monolithic societal or hegemonic reactions' since 'they could not possibly take account of the labyrinthine web of determining relations which now exist between social groups and the media, "reality" and representation' (McRobbie and Thornton 1995: 560).

The existence of multiple arenas is not in dispute. Youth cultures have developed modes of expression beyond the control and frequently under-standing of adult society. Their representations of such lifestyle options as sexuality and drug consumption run counter to the mainstream press. More conventional pressure groups have also proliferated and intervened successfully to prevent the demonization of specific groups, like the single mothers cited by McRobbie and Thornton (1995). All this ought to make the construction of moral panics more difficult but classic moral panics show no signs of abating. It may be less their frequency or intensity which is affected than the terrain they inhabit, now more likely to be childhood than youth. The capacity of mainstream media to deny ambiguity and sup-press opposition should not be underestimated. Ultimately they retain the power to define issues in their own terms. They also connect directly with opinion and law makers which new media and most pressure groups cannot. We may think of media and political power as comprising a tra-ditional centre and an innovative periphery. At times of perceived crisis, the centre holds sway.

Critical overview

Dividing criticisms of moral panics into separate issues dilutes the full force of some of the more comprehensive reviews. For Miller and Kitzinger (1998) the model collapses crucial distinctions into the 'control culture' and cannot explain why AIDS did not become a moral panic. For Watney (1988) the model does not establish the vital connections. The complex set of discourses around AIDS and sexuality is excessively simplified by narrow conceptions of the state or social reaction and, above all, by the insistence on seeing moral panics as discrete entities rather than a continuous discursive flow. For McRobbie and Thornton (1995) the model is unable to recognize the complexities of modern debates about social problems, the suffusion of youth culture or the networks of media and pressure groups. The cumulative implication of such critiques is that the model should be abandoned, at least until or unless it has been revised to take account of its deficiencies.

> This leads us to query the usefulness of the term 'moral panic' – a metaphor which depicts a complex society as a single person who experiences sudden fear about its virtue. The term's anthropomorphism and totalization arguably mystify more than they reveal. Its conception of morals overlooks the youthful ethics of abandon and the moral imperatives of pressure groups and experts. In the 1990s, we need to acknowledge the perspectives and articulations of different sectors of society. New sociologies of regulation need to shift attention away from the conventional points in the circuit of amplification and control and look instead to these other spaces.
> (McRobbie and Thornton 1995: 567)

Such exhortation has had little effect. Only Sumner (1990) has offered a specific alternative in a 'sociology of censure'. The question remains whether the models are beyond redemption or can be revised to take account of valid criticisms, so remaining 'a helpful heuristic device' (Weeks 1993: 25).

Towards a synthesis

This book has rigorously tested moral panic models against a range of British examples and their equivalents elsewhere, an explicit attempt to meet the criticisms of Ungar (2001). He argues that 'knowledge about moral panics is fundamentally tainted' because research has focused on 'authentic' moral panics. The lack of attention to failed panics means that 'conclusions about key variables amount to asserting that what transpired (more or less) had to' (Ungar 2001: 278). This we have tried to avoid, one reason why the 'failed' case of AIDS was included. We now consider whether or how the original model can be reformulated to take account of all the variations in the case studies and the substantive reservations of critics. The strategy is to revise Cohen's (1973) model, retaining essentially the same processes but providing a critical commentary. The attributional model seems less satisfactory and can be abandoned, except for some important insights. We consider first why Goode and Ben-Yehuda's (1994) model is unsatisfactory and what might be salvaged from it.

Attributional model

One: concern: among whom; how widespread; forms of expression. The persistent problem was the sparse evidence of public concern. Polls showed public opinion to follow media coverage. It was concluded that public opinion was not necessary to the creation of a moral panic. If necessary, it can be created or invoked. What does matter is concern among elites in the media and in politics, stimulated by claims-making activity. We need to trace and understand why opinion leaders and makers come to be convinced about the nature and dimensions of a social problem.

Two: hostility; enemy, threat, folk devil. This was simply not true of the issues we have examined. Only the paedophile was unequivocally a folk devil. In other issues of child abuse there was a largely unsuccessful attempt to create folk devils out of professional groups, such as social workers or doctors. Rave/ecstasy produced a largely mythical folk devil, the drug pusher. Video nasties had an object, the horror film, as its focus. If we assume a moral panic to require folk devils, we make a serious empirical mistake.

Three: consensus: clarity, among whom, organized opposition. The same problem occurs over consensus as over concern, to specify its scope. The original formulation referred to 'a certain minimal measure of consensus in the society as a whole – or *in designated segments of it*' (Goode and Ben-Yehuda 1994: 35, emphasis added). This points us again towards a consensus among elites across pressure groups, the media and politicians, initially outside then inside government. This may not happen, as Goode and Ben-Yehuda realize, if there is any organized opposition to the emerging consensus. AIDS was the most obvious example of such opposition and paedophilia of its absence. Video nasties achieved such consensus temporarily but sufficiently. The consensus on rave/ecstasy was slowly undermined by the realization that drug taking has become normalized in youth culture. There was consensus about the need to improve social workers'

competence to handle physical abuse but less on whether they should be pil-
loried. Ritual abuse was permanently contested. The extent and nature of
opposition within elite opinion is an important determinant of the outcome
of a potential moral panic. Any revised model should retain this insight.

*Four: disproportionality: dimensions and implications; claims versus
reality.* We have found that in many cases disproportionality was present.
The threat was exaggerated beyond what any objective measure would warrant. Not only the magnitude is exaggerated but also the causes and effects
are distorted. It is not enough to say that concern was disproportionate,
since simple exaggeration is not the only issue (Goode 1990). Other kinds of
distortion are equally important. Thus modified, this general idea should
also be retained.

Five: volatility: length; speed of emergence and decline. This has proved
difficult to test because it is so vague. Many of the panics examined lasted
years, not months or weeks. Though punctuated by shorter, more intense
episodes, they could scarcely be described as volatile. That moral panics do
erupt and subside rapidly is a different proposition. Volatility has not proved
to be a useful or testable attribute.

*(Six): claims makers: principal claims and counter claims makers; motives
and strategies; degree of success.* This was added because it is foregrounded
in all social constructionist work which identifies who claims makers are,
where they are lodged and the strategies they adopt. They can be within the
state or outside it. They may be already in existence or formed in response
to the specific issue. The most important point, which generally has passed
social constructionists by, is that the media themselves, especially the popular press, can become active claims makers with or without other groups to
back them up.

From the constructionist attributional model, we want to drop all reference
to public opinion. Elite opinion, interacting with claims makers, constructs
concern and consensus. But there is no need for a folk devil nor is it helpful
to stress volatility. Cohen's model will be revised along these lines.

Processual model

One: emergence: form, novelty, threat. In his opening paragraph Cohen
(1973) does not mention a folk devil, defining the object of a moral panic as
a 'condition, episode, person or group of persons'. That is more accurate for
our case studies than the imputation of a folk devil evident in the rest of his
book. Dispensing with the necessity of a folk devil does not resolve the problem of how and why moral panics start. The evidence does not support the

idea that there is invariably a precipitating or key event. These do not always occur and, when they do, may be found in the middle rather than at the beginning of the moral panic narrative. An issue can take many different forms, such as a concerted campaign, a dramatic death or an official inquiry. It is less the event itself which is important than what it is taken to symbolize. The news value of James Bulger's death was his brutal murder by two other children but its ideological value was what it 'said' about the state of childhood. Such judgements can be made only in retrospect, since symbolization cannot be anticipated.

Two: media inventory: stylization and stereotyping; exaggeration, distortion, prediction and symbolization; sensitization; folk devil. We need to put more emphasis than Cohen on variation within and between the media discussed in Chapter 9. The requirement is for the stylization, stereotyping, exaggeration and distortion characteristic of mid- and downmarket press to be reproduced by the upmarket press and then broadcasting. The media as a whole need to be sensitized to the issue for 'symbolization' to occur. This is what happened in many of our case studies: rave/ecstasy, video nasties and paedophilia. What started as a sectional interest became a common media agenda. A 'tabloid' agenda will not attract sufficient support unless it can compel or persuade other media to accept it, as happened in the *News of the World*'s campaign over Sarah's Law. Cohen was accurate about the methods of media portrayal but it may be important to establish its scope.

Three: moral entrepreneurs: significant actors; relationship to media; orientations, images and causal explanations. Since the press has the power to instigate moral panics on its own, moral entrepreneurs are not necessary but always useful. Claims makers appear less important in Britain than constructionists suggest but the term is more precise than either moral entrepreneurs or pressure groups. It specifies groups organized to make claims about an issue, whose own interests are served by its prominence. In our case studies the two most prominent were the NVLA and the NSPCC. In their respective fields, they established a permanent presence, constantly propagandizing on the issue and thus able to capitalize when an event triggered media attention. Elsewhere significant groups did not easily fall into the claims making category. The distinction between claims makers, quasi-authoritative groups and experts is not easy to make.

Four: experts: who; grounds for claims; media accreditation. Experts were not prominent in the case studies, AIDS excepted. In some cases the panic depended upon suppressing the views of those who might claim expertise, academics on media violence or those working with young people on drug taking. In child abuse legal experts were called in to conduct judicial inquiries whose findings were misrepresented in the media. Much more common in the press was accrediting claims makers with expertise, so that Christian fundamentalists became experts on horror movies and the NSPCC on paedophilia. In these instances expertise was not an inherent attribute of any individual or group but something bestowed by the media. In the upmarket press more credibility was habitually given to professional experts but overall their influence was marginal. Durham (1989) and MacGregor (1999) have commented on the limited and declining role of experts in public discussion of social problems, an area that needs further investigation.

(New) Five: elite consensus and concern based on distortion. Probably between old stages four and five, we need to incorporate the insights derived from Goode and Ben-Yehuda (1994). For a panic to develop, there must be constructed a sufficient level of concern and consensus among elites, more likely in the absence of organized opposition. This is generally achieved by a distortion of the issue, both its magnitude (disproportionality) and its causes and effects.

Six: coping and resolution: proposed solutions, measures adopted; procedural/legal; effective/symbolic. Findings on this have been consistent. We do know why and how moral panics end, with a change in the law or in procedures governing its application. This was true of Cohen's original study of Mods and Rockers and consistently so through to paedophilia. Using Gusfield's (1967) terms, some laws (all Children Acts since 1973 and the Sex Offenders Act 1997) were instrumental, others, on rave and video censorship, largely symbolic. We suggested in Chapter 9 that such resolutions are forms of narrative closure.

Seven: fade away: timing, recurrence; subsequent status. Why moral panics decline is explained by how they end. Once the law is passed, the problem loses impetus. It may be renewed by fresh events, such as the murders of James Bulger and Sarah Payne. Otherwise, it will be routinized into existing frameworks for dealing with social problems, an example being ecstasy's eventual status as another recreational drug.

Eight: legacy: long-term effects; relationship to other issues. Moral panics may result in new laws which have a material effect upon state agencies, from police to social workers. As or more important are their cultural and ideological effects. The deaths of Maria Colwell, Leah Betts, James Bulger and Sarah Payne comprise an iconography of childhood tragedy. Cohen (1973) was perspicacious in saying that one effect may be to 'bring about changes in the way society conceives itself'.

It would be unwise to condense these modifications into an equivalent of Cohen's opening paragraph. This is work in progress. The commentary is far from definitive. The case studies informing the generalizations are limited in number and skewed towards issues of childhood. Finally we should remember that moral panic is an ideal type. It does not have to be perfect or fit all known cases. The critics did not always appreciate the usefulness and limitations of the model. They seemed to want it to provide a full explanation when it is more properly seen as an heuristic device. It is enough if the model reveals commonalities and differences between issues.

The model still remains extraordinarily relevant. Where an issue, in whatever form, emerges as a symbolic threat; where the media as a whole accept a single definition of the problem; where there are organized groups supporting the panic and none disputing it; where expert opinion does – or can be presented to – support the diagnosis of the problem; where the state, however laggardly, does institute repressive measures, then we have the basic requirements of the ideal type fulfilled. That happened, not perfectly but very nearly, with video nasties and paedophilia. Where there is substantial variation from the ideal type but with some basic elements intact, then we have a confused pattern of reaction, as happened with physical or sexual abuse in families, or a panic which succeeds only at the expense of isolating the issue over which there was consensus (raves) and ignoring that which was more intractable (ecstasy). Where there is variation and intervention at almost every stage, then the panic is thwarted, essentially what happens with AIDS. It remains to be tested whether other panics can be successfully assigned to one of these three basic categories. No model, however, will account for underlying themes discussed in the sections on each case study deliberately labelled 'beyond' moral panics. The selected case studies pointed inexorably to one predominant theme, the status of childhood. The next chapter attempts to tease out its significance.

Further reading

Buckingham, D. (1996) *Moving Images: Understanding Children's Emotional Responses to Television*. Manchester: Manchester University Press.

McRobbie, A. (1994) Moral panics in the age of the postmodern mass media, in A. McRobbie, *Postmodernism and Popular Culture*. London: Routledge.

Miller, D. and Kitzinger, J. (1998) AIDS, the policy process and moral panics, in D. Miller, J. Kitzinger, K. Williams and P. Beharrell, *The Circuit of Mass Communication: Media Strategies, Representation and Audience Reception in the AIDS Crisis*. London: Sage.

Watney, S. (1988) AIDS, 'moral panic' theory and homophobia, in P. Aggleton and H. Homans (eds) *Social Aspects of AIDS*. London: Falmer.

11

MYTH APPROPRIATION:
THE CHILDHOOD THEME

Introduction

The dominant discourse in the moral panics we have studied – what Watney (1988) would call the 'overhead narrative' – is a discourse about childhood. In the 1960s and 1970s the folk devils of British moral panics tended to be young people, specifically working-class males: Teddy boys, Mods and Rockers, skinheads, football hooligans, punks, muggers. But, with the exception of raves, there is a clear shift in the 1980s and 1990s. Instead of youth *as* folk devils, we have children as *the victims* of folk devils. Most transparently in the case of child abuse and paedophilia, moral panics are irresistible when they present threats to children. As Buckingham (2000: 3) notes, 'the figure of the child has always been the focus of adult fears, desires and fantasies' but more recently 'debates about childhood have become invested with a growing sense of anxiety and panic'.

The subject of this chapter is how and why this has happened. Sources are limited since 'there has been little work on childhood in this area, despite the pervasiveness of anxiety about risks to children' (Jackson and Scott 1999: 86). We look first at how moral panics mobilize the need to protect children through increased regulation, supported by the way childhood is socially constructed. Two explanations for the increased anxiety about children are examined, the psychological needs and definitions of adult society and recent changes in the status of children. In the conclusion we propose an alternative account of why childhood has emerged as such an important theme of contemporary moral panics.

Childhood and moral panics

Moral panics about childhood rest on the proposition that children need to be protected by increased regulation of adult activity. Children need to be protected from exposure to video nasties and the dangers of physical and sexual abuse within families or from paedophiles. Childhood is 'a precious realm under siege from those who would rob children of their childhoods' (Jackson and Scott 1999: 86). Children are vulnerable and underdeveloped, incapable of informed choice about mass media use or sexual activity. Adults are able to make these choices; children are not. Children are threatened by those adults who seek to exploit their vulnerability and corrupt their innocence. What therefore has to be done is to *regulate childhood*. Measures – from the certification of videos to the monitoring of released paedophiles – protect children's vulnerability by prohibiting adults from having access to them. Those who ought properly to be responsible for this regulation of childhood are held accountable: video distributors and film censors, social workers and the police or occasionally parents. To validate this intervention on behalf of children, adult society has to construct an image of childhood: what it means to be not adult and why such a status requires protection.

Childhood as social construction

Adults construct who are children and what childhood is. 'Childhood is a shifting, relational term, whose meaning is defined primarily through its opposition to another shifting term, "adulthood"' (Buckingham 2000: 7). Jackson and Scott (1999) have usefully identified three different levels at which childhood is constructed:

- *structural*, incorporating the family, education system and state policies
- *discursive*, where psychologists and child experts predominate
- *situated*, everyday interaction where generalized understandings about children guide adult interactions with them.

An example at the structural level is legal definition. Laws prescribe the ages at which it is lawful to be held responsible for criminal actions, undertake sexual activity, leave home or school, drive a motor car or drink alcohol in a pub or bar. A judgement is being made about the age at which these activities become not just possible but competently undertaken and thus legal. 'The separate condition of the child has never been so bounded by thinking, so established in law as it is today' (Warner 1994: 35).

Discursive constructions are undertaken by professionals directly or indirectly employed by the state. Psychologists and educators, counsellors and social workers – all creations of the twentieth century – inherit and apply models of childhood. 'Developmental psychology has come to dominate professional, and indeed lay, ideas about childhood and so about the responsibilities of parenthood' (White 1998: 268). The capacity of children to think logically, make moral judgements and handle their emotions proceeds through a series of stages which professionals are trained to identify. They assess whether a child has reached their appropriate stage of development. The media also produce discourses about childhood (Hartley 1998). Images of childhood circulate in novels, plays, films, news stories and advertisements. Visual images are indicative (Holland 1992; Davies 1997). Some are representations to children, others representations of childhood to adults. Some produce conventional idealized portraits of childhood; others explore its darker, more ambiguous side. Stainton Rogers and Stainton Rogers (1992: 162) note a contradiction: 'As a culture we voice concern that children should not become the objects of sexual abuse by adults and yet evince a fascination with the sexuality of the young.'

Of the 'situated' level of everyday interactions we know little outside our own experience though Mayall (1994) is an exception. How the status of childhood is mobilized by adults and children in the family remains essentially private. There is evidence that on such activities as watching adult television programmes and films, drinking alcohol and sexual activity, parents are considerably more lax than the law. Childhood is negotiated in families but being a child cannot be practised outside the structures of the law, the education system and the mass media. Largely they forbid children from areas of activity. The consequence is that 'in the recent history of industrialized countries, childhood has essentially been defined as a matter of *exclusion* . . . children are primarily defined in terms of what they are *not* and in terms of what they *cannot* do' (Buckingham 2000: 13, original emphases).

This exclusion is for their own good. Childhood is a process, as yet unrealized, of becoming adult. Adults understand the consequences of their actions in a way that children do not. They are sophisticated; they know that this is only a horror film, that excessive intake of alcohol or psychotropic drugs makes them dysfunctional, that they have the right not to be sexually interfered with. Children only half understand these things. The aim therefore is to enhance their understanding of, and prevent their exposure to, danger from predatory adults. This involves 'the imputation of "specialness" to children (as particularly cherished beings) and childhood (as a cherished state of being)' (Jackson and Scott 1999: 86). Adult society constructs a view of childhood which validates protective measures. 'The notion that children are precious, that they need protection from a harmful adult world, is basic to contemporary understandings of childhood' (Best 1990: 182). Children are precious not only in themselves but also for what they represent.

Childhood as symbol

Jenks (1996) suggests that four themes have historically emerged in the social construction of childhood. Childhood is seen as temporally separated, closer to nature, innocent and vulnerably dependent: 'a dominant modern discourse of childhood continues to mark out "the child" as innately innocent, confirming its cultural identity as a passive and unknowing dependant' (Jenks 1996: 124). This modern discourse is institutionalized in legal and social practices, globalized according to a western norm and protectionist, advocating adult intervention to protect the interests of children. The protectionist tendency is clearly mobilized by moral panics. The grounds are that children are increasingly, to use a social work term, 'at risk'. The environment is monitored for its sources. All moral panics about childhood identify a risk from adults; define children as vulnerable to them; proclaim the need to defend innocence of childhood against corruption; and require authority to intervene to protect children. 'The degree of anxiety generated by risks to children is associated with a particular construction of childhood as an age of innocence and vulnerability which adults have a duty to protect' (Jackson and Scott 1999: 95).

Moral panics select inappropriate or illusory targets for action. The concern is, to use Goode and Ben-Yehuda's (1994) term, systematically disproportionate. There are some real difficulties about children's access to and use of a media-rich environment but these are not recognized or resolved by periodic panics about video material or more recently the Internet. There are genuine problems about sexual abuse of children but these are more likely to occur in and around the family than from predatory paedophiles. Many of the documented dangers to children, physically from accidents (Roberts et al. 1995) or emotionally from parental divorce, are to all intents and purposes ignored. Moral panics seize on issues which are comparatively minor but are perceived as preventable. Why some objects, experiences and people are seen to pose threats to children while others do not, and why the campaign operates with such intensity, raises questions about the sources of this exaggerated concern with the welfare of children and the discourses which support it. Such questions, commonly raised (Best 1990; Cox 1996), ask 'what it is that elevates these issues to absolute centrality and renders them so pressing' and 'why childhood itself has become such a newly contested terrain' (James et al. 1999: 197).

Jenks (1996) provides three kinds of answers to this problem. The first is that the child is symbolic of the social order; the second that adult anxieties are projected onto children; the third that the first two are themselves reactions to perplexing changes in adult experience. In the first version, the child symbolizes the social order. What happens to them, or what they do, tell us what kind of society we have become or are becoming: ' "the child" has become a way of speaking about sociality itself. Any assault on what the child is, or rather what the child has evolved into, threatens to rock the social base' (Jenks 1996: 130). In the second version, adults evoke 'an imagined past in which children played safely throughout a carefree innocent childhood' (Jackson and Scott 1999: 87). Childhood is constructed through the prism of adult nostalgia: 'the concept of "childhood" serves to articulate not just the status of the young within modern society but also the projections, aspirations, longings and altruism contained within the adult experience' (Jenks 1996: 137).

In the third interpretation, adults have become so concerned about the safety of children because 'children have become our principal concern, we have become their protectors and nurturers and they have become our primary love objects, our human capital and our future' (Jenks 1996: 99). There is a recurrent suggestion that adult anxieties about their own identities (Drotner 1992) or the pace of social change (Best 1990; Buckingham 1997) are projected onto children and childhood. Furedi (1997) goes even further. Modern society is characterized by the collapse of all forms of solidarity or mediating experiences between the isolated individual and the abstraction of society. Not only the family but also community life of all kinds has declined. The isolated adult clings, literally and metaphorically, to children as an ideal. This is made more complex by changes in the reality of childhood.

Childhood and change

Buckingham (2000) has argued that changing perceptions of childhood status reflect some real changes in the lives of children in British society: 'children's lives – and hence the meanings we attribute to childhood – have indeed changed significantly in the past two or three decades' (Buckingham 2000: 62). He identifies three areas of change. In family life, children's experience has been changed by the disruption of the conventional nuclear family, the trend towards smaller families and increases in working mothers.

Children's economic importance as producers has been 'replaced by an emphasis on their psychological and particularly *emotional* value for parents' (Buckingham 2000: 65, original emphasis). In the second area, education and employment, earlier nursery care and larger numbers in higher education or compulsory training have meant that 'the institutionalization of childhood appears to be starting earlier and ending later' (Buckingham 2000: 6). In the third area, leisure opportunities have increased but within the confines of the home; children have more to do but fewer spaces in which to do it. Many activities and spaces outside the home are seen as dangerous. There is both more individual choice in and more control of children's leisure. While they have more access to some adult experiences, for example through the mass media, they are cut off from others, especially those of public space. The consequence is that childhood has changed and become more ambiguous. 'Arguably, we are witnessing contradictory trends – both towards the autonomy of children, domestic democracy and individualization of childhood and towards increased regulation and risk management of children by adults' (Livingstone 1998: 444).

Furedi (1997) stresses one side of this equation: the movement towards surveillance.

> During the past twenty years, concern with the safety of children has become a constant subject of attention. Children are portrayed as permanently at risk from danger . . . concern for the security of children has led to a major reorganization of the childhood experience. Childhood activities such as roaming about with friends or walking to and from school are becoming increasingly rare experiences. There is now a well-established consensus that children should not be left on their own. Middle-class children in particular are now subject to constant policing.
>
> (Furedi 1997: 115)

There are 'decreasing opportunities for children to develop autonomy and self reliance' (Jackson and Scott 1999: 94). Parents must be eternally vigilant and guard their children against known and unknown dangers. 'The combined effect of children's restriction and parental anxiety is a poorer quality of family life for all' (McNeish and Roberts 1995: 3).

The politics of childhood

We have explored why childhood has become such a consistent focus of moral panics, how images of vulnerability and threat have been mobilized to justify increased regulation. It seems generally true that 'the cultural significance of children, which prompts such quick response from alarmed parents, has not been fully appreciated by social scientists' (Stevens 1991: 29). Changes in the status and experience of children do not of themselves explain the obsession with risks to children and childhood. The change is less in the objective condition of children than in the subjective perception of adults; 'the anxieties specific to childhood are part of a general sense that the social world itself is becoming less stable and predictable' (Jackson and Scott 1999: 88). The moral intensity of the concern with risks to children justifies extreme measures. The protection of 'childhood acts as a focus for broader concerns about social change, "indiscipline" and moral collapse – and hence as a justification for more authoritarian social policies' (Buckingham 2000: 76). Panics around children have produced coercive controls of both children and adults (Pilcher and Wagg 1996; Scraton 1997).

Much of this argument is frankly speculative. Anxiety about children is hypothetically constructed. Because anxiety is evident at the public visible level, in the discourse of politics and the media, it is assumed that this is prevalent throughout society. Thus established as a characteristic of the whole society, an explanation is sought in the conditions of late modernity or postmodernity which are thought to have increased uncertainty. We are here in the realm of what is at best intelligent speculation and at worst claims which are not amenable to proof. It is difficult to know what to make of this kind of statement. 'The shrill cry of abuse is a cry of our own collective pain at the loss of our social identity' (Jenks 1994: 120).

Perhaps we should suspend speculation and recognize that what has to be explained is not what people actually think about children but how childhood is constructed, why it is, if it is, that 'the endangered child is a powerful symbol for almost all Americans' (Best 1990: 181). Childhood may be less a psychological projection of all adults than a discourse mobilized by elites, evident in claims makers' 'rhetoric of unreason'.

Certain categories of persons are understood to require greater vigilance in regard to the issues encapsulated by this kind of discourse. Those who can be said to be *trusting, naive, innocent, uneducated, uninformed, desperate,* and so forth can be 'taken advantage of' *as easy prey, vulnerable* to being manipulated by persons or institutions of greater power or authority. 'Children' provides a paradigmatic version for articulating this rhetorical idiom. Playing off the understanding that they are as yet 'unformed', interjecting into social problems the suggestive question, What about the children? directs auditors to extrapolate the worst-case scenario: What a child would 'end up like' were s/he to mature under the tutelage of influence of the pernicious agents.

(Ibarra and Kitsuse 1993: 40–1, original emphases)

Three points can be made about this lengthy passage. First, it is a very accurate portrait of the rhetoric about childhood evident in some case studies: video nasties, physical and sexual abuse in families and paedophilia. Second, the rhetoric is designed to appeal through its inherent undeniability. It does not depend upon adult anxiety but on a particular construction of both vulnerability and threat. Its internal logic is what matters. Third, the closed nature of this rhetoric about children takes us back to the problem with which we began, why there has in moral panics been a shift away from youth towards childhood. One answer would be that youth has now become a contested terrain, not least by youth culture itself. Attempts to portray youth as vulnerable to external threat are less viable if youth culture and its allies deny both the vulnerability and the threat, persisting in voluntary participation in activities which adult society tries to define as dangerous. From this perspective, the concentration on childhood is not rooted in the social psychology of postmodernity but in the shifting terrain of moral regulation. Dislodged from their advanced position, the army of claims makers has retreated to safer ground where its moral concerns are unlikely to be challenged. Children are 'seen as the weak link through which external threats make their entry' (Livingstone 1998: 447).

As will be discussed in Chapter 12, similar considerations apply to that line of argument which connects concern about childhood with an increased consciousness of risk. 'Risks to children are presented as inherently more grave than risks to adults: it is almost beyond debate that we should "protect" children, that any potential risk to them should be taken seriously' (Scott et al. 1998: 691). The question is whether this construction of children as 'at risk' is a feature of public cultural discourse or the collective psychology of postindustrial societies. Comparative study makes either generalization hazardous. While issues around childhood have become globalized (James et al. 1999), its precise definition remains local. 'Within Europe there are marked differences in the structures of childhood' (Livingstone 1998: 446). There are also differences in cultural perception. Scandinavian and Nordic countries appear to exhibit less anxiety about childhood than Britain and the USA (Jackson and Scott 1999). As Chapter 8 showed, in other countries like France child abuse is, rightly or wrongly, not such a public issue.

We must therefore make a distinction between public discourses and private practices about childhood and risk. Clearly parents do worry about risks to their own children (McNeish and Roberts 1995), which they deduce from their own experience and messages about risks from authoritative sources. These messages actually lead them to worry about the least likely threats and ignore the most likely. So, rather than private anxieties informing public debates, public debates structure private anxieties. As in moral panics generally, debates about childhood are constructed in the public arena by elite groups or those permitted entry to them. Two features of such contemporary debates now require our attention: their status as discourses and their construction of risk.

Further reading

Best, J. (1990) *Threatened Children: Rhetoric and Concern about Child Victims.* Chicago: University of Chicago Press.
Furedi, F. (1997) *The Culture of Fear: Risk-taking and the Morality of Low Expectation.* London: Cassell.
Jenks, C. (1996) *Childhood.* London: Routledge.

12

UNDERWRITING RISK: MORAL PANICS AND SOCIAL THEORY

Introduction

Kenneth Thompson (1998) has suggested that moral panic models can be connected to two of the most important sociological ideas of the 1990s: the risk society and discourse analysis. Our case study material validates this suggestion. Risk emerged as a fundamental issue across the case studies, in ways not captured by existing models. AIDS involved estimating who was at risk and how they placed themselves at risk. Rave/ecstasy was deplored for posing risks to participants. Video nasties posited the risk that children might be disturbed by, and even imitate, violence in horror films. The image of children at risk inside and outside families, which authorities should minimize, was central to child abuse. Discourses were consistently found 'beyond' the confines of conventional moral panic analysis. These were often specific to the issue: sexuality to AIDS, dangerous hedonism to rave/ecstasy and demonic children to video nasties. Child abuse generated discourses about childhood innocence or vulnerability. Some discourses were conspicuous by their absence. Discourses about masculinity did not appear in child abuse, even though virtually all the perpetrators were men.

Our concerns with risk and discourse theory are quite specific, whether risk can help identify how specific groups of people, objects or activities become defined as posing a risk to the moral order or discourse analysis illuminate the rhetorical evident in moral panics. It may even be useful to rethink moral panics as discourses about risk. It is not easy to relate the abstract concerns of risk theorists or the empirical examples of discourse analysts to the definition of social problems, much less the extreme case of moral panics. We need some intermediaries and some relevant cases to make the connections, provided for risk by Lupton (1999) and for discourse analysis by Mills (1997).

Risk

The risk society

Lupton (1999) outlines how Beck (1992) and Giddens (1991) have argued that modern society has become extremely risk conscious. Constant change and flux in politics, economy and culture, the compression of time and space in a globalized world, the collapse of traditional authority and sources of identity, all serve to remove any sense of stability. There is insecurity in the life passages which once predetermined individual biographies, such as routes through education, work and family life, or self-definitions in terms of class, gender and ethnicity. The result, that we are thrown more and more upon our own resources to make our own lives, necessarily produces 'high levels of anxiety and insecurity' so that 'life becomes less certain even while it is placed more under one's control' (Lupton 1999: 71). Risk theorists assume that risk is now a pervasive aspect of human existence, seen as manageable, associated with individual choice and responsibility and central to human subjectivity. The risk society has produced 'a particular way of understanding the self and the world that differs dramatically from other eras' (Lupton 1999: 11). The two crucial aspects are reflexivity, the constant consciousness of and about risk, and individuation, the definition and achievement of identity by individual action.

Risk theory has been little applied to the public construction of social problems except indirectly by anthropologist Mary Douglas (1966). Her concern with the sources, forms and functions of taboos in simple societies focused on the representation of dirt and impurity as morally defined, since 'the risks that receive most attention in a particular culture are those that are connected with legitimating moral principles' (Lupton 1999: 45). Attributing risk is a political act, identifying the source of impurity in 'an Other who is positioned as posing a threat (and thus a risk) to the integrity of self' (Lupton 1999: 40). Since conduct defined as deviant transgresses the basic rules of the community, responses are intense.

> In this approach, 'risk' may be understood as the cultural response to transgression: the outcome of breaking a taboo, crossing a boundary, committing a sin. At the heart of these 'risks' are the emotional dimensions of transgression: anger, anxiety, frustration, hatred, rage, fear.
>
> (Lupton 1999: 45)

In modern societies there is an increasing emphasis on preventing risks. They should not occur so somebody is held accountable, producing a new 'blaming system' assuming a problem to be somebody's fault. This modern view appears to secularize risk but retains religious traces of sin. Of the risk theories Lupton reviews, this is the only one to suggest why risk is a recurrent motif in moral panics but it is very indirect, by analogy with simple societies. Others have attempted to apply the risk framework to contemporary social problems in modern societies.

Risk and childhood

Jackson and Scott (1999) have applied risk analysis to current anxieties about children and childhood.

> Because children are thus constituted as a protected species and childhood as a protected state, both become loci of risk anxiety: safeguarding children entails keeping danger at bay; preserving childhood entails guarding against anything which threatens it. Conversely, risk anxiety helps construct childhood and maintain its boundaries – the specific risks from which children must be protected serve to define the characteristics of childhood and the 'nature' of children themselves.
>
> (Jackson and Scott 1999: 86)

There is a symbiotic relationship between prevailing ideas about childhood and those about risk. The sensibility shaping these ideas is that of adult society, whose social world has become less stable and predictable. Such a 'preoccupation with prevention' shows how 'risk management' underlies 'the social construction of childhood and the everyday experiences of children' (Jackson and Scott 1999: 90). Children are regarded as incapable of assessing risks so adults must do it for them. Adults 'know' but children do not that other adults pose a risk. Since we cannot know exactly who does and who does not pose a risk, we must prevent all interaction with unknown adults. Any stranger is a potential danger. Risk here is made relevant to moral panics. Links are made between a generalized consciousness of risk, the way childhood is constructed, actual daily practices of parenting and the moral panics about child abuse. The concept of risk here does identify and clarify how modern conceptions of childhood are indivisible from a pervasive sense of risk.

It is, however, an unusual application of risk theory. Many publications on risk are entirely confined to environmental and technological risks (Adams 1995), including Douglas's (1985) subsequent work. Hill (2001) applies the concept of the 'social amplification of risk', developed to explain reaction to environmental issues, to explore a series of moral panics about screen violence, including video nasties. Suggestive but essentially an analysis of claims making, it is unclear what is achieved by applying 'the master-frame of environmental discourse to a non-risk area' (Hill 2001: 210) or conceptualizing media violence as 'an environmental hazard' (Hill 2001: 213). Other work actually emphasizes the distinctiveness of 'scientific' risks. Kitzinger and Reilly (1997) argue that risk issues are not attractive for the media. They are ambiguous, often fail to provoke governmental response and involve projections into future rather than risks in the here and now. None of this is true of moral panics. Ungar (2001) rejects moral panic frameworks as inadequate to understanding the dimension or processes of problem definition in the risk society, though Hier (2001) disputes this. Scott et al. (1998) suggest that moral panics and risk anxiety are analytically distinct. Moral panics are short-lived campaigns about public issues requiring management by authorities. Risk anxiety is constant, private and has to be managed by individuals. The case for seeing moral panics as particular forms and expressions of risk consciousness has yet to be made.

Discourse

Discourse analysis

Discourse is a slippery word, subject to 'terminological confusions' (Potter and Wetherell 1987: 6). It is rarely defined with any accuracy or consistency, being often 'vague and sometimes obfuscatory' (Mills 1997: 1). Moreover, it is used in quite different ways in three distinct academic areas: cultural theory, social psychology and linguistics, so that 'their definitions of discourse differ significantly, and the types of analyses which they produce vary greatly from one to another' (Mills 1997: 135). All variants of discourse analysis reject the view that language is simply the vehicle for the expression of ideas. Language is a system with its own rules and constraints, which structure how we think and express ourselves. 'Social texts do not merely *reflect* or *mirror* objects, events and categories pre-existing in the social world. Rather, they actively *construct* a version of those things. They do not describe things; they *do* things' (Potter and Wetherell 1987: 6, original emphases). This is what is sometimes called the 'linguistic turn' in the social sciences which insists on the primacy of language.

Most discussions of discourse eventually lead to French philosopher Michel Foucault (1978, 1979, 1982). His enormously complex and massively influential work has at least three general implications for moral panic analysis. First, it is directly concerned with how deviant outgroups, such as criminals or the insane, are socially constructed to justify new forms of institutional intervention. Second, many of his key concepts, such as governmentality, disciplinary regimes or biopower, explore how mechanisms of social control are internalized in the ways we regulate our own social behaviour. Third, he explicitly discusses ambiguities in themes central to our cases studies, notably child sexuality and bodily pleasure. In what amounts to an attempt to rewrite the history of western civilization, it is doubtful whether moral panics would rate more than a footnote but the connections are there to be made, if an analyst can be found interested in both Foucault and moral panics.

To appropriate only discourse from Foucault is legitimate but partial. Mills (1997) suggests that discourse for Foucault is not a theory or even a concept but a tool for analysis. The model of the state promulgating a single ideology is replaced by multiple sites of contending discourses: 'there may be several different discourses at work in the construction of a particular text, and these discourses are often in conflict with one another' (Mills 1997: 100). Discourse in general has three basic characteristics: it is related to the institutional contexts in which it occurs; it has identifiable effects on 'our sense of reality and our own identity' (Mills 1997: 15); and, crucial for our purposes, it operates as an exclusionary device. There are some people whose discourse can be disregarded (the insane) and others who are discursively constructed as outside the category of human (the Other). Discourse is effective. It delimits the field, what is and is not being talked about. It establishes the writer or speaker's right to speak about it. It prescribes the way in which it is possible to speak about it, 'the parameters of the possible ways in which future statements can be made' (Mills 1997: 51).

Foucault's essential characteristics of discourses are relevant to moral panics. Moral panic discourses are located in institutional contexts (Parliament, the mass media, pressure groups), include and exclude topics and groups (folk devils are invariably excluded from society), affect the way we perceive the problem (there is now no other way to talk about the mistreatment of children other than as abuse). Discussion of moral panic issues precisely delimit the field (paedophilia, not sexual abuse in families) establish the right to speak (on behalf of a concerned public) and, perhaps most crucially of all, lay down the rules for the ways in which the problem can be talked about (as a self-evident threat to the moral order). Discourse analysis has the potential to analyse the ways in which linguistic strategies serve to validate the definitions and responses characteristic of moral panics. Its realization is evident in two studies of drug taking.

Discourses about drugs

Bell (1985) has applied a discourse approach to the way the mass media cover drug issues. He explicitly sets out to criticize what he sees as the consensual paradigm, represented mainly by Young (1974), but also typical of Cohen (1973) and Hall et al. (1978). This paradigm sees the media portrait of deviants in general and drug takers in particular as contrasting the normal 'us' with a deviant 'them', so constructing an ideological consensus. Bell aims to demonstrate that this approach is inadequate. He performed a content and then semantic analysis on 1300 stories from New South Wales newspapers in 1980 and 1981. Much of what he discovered was apparently compatible with the consensual paradigm. Drug takers were stereotyped and their behaviour disconnected from any social or economic context. Most news stories did come from official sources. Linguistic analysis demonstrated more precisely how drug takers were 'nominalized', presented as passive victims rather than active agents. The stories were structured around 'heroes' who diagnose and help the 'victims' of drugs and rescue them from the 'villains' who deal in them.

News coverage was less about drug takers themselves than the state and its agencies, with an 'overwhelming presence of scientific, bureaucratic-administrative, and medical discourses' (Bell 1985: 310). Citing Foucault, Bell interprets this drugs discourse as actually about the regulation of the body. It involves a focus on the body as a source of health and pleasure, on pedagogy – information and education about drugs – and on the need for surveillance by medical, legal and educational agencies of the state (Bell 1985: 318). Hence 'the interpretive frameworks into which drug issues are integrated frequently concern the administering, social-welfare interventionist arm of the state' (Bell 1985: 308). The specifics of this discourse cannot be recognized by the consensual paradigm which 'implies too monolithic an "inferential structure" in the media' (Bell 1985: 319), unable to appreciate that in this discourse 'the construction of deviance' is less important than 'the positive representation of the interventionist state' (Bell 1985: 318). The role of the media is to legitimize state intervention, constructing its readers as consenting subjects.

Mugford (1993) has also argued that drugs policies need to be situated within models of state activity and regulatory regimes. Foucault identified a historical shift in social control from the corporal, where bodily punishment is carried out in public, to the carceral, where punishment and surveillance of the body is achieved through incarceration. Mugford suggests there is now a third stage of risk management, where the bodies of defined populations are pragmatically controlled. Overall there is 'a shift away from punitive models emphasising surveillance towards a system of monitoring underpinned by the organization of pleasure' (Mugford 1993: 373). A distinction is made between the marginalized addict who requires disciplinary measures and the 'mainstream person' in search of pleasure, whose risk taking behaviour needs to be managed. In this perspective, changes in drugs policy are less the outcome of contest in public arenas or even the intractability of the recreational drugs problem than fundamental changes in the ways the state seeks to regulate bodily behaviour. By contrast, Giulianotti (1997) has argued that applying Foucault's concept of an 'archaeology' to discourses about drugs in British media shows them to be fundamentally ambiguous.

Such application of Foucault's ideas to moral panic discourses is rare. Many Foucauldian analyses of events covered in this book talk past or over any concern with moral panics (Ashenden 1996). Constructionist analysis of the rhetoric used in moral panics, especially by political leaders (Hawdon 2001), is often more relevant. Most relevant of all is the discourse analysis of critical linguistics.

Critical linguistics, discourse and the press

Critical linguists are 'concerned with a more ground-level approach than Foucault; they thus provide more working models and concrete examples of how texts work to create inequalities of power, and are more concerned with the mechanics of discursive functioning' (Mills 1997: 134). Such work has discussed the general nature of media discourses (Fairclough 1995; Bell and Garrett 1998) but for our interest in news coverage of social problem issues, especially in the press, the most useful guide is Fowler (1991). He sees critical linguistics as filling in a crucial gap in the study of news: the role of language, 'the discursive structure of the medium itself, the power of the structural minutiae of images and words to impose a value-laden organization on the news in the process of articulating it'. To achieve this requires 'extra components of theory' and 'a more powerful technical apparatus for practical textual analysis' (Fowler 1991: 222). Discourse is the key concept, following the definition provided by Kress (1985):

> Discourses are systematically-organized sets of statements which give expression to the meanings and values of an institution. Beyond that, they define, describe and delimit what it is possible to say and not possible to say (and by extension what it is possible to do or not to do) with respect to the area of concern of that institution, whether marginally or centrally. A discourse provides a set of possible statements about

a given area, and organizes and gives structure to the manner in which a particular topic, object, process is to be talked about. In that it produces descriptions, rules, permissions and prohibitions of social and individual actions.

(Kress 1985, cited in Fowler 1991: 42)

For Fowler, discourse does not supplant but is an elaboration of ideology. He accepts the concept of consensus but insist that it is 'a *linguistic* practice' (Fowler 1991: 49, original emphasis). The use of such pronouns as 'we', 'us' or 'our' is a mechanism which 'assumes and in times of crisis actually *affirms,* that there is no difference or disunity in the interests and values of any of the population, or of any institution' (Fowler 1991: 49, original emphasis). The press translates bureaucratic into public language, mediating between government and populace. The language of newspaper editorials embodies assumptions about the speaker, the audience and the issue, addressed in a 'vocabulary of categories'. The press inevitably use a form of cultural shorthand, instantly recognizable to journalists and to their audience, so that 'stereotypes are the currency of negotiation' (Fowler 1991: 17). Directed against an outgroup, their power to justify discrimination is enormous. 'Language provides names for categories, and so helps to set their boundaries and relationships; and discourse allows these names to be spoken and written frequently, so contributing to the apparent reality and currency of the categories' (Fowler 1991: 94). The language of news has to be studied in detail using the key terms of critical linguistics: transitivity, syntactic transformations, lexical registers, modality and speech acts.

One of his case studies is particularly indicative: the salmonella in eggs affair of late 1988 and early 1989. Though in our terms a food scare and not a moral panic, this nevertheless indicates how critical linguistics can uncover the mechanics of a specific discourse. The details of this issue, in which it was alleged that mass produced eggs contained salmonella poisonous to humans, need not detain us. Revealing is his emphasis on hysteria.

Fowler suggests that over five months there developed 'an hysterical episode of massive proportions built up in the British media' (Fowler 1991: 146). The massive scale of reportage, its emotive nature and its eventual exaggeration into a generalized threat of poisoned food was a form of hysteria.

Hysteria requires an expressive system, a mode of discourse, and, established, exists within that mode of discourse independent of empirical reality. Since expressive systems are shared among the members of a community, hysteria can be intersubjective: mass hysteria. Such was the status of listeria hysteria/the great egg scare: once established in the discourse of the media, it persisted autonomously within that discourse, going on and on at an increased pitch independent of the factual unfolding of the matter. The great egg scare was not a medical phenomenon, not an epidemic; it was a construct of discourse, a formation and transformation of ideas in the public language of the newspapers and television.

(Fowler 1991: 148)

This hysteria was located in and confined to the press with no reliable evidence that the public shared it. Headlines transparently revealed the 'hysterical style' of press discourse. In the dominant vocabulary, terms of risk (danger, hazard, threat, menace) were presented as leading to emotional reactions (fear, confusion, anxiety) which the use of alien medical terms exacerbated. The issue was dramatized; 'bugs' became threatening life forms against which humans had to wage a battle. Finally there was the 'rhetoric of quantification' which was 'really the dominant stylistic feature of the discourse' (Fowler 1991: 166). The epic scale of the problem was conveyed by the choice of verbs and adverbs (astronomical increase, large and accelerating rise, rampant rise, sudden and exponential leap).

These discursive strategies expressed and legitimized a reaction far in excess of anything justified by the actual issue. But then, suggests Fowler, much of this was not about salmonella in eggs at all: 'the real subject of discourse is not objective phenomena such as salmonella or eggs, but abstractions and subjective states such as crisis, danger, alarm' (Fowler 1991: 172). The 'stylistic template' of the media conflated otherwise unconnected issues, such as the deliberate contamination of baby foods on supermarket shelves, into a generalized anxiety about threats in and from food. Though he does not use the term, it would not be difficult to interpret such reaction as an extreme, perhaps hysterical, expression of risk consciousness.

Moral panics and risk discourses

Risk and discourse analysis have only occasionally been synthesized in moral panic analysis. In a polemical work, Furedi (1997) has outlined the logic behind the discourse of fear.

One of the most far-reaching consequences of these forms of thinking is to obscure the social causation of many of the problems people face . . . Behind the people who are out of control is a society which has lost its way. The effect of concentrating on degraded people rather than on society is to abandon any hope of finding solutions, because it is only possible to conceive of effective intervention in relation to a social problem. After all, a problem created by humans ought to be subject to their solutions. But the degraded person is not susceptible to effective intervention. The problem is caused by a moral flaw – and the only thing to be done is to punish and pray.

(Furedi 1997: 171)

In a more elaborate version, Hollway and Jefferson (1997) have argued that

fear of crime is a peculiarly apt discourse within the modernist quest for order since the risks it signifies, unlike other late modern risks, are *knowable*, *decisionable* (*actionable*) and potentially *controllable*. In an age of uncertainty, discourses that appear to promise a resolution to ambivalence by producing identifiable victims and blameable villains are likely to figure prominently in the State's ceaseless attempts to impose social order. Thus the figure of the 'criminal' becomes a convenient folk devil and the fear of crime discourse a satisfying location for anxieties generated more widely.

(Hollway and Jefferson 1997: 265, original emphasis)

Any revised model of moral panics needs to incorporate the dimension of discourse. While discourses are usually multiple, contradictory and contested, moral panics are distinctive in their production of singular, consistent and incontestable discourses. At least those which most approximate to the ideal type are, with paedophilia the archetypal case. Elsewhere, most obviously around AIDS but also sexual abuse in families, there was substantial evidence of competing discourses. Moral panics may thus be seen as a struggle to impose one closed definition on the issue, to prevent other ways of speaking about it. This struggle is not always successful, even when severe remedial action is taken. On the issue of recreational drugs, the harm reduction discourse has slowly won out over the repressive discourse to the point where the law may now be reformed.

Despite shifts over time as well as immediate contestation of discourses (Barak 1994), the initial impetus is to construct a unified discourse about the presenting social problem. We can predict what it will look like. It will have the following discursive elements:

- *the source of the threat* explained sociologically (the permissive society), psychologically (pathological behaviour) or morally (corroded values)
- *the nature of the threat* to the moral order – who or what poses it and why if left unchecked it will destroy the fabric of society

- *the victims of the threat* likely to be innocent and/or naive but essentially ordinary, anybody's child
- *campaigners against the threat* with impeccable motives: pressure groups, individual experts, politicians outside government and, of course, the media themselves
- *the remedy to the threat*, invariably measures to protect victims and punish perpetrators
- *the ultimate responsibility for protection from the threat*, the state or its agents, with novel legal powers.

That is an ideal type of the discourse about any new social problem. It is contestable in each element: the threat may be denied, its causes disputed; victims may be seen as making informed choices or restricted to segments of the population; claims makers may be opposed by counter claims makers; repression may be defined as counterproductive and legislative change as unwarranted. The course of the moral panic is shaped by the outcome of such discursive contest among elites. Where the discourse is successful, or successful enough, then the specific social problem will be inserted into a different overriding order of master discourse. This is a discourse about evil. Evil is a generalized threat which happens to take particular forms. Evil cannot be reformed or remedied except by being cast out. There can be no debate about evil; it has to be confronted, not understood. If evil is externalized, it is a justification for war. Internalized, it justifies exceptional measures beyond the normal processes of social and legal control. Essentially what distinguished paedophilia from virtually all the other panics was its embodiment of evil.

It is an exceptional outcome and by no means an inevitable one. The language of evil will be present from the very beginning in the denunciation of a 'social evil'. But such a definition will not always succeed. Discourse analysis reminds us that definitional processes are problematic and risk analysis that the level and nature of risk have to be debated. Such debates take place principally within the media. The development of a closed discourse in the media is a hallmark – now, a constitutive element – of a moral panic. At the point where there is only one way of 'speaking about' an issue, when other ways of speaking are excluded, then we have a discursive precondition for the emergence of a moral panic. Its emergence depends on such contingent factors as whether the media as a whole legitimize this discourse and whether there are other powerful competing discourses. This is in principle wholly compatible with a model of moral panic based upon stages and processes which could enable us to specify why some discourses achieve legitimacy and others do not. Much depends on the authority attributed to discourses and the degree of contestation between them.

Though discovered in quite another context, we might want to take up Astroff and Nyberg's (1992) concept of a 'hierarchy of discourses'. At the bottom and to be found in the earliest stages of a moral panic is a discourse about the specific problem, what it is taken to be and represent. At the next level is the discourse about risk, the extent to which the problem extends to the innocent and constitutes a threat to the moral order as a whole. At the apex is a discourse about evil. All three levels may be apparent at any one time but as an issue moves up the hierarchy the importance of the level below declines. The discourse becomes less specific and more generalized. The threat is no longer localized; we are all at risk; we confront not people mostly like us but the Other embodying evil. The pressure for action becomes unbearable. This may not happen but, when it does, society is in the throes of a moral panic. That is how the theories of risk society and the analysis of discourse indicate that moral panics should now be understood. The consequent reforms in how to conceptualize moral panics are outlined in the Afterword.

Further reading

Fowler, R. (1991) *Language in the News: Discourse and Ideology in the Press.* London: Routledge.
Lupton, D. (1999) *Risk.* London: Routledge.
Mills, S. (1997) *Discourse.* London: Routledge.

AFTERWORD

This book was finished in the first three months of 2002. The major news stories in that period showed traces of our moral panic case studies. The British Medical Association reported sexually transmitted diseases, including HIV/AIDS, to be on the increase. A survey of ecstasy users identified possible long-term effects on mental health; a Home Office guide to Safe Clubbing recommended fresh water supplies and 'chill out' areas. The retiring president of the British Board of Film Classification was noted to have liberalized censorship. The ongoing inquiry into the death of Victoria Climbié was covered regularly and the final report was issued into the death of 6-year-old Lauren Wright in 2000. There were paedophile scandals in the Catholic Church in Boston (USA), Poland and Australia, obliquely mentioned by the Pope. But the biggest issue by far was street crime, especially an increase in mobile phone muggings. The British government drove the issue. It admitted there was a problem and instituted an immediate response: more effective policing, longer sentences and extended tagging of young criminals. This was a telescoped moral panic, with the Home Secretary as its primary definer. It reproduced the same essential elements, including racial overtones, as the original emergence of mugging in the 1970s (Hall et al. 1978).

This reminds us of the difficulties of generalizing about moral panics. The case studies in this book often portrayed governments as reluctant to act, with divisions between state agencies. Consequently, our discussion of the role of the state in moral panics acknowledged complexity and variability. Yet here, as the project approached its end, was a clear example of government activating a moral panic for transparently political reasons, to prevent the main opposition party from capitalizing on law and order issues. It is nevertheless possible to hazard some generalizations about moral panics. Initially, we can dispose of two misconceptions. Moral panics do not have to have personified folk devils, though it is an advantage if they do. Future analysis of moral panics should not assume the indispensability of folk devils. The other misconception is that moral panics depend on support from public opinion. It is enough if those involved feel able to speak on behalf of the public. Moral panics are triggered among elite groups: politicians, pressure groups and the media, especially the popular press. Public opinion is constructed, not activated.

These are the major revisions required of moral panics as an ideal type. In the course of this book it has become evident that this processual model, though useful, is inadequate. Part III identified areas where further refinement is necessary to understand where moral panics vary across national contexts, how the media are implicated in them and why childhood has emerged as such a central theme. Two other dimensions of moral panics should be allied to the processual model. One, discussed in Chapter 12, is that moral panics mobilize sets or hierarchies of discourses. At their most successful, they achieve hegemony by constructing a single, incontestable discourse. Future analysis should specify discourses evident in moral panics and their relationship to perceptions of risk.

In addition to processes and discourses, there is a third dimension to moral panics which this book has underrepresented. Moral panics reaffirm the moral boundaries of society by nominating people or activities as beyond the pale. This is hardly a new insight. It has informed a whole strand in studies of deviance, from Durkheim's ([1895] 1964) original analysis of crime and the collective conscience to Erikson's (1966) analysis of how seventeenth-century New England settlers solidified an uncertain moral order by discovering the Devil in their midst. Sutherland (1950) demonstrated the construction of the sexual psychopath as a modern monster in post-war USA. So obvious as to be taken for granted, this function of moral panics should not be underestimated. Moral panics are moments when, in an otherwise dynamic and contradictory context of social change, moral certainty becomes achievable. Consensus about 'normal' sexuality or sexual behaviour is no longer viable but we can all condemn paedophiles. Such an 'ideal' moral panic offers a stark contrast between normal and deviant, good and evil, us and them.

The overall conclusion is that moral panics need to be understood in terms of these three dimensions, as identifiable processes, sets of discourses and an expression of irreducible moral values. We should no longer operate with the simplistic notions that moral panics require folk devils, mobilize public opinion or are instigated by the state. Cohen's first paragraph need no longer be cited as indicating, without further discussion, what a moral panic is. As has been consistently argued throughout this book, moral panic analysis is not an end but a beginning. An ideal type of moral panic goes only part of the way towards a comprehensive understanding of how social problems come to be defined as a threat to the moral order. It may well be that, as work progresses, the heuristic value of the moral panic concept declines. At the moment, the judgement has to be that it remains a necessary but not sufficient explanation. We cannot yet do without it.

GLOSSARY

Agenda setting: the process through which problems are recognized as requiring remedial action. The media are held to be strategic in setting the problem agenda for political elites and the public.

AIDS (acquired immune deficiency syndrome): a condition in which the body's immune system breaks down so that sufferers become gravely ill and may even die as a result of comparatively minor infections. It is caused by a virus, HIV (human immunodeficiency virus), which is transmitted by bodily fluids. The transition from HIV positive to AIDS is not inevitable and may now be delayed by drug therapy.

British Board of Film Classification (BBFC): any films shown publicly in Britain must have a certificate from the board indicating which age groups can see it. The board also issues certificates for sold and rented videos where the classifications are applied more strictly.

Child abuse: a generic term for all forms of maltreatment of children. Originally referring to physical injury, it came to encompass sexual exploitation. In childcare professions it has an even wider meaning, as in emotional abuse.

Claims makers: those groups or individuals who systematically make claims about the seriousness of a given social problem.

Class A drug: under British law, all illegal substances are classed as belonging to one of three groupings, Class A being the most serious, Class B intermediate and Class C the least serious. The classification of any drug determines the penalties for manufacture, possession or dealing. **Ecstasy** is at the time of writing a Class A drug and cannabis Class B.

Daily Mail: one of Britain's nine daily papers, excluding the specialist concerns of the *Financial Times* and *Daily Sport*. These are usually divided into quality broadsheets and popular tabloids but a more accurate distinction would be between four upmarket papers (*Guardian, Independent, Telegraph, Times*), two mid-market papers (*Express, Mail*) and three downmarket (*Mirror, Star, Sun*). While produced in a tabloid format, the *Daily Mail* places less emphasis than downmarket papers on sex, scandal and show business. Owned by Associated Newspapers, its politics are solidly right wing, never deviating from overt support for the Conservative Party. It currently sells 2.35 million copies a day, more than all the upmarket papers combined and 1 million less than the biggest selling paper, the *Sun*.

Deviance: strictly speaking, this describes any conduct which breaches social norms. Social scientists now generally agree that deviance is rarely an inherent property of an act or person but a process of definition and labelling which is often inconsistent and sometimes arbitrary.

Diffusion: the process by which an idea spreads from its original source to become more widely accepted. Ideas can diffuse from small groups to large groups and from one nation to another.

Discourse: difficult to define precisely but generally taken to mean a way of speaking about an issue, both the language habitually employed and the assumptions on which it rests.

Dunblane murders: in March 1996 a local man, Thomas Hamilton, shot and killed 16 children, their teacher and then himself in a primary school in the Scottish village of Dunblane. Hamilton had been banned from working with children after suspicions of sexual interference. Following arguments about how Hamilton had obtained a gun licence, the law relating to licences for firearms was tightened by Parliament later in the same year, effectively prohibiting private citizens from owning handguns.

Ecstasy: the street name for the **Class A drug** MDMA (methyleledioxyamphetamine) which induces temporary euphoria. Widely used at **raves** in the 1980s and 1990s, it is still frequently consumed in clubs. Little is understood about its long-term effects.

Federalism: a system in which power is decentralized. The centre of power is a federation of regional or locality based groupings. Most Anglophone and European political systems are of this type. Britain is unusual in its degree of centralized power in both politics and the mass media.

Hegemony: a situation where the definitions of social reality promulgated by a small, powerful group come to be accepted as normal and natural in a wider group or whole society.

HIV: see **AIDS**.

Ideal type: a concept used in sociology to construct what a social institution or process would look like, taken to its logical extreme. This is used to assess how and why actual institutions and processes vary from it.

Inferential structures: a set or system of interpretations of the meaning of a news event or issue, used by journalists and conveyed to audiences.

Key events: happenings which come to symbolize problems or issues, triggering extensive preoccupation with their alleged causes and effects.

Mods: a youth subculture emergent in Britain in the early 1960s. Its key elements were sharp dressing, scooters, parka coats, rhythm and blues music and the use of amphetamines. It was the first such style to attract female adherents. See also **Rockers**.

Moral entrepreneurs: those who seek to take a lead on moral issues, initiating campaigns to suppress or outlaw perceived immorality.

Mugging: now in everyday use but with no legal meaning, it implies robbery in public with the use or threat of force.

National Society for the Prevention of Cruelty to Children (NSPCC): founded in the nineteenth century as part of the child-saving movement, it has a long history of intervening in cases of child maltreatment, its officers originally wearing uniforms. It remains the only non-governmental body able to initiate care proceedings. With the decline of its casework functions, its campaigning role on all forms of child abuse has increased. As a charity, it enjoys royal patronage and considerable public support, though its reputation among professionals is more mixed.

National Viewers' and Listeners' Association (NVLA): originally founded in the 1960s as a 'Clean Up Television' campaign, it adopted the NVLA title to broaden its appeal. Its focus was on what it regarded as excessive violence, sex and bad language on television and in the media generally. Its founder, Mary Whitehouse, and other leaders were motivated by a fundamentalist Christian agenda. It now calls itself Mediawatch-UK.

New Age Travellers: a subculture especially prominent in the mid-1980s. Groups of young adults rejected the materialism of consumer society in favour of alternative lifestyles, often living in converted vehicles in which they travelled around the countryside.

News attention cycle: the idea that it is inherent in the nature of news for novel events and issues to be taken up for brief and intensive exploitation by the media. Unless there is something to sustain them, they will be dropped as a fresh issue is identified.

News of the World: one of Britain's nine main Sunday papers. These are usually divided into quality broadsheets and popular tabloids but a more accurate distinction would be between four upmarket papers (*Independent, Observer, Telegraph, Times*) two mid-market papers (*Express, Mail*) and three downmarket (*Mirror, People, News of the World*). The *News of the World* concentrates almost entirely on sex, show business and sport, specializing in scandal. Owned by Rupert Murdoch's News Corporation, its politics are extremely right wing. Its circulation, 4 million copies a week, is the largest of any Sunday paper.

News values: a set of working criteria by which the newsworthiness of an issue or event is assessed. Rarely written down, they are integral to the occupational culture and socialization of journalists.

Paedophile: any adult with a sexual interest in children, used more specifically to refer to men who seek sexual gratification from children by persuasion or force. Some are regarded as distinctive and classed as 'predatory' or 'fixated' but otherwise the term paedophile is applied indiscriminately.

Primary definers: those individuals or groups with established authority or expertise who have the power to define the terms of the debate about a social problem.

Rave: a new kind of dance-based event emergent in the late 1980s characterized by mass venues, fast (techno, garage and house) music, extensive special effects, distinctive dress codes and ubiquitous use of drugs such as **ecstasy**. Eventually outlawed, the rave was incorporated into mainstream clubbing.

Risk (society): the proposition that modern society has become more conscious of the insecurity involved in all spheres of social life, highly sensitive to any indications that the level and nature of risk has been misrepresented, especially by those in authority.

Ritual abuse: sexual acts performed on children with allegedly ritualistic elements, often attributed to Satanist practices, involving Devil worship.

Rockers: a youth subculture emergent in Britain in the early 1960s. Its key elements were leather jackets and jeans, motorbikes, rock and roll music and heavy drinking. Females were peripheral and subordinate. See also **Mods.**

Sensitization: the process whereby the media and other agencies of social control recognize a new problem or issue and begin to see its symptoms as rife, classing otherwise unremarkable events or trends as evidence of the spread and seriousness of the problem.

Social anxiety: a psychological reaction to unsettling social change, in which concern about apparently uncontrollable changes in major social institutions becomes displaced onto outgroups who symbolize social decline.

Social constructionism: a school of thought apparent in several social science disciplines which argues that what we take to be social reality is not self-evident but a selective interpretation. Applied to social problems, it requires focus on how and by whom the problem is constructed.

Social reaction: the ways in which the media, concerned groups, legal institutions and politicians define the nature, causes and resolutions of a new and problematic group or activity.

Template (media): the pattern of themes or conflicting groups established in news coverage of a key event or issue, which provides a model for subsequent treatment of apparently similar events or issues.

The Times: one of Britain's nine daily papers, excluding the specialist concerns of the *Financial Times* and *Daily Sport*. These are usually divided into quality broadsheets and popular tabloids but a more accurate distinction would be between four upmarket papers (*Guardian, Independent, Telegraph, Times*), two mid-market papers (*Express, Mail*) and three downmarket (*Mirror, Star, Sun*). Owned by Rupert Murdock's News Corporation, *The Times* is predictably right wing though less hostile to New Labour than it was to Old Labour. It currently sells 650,000 copies a day and remains highly influential with political elites.

Video nasty: the origins of this phrase have been variously attributed to a *Sunday Times* journalist or the **NVLA**. Early on it was restricted to films which the **BBFC** would not have granted a certificate to but later expanded to include most horror films.

REFERENCES

Adams, J. (1995) *Risk*. London: UCL Press.

Agger, B. (1993) The problem with social problems: from social constructionism to critical theory, in J.A. Holstein and G. Miller (eds) *Reconsidering Social Constructionism*. New York: Aldine de Gruyter.

Albert, E. (1986) Acquired Immune Deficiency Syndrome: the victim and the press, *Studies in Communication*, 3: 135–58.

Aldridge, M. (1990) Social work and the news media: a hopeless case, *British Journal of Social Work*, 20(6): 611–20.

Aldridge, M. (1994) *Making Social Work News*. London: Routledge.

Aldridge, M. (1995) Contemplating the monster: UK national press treatment of the Frank Beck affair, *Sociological Review*, 43(4): 658–74.

Aldridge, M. (1999) Poor relations: state social work and the press in the UK, in B. Franklin (ed.) *Social Policy, the Media and Misrepresentation*. London: Routledge.

Altheide, D.L. (1997) The news media, the problem frame, and the production of fear, *Sociological Quarterly*, 38(4): 647–68.

Altman, D. (1986) *AIDS and the New Puritanism*. London: Pluto.

Altman, D. (1988) Legitimation through disaster: AIDS and the gay movement, in E. Fee and D.M. Fox (eds) *AIDS: The Burdens of History*. Berkeley, CA: University of California Press.

Ames, M.A. and Huston, D.A. (1990) Legal, social and biological definitions of pedophilia, *Archives of Sexual Behavior*, 19(2): 333–42.

Appleyard, B. (1998) Lost in the dark shadows of child abuse, *Sunday Times*, 31 May.

Ashenden, S. (1996) Reflexive governance and child sexual abuse: liberal welfare rationality and the Cleveland Inquiry, *Economy and Society*, 25(1): 64–88.

Astroff, R.J. and Nyberg, A.K. (1992) Discursive hierarchies and the construction of crisis in the news: a case study, *Discourse and Society*, 3(1): 5–24.

Atmore, C. (1991) Essential fictions, fictional essences: some recent media constructions of child abuse, *New Zealand Women's Studies Journal*, 7(1): 29–54.

Atmore, C. (1996) Cross-cultural media-tions: media coverage of two child abuse controversies in New Zealand/Aoterea, *Child Abuse Review*, 5: 334–45.

Atmore, C. (1997) Rethinking moral panic and child abuse for 2000, in J. Besant and R. Hil (eds) *Youth, Crime and the Media*. Melbourne: National Clearing House for Youth Studies.

Barak, G. (1994) Media, society and criminology, in G. Barak (ed.) *Media, Process, and the Social Construction of Crime*. New York: Garland.

Barker, M. (1984a) Introduction, in M. Barker (ed.) *The Video Nasties*. London: Pluto.

Barker, M. (1984b) Nasty politics or video nasties?, in M. Barker (ed.) *The Video Nasties*. London: Pluto.

Barker, M. (1997) The Newson report, in M. Barker and J. Petley (eds) *Ill Effects: The Media/Violence Debate*. London: Routledge.

Barker, M. and Petley, J. (1997) Introduction, in M. Barker and J. Petley (eds) *Ill Effects: The Media/Violence Debate*. London: Routledge.

Barlow, G. and Hill, A. (eds) (1985) *Video Violence and Children*. Sevenoaks: Hodder and Stoughton.

Bayer, R. and Kirp, D.L. (1992a) An epidemic in political and policy perspective, in D.L. Kirp and R. Bayer (eds) *AIDS in the Industrialized Democracies: Passions, Politics and Policies*. Montreal: McGill-Queen's University Press.

Bayer, R. and Kirp, D.L. (1992b) The United States: at the centre of the storm, in D.L. Kirp and R. Bayer (eds) *AIDS in the Industrialized Democracies: Passions, Politics and Policies*. Montreal: McGill-Queen's University Press.

Bean, P. (1993) Cocaine and crack: the promotion of an epidemic, in P. Bean (ed.) *Cocaine and Crack*. London: Macmillan.

Beck, U. (1992) *Risk Society: Towards a New Modernity*, trans. M. Ritter. London: Sage.

Becker, H. (1963) *Outsiders: Studies in the Sociology of Deviance*. New York: Free Press.

Becker, H. (1966) Introduction, in H. Becker (ed.) *Social Problems: A Modern Approach*. New York: John Wiley.

Beharrell, P. (1993) AIDS and the British press, in J. Eldridge (ed.) *Getting the Message Across: News, Truth and Power*. London: Routledge.

Beharrell, P. (1998) News variations, in D. Miller, J. Kitzinger, K. Williams and P. Beharrell, *The Circuit of Mass Communication: Media Strategies, Representation and Audience Reception in the AIDS Crisis*. London: Sage.

Bell, A. and Garrett, P. (eds) (1998) *Approaches to Media Discourse*. Oxford: Blackwell.

Bell, P. (1985) Drugs as news: defining the social, in M. Gurevitch and M.R. Levy (eds) *Mass Communication Yearbook*. London: Sage.

Bell, S. (1988) *When Salem Came to the Boro: The True Story of the Cleveland Child Abuse Crisis*. London: Pan.

Bell, V. (2002) The vigilante parent and the paedophile, *Feminist Theory*, 3(1): 83–102.

Berridge, V. (1992) AIDS, the media and health policy, in P. Aggleton, P. Davies and G. Hart (eds) *AIDS: Rights, Risk and Reason*. Bristol: Falmer.

Berridge, V. (1996) *AIDS in the UK: The Making of Policy 1981–1991*. Oxford: Oxford University Press.

Best, J. (1990) *Threatened Children: Rhetoric and Concern about Child Victims*. Chicago: University of Chicago Press.

Best, J. (1993) But seriously folks: the limitations of the strict constructionist interpretation of social problems, in J.A. Holstein and G. Miller (eds) *Reconsidering Social Constructionism*. New York: Aldine de Gruyter.

Bibby, P.C. (ed.) (1996) *Organised Abuse: The Current Debate*. Aldershot: Arena/Ashgate.

Blumer, H. (1971) Social problems as collective behavior, *Social Problems*, 18(winter): 298–306.

Boethius, U. (1994) Youth, media and moral panics, in J. Fornas and G. Bolin (eds) *Youth Culture in Late Modernity*. London: Sage.

Bromley, D. (1991) Satanism: the new cult scare, in J.T. Richardson, J. Best and D. Bromley (eds) *The Satanism Scare*. New York: Aldine de Gruyter.

Brosius, H. and Eps, P. (1995) Prototyping through key events: news selection and the case of violence against aliens and asylum-seekers in Germany, *European Journal of Communication*, 10(3): 391–412.

Brown, B. (1984) Exactly what we wanted, in M. Barker (ed.) *The Video Nasties*. London: Pluto.

Bryman, A. (2001) *Social Research Methods*. Oxford: Oxford University Press.

Buckingham, D. (1996) *Moving Images: Understanding Children's Emotional Responses to Television*. Manchester: Manchester University Press.

Buckingham, D. (1997) Electronic child abuse?, in M. Barker and J. Petley (eds) *Ill Effects: The Media/Violence Debate*. London: Routledge.

Buckingham, D. (2000) *After the Death of Childhood*. Cambridge: Polity.

Butler-Sloss, Lord Justice (1988) *Report of the Inquiry into Child Abuse in Cleveland*. Short Version. London: HMSO.

Campbell, B. (1987) *Unofficial Secrets: Child Sexual Abuse – the Cleveland Case*. London: Virago.

Carment, A. (1987) The media and the 'discovery' of child abuse: bringing the monster back home, *Australian Journal of Law and Society*, 4: 7–41.

Check, W.A. (1987) Beyond the model of reporting: non-specific symptoms in media reporting about AIDS, *Review of Infectious Diseases*, 9(5): 987–99.

Chermak, S. (1994) Crime in the news media: a refined understanding of how crimes become news, in G. Barak (ed.) *Media, Process, and the Social Construction of Crime*. New York: Garland.

Chibnall, S. (1977) *Law and Order News*. London: Tavistock.

Clapton, G. (1993) *The Satanic Abuse Controversy: Social Workers and the Social Work Press*. London: University of North London Press.

Clyde, Lord (1992) *The Report of the Inquiry into the Removal of Children from Orkney in February 1991*. London: HMSO.

Cohen, S. (1973) *Folk Devils and Moral Panics*. St Albans: Paladin.

Colby, D.C. and Cook, T.E. (1991) Epidemics and agendas: the politics of nightly news coverage of AIDS, *Journal of Politics, Health and Law*, 16(2): 215–49.

Collier, R. (2001) Dangerousness, popular knowledge and the criminal law: a case study of the paedophile as sociocultural phenomenon, in P. Alldridge and C. Brant (eds) *Personal Autonomy, the Private Sphere and the Criminal Law*. Oxford: Hart.

Collin, M. with Godfrey, J. (1998) *Altered State: The Story of Ecstasy Culture and Acid House*, 2nd edn. London: Serpent's Tail.

Cooper, C. (1995) Child abuse, in G. Pearson (ed.) *Scare in the Community*. London: Community Care.

Costin, L.B., Karger, H.J. and Stoetsz, D. (1996) *The Politics of Child Abuse in America*. New York: Oxford University Press.

Cox, R. (1996) *Shaping Childhood*. London: Routledge.

Craib, I. (1992) *Modern Social Theory*. Hemel Hempstead: Harvester Wheatsheaf.

Critcher, C. (2000a) 'Still raving': social reaction to ecstasy, *Leisure Studies*, 19(2): 145–62.

Critcher, C. (2000b) *Madness in their Methods: Moral Panics and the Mass Media*. Sheffield: Sheffield Hallam University School of Cultural Studies.

Critcher, C. (2002) Media, government and moral panic: the politics of paedophilia in Britain 2000–1, *Journalism Studies*, 3(4): 520–34.

Davies, S. (1997) A sight to behold: media and the visualisation of youth, evil and innocence, in J. Besant and R. Hil (eds) *Youth, Crime and Media*. Melbourne: National Clearing House for Youth Studies.

Dearing, J.W. (1992) Foreign blood and domestic politics: the issue of AIDS in Japan, in E. Fee and D.M. Fox (eds) *AIDS: The Making of a Chronic Disease*. Berkeley, CA: University of California Press.

Dearing, J.W. and Rogers, E.M. (1996) *Communication Concepts 6: Agenda-Setting*. Thousand Oaks, CA: Sage.

deYoung, M. (1998) Another look at moral panics: the case of satanic day care centers, *Deviant Behavior*, 19(3): 257–78.

Dingwall, R. (1986) The Jasmine Beckford Affair, *Modern Law Review*, 48: 489–507.

Donaldson, L.J. and O'Brien, S. (1995) Press coverage of the Cleveland sexual abuse enquiry: a source of public enlightenment?, *Journal of Public Health and Medicine*, 17(1): 70–6.

Douglas, M. (1966) *Purity and Danger: An Analysis of Concepts of Pollution and Taboo*. London: Routledge and Kegan Paul.

Douglas, M. (1985) *Risk Acceptability according to the Social Sciences*. New York: Russell Sage Foundation.

Downes, D. and Rock, P. (1998) *Understanding Deviance*. Oxford: Oxford University Press.

Downs, A. (1972) Up and down with ecology: the 'issue-attention' cycle, *The Public Interest*, 28: 38–50.

Doyle, K. and Lacombe, D. (2000) Scapegoat in risk society: the case of pedophile pornographer Robin Sharpe, *Studies in Law, Politics and Society*, 20: 183–206.

Drotner, K. (1992) Modernity and media panics, in M. Skovmand and K.M. Schroder (eds) *Media Cultures*. London: Routledge.

Dunn, M. (1994) From Colwell to Cleveland, in S. Richardson and H. Bacon (eds) *Child Abuse: Whose Problem? Reflections from Cleveland*. London: Venture Press.

Durham, M. (1989) The Thatcher government and the 'moral right', *Parliamentary Affairs*, 42(1): 58–71.

Durkheim, E. ([1895] 1964) *The Rules of Sociological Method*. New York: Free Press.

Dwyer, T. and Stockbridge, S. (1999) Putting violence to work in new media policies, *New Media and Society*, 1(2): 227–49.

Earle, F., Dearling, A., Whittle, H., Glasse, R. and Gubby (1994) *A Time to Travel?* Lyme Regis: Enabler.

Edwards, S.S.M. and Soetenhorst-de Savornin Lohman, J. (1994) The impact of 'moral panic' on professional behavior in cases of child sexual abuse: an international perspective, *Journal of Child Sexual Abuse*, 3(1): 103–26.

Eldridge, J., Kitzinger, J. and Williams, K. (1997) *The Mass Media and Power in Modern Britain*. Oxford: Oxford University Press.

Ericson, R.V., Baranek, P.M. and Chan, J.B.L. (1987) *Visualizing Deviance: A Study of News Organization*. Milton Keynes: Open University Press.

Erikson, K. (1966) *Wayward Puritans: A Study in the Sociology of Deviance*. New York: John Wiley.

Fairclough, N. (1995) *Media Discourse*. London: Edward Arnold.

Feldman, E.A. and Yonemoto, S. (1992) Japan: AIDS as a 'non-issue', in D.L. Kirp and R. Bayer (eds) *AIDS in the Industrialized Democracies: Passions, Politics and Policies*. Montreal: McGill-Queen's University Press.

Fischer, B. (1998) Prohibition as the art of political diplomacy: the benign causes of the 'war on drugs' in Canada, in E.L. Jensen and J. Gerber (eds) *The New War on Drugs: Symbolic Politics and Criminal Justice Policy*. Academy of Criminal Justice Sciences, Highland Heights, KY: Northern Kentucky University.

Fitzpatrick, M. and Milligan, D. (1987) *Truth about the AIDS Panic*. London: Junius.

Foucault, M. (1978) *The History of Sexuality: An Introduction, Volume 1*. Harmondsworth: Penguin.

Foucault, M. (1979) *Discipline and Punish: The Birth of the Prison*. New York: Vintage/Random House.

Foucault, M. (1982) *Madness and Civilization: A History of Insanity in the Age of Reason*. London: Tavistock.

Fowler, R. (1991) *Language in the News: Discourse and Ideology in the Press*. London: Routledge.

Frankenberg, G. (1992) Germany: the uneasy triumph of pragmatism, in D.L. Kirp and R. Bayer (eds) *AIDS in the Industrialized Democracies: Passions, Politics and Policies*. Montreal: McGill-Queen's University Press.

Franklin, B. and Parton, N. (1991) Media reporting of social work: a framework for analysis, in B. Franklin and N. Parton (eds) *Social Work, the Media and Public Relations*. London: Routledge.

Franklin, B. and Petley, J. (1996) Killing the age of innocence: newspaper reporting of the death of James Bulger, in S. Wagg and J. Pilcher (eds) *Thatcher's Children: Childhood, Politics and Society in the 1990s*. London: Falmer.

Fritz, N.J. and Altheide, D.L. (1987) The mass media and the social construction of the missing children problem, *Sociological Quarterly*, 28(4): 473–92.

Furedi, F. (1997) *Culture of Fear: Risk-taking and the Morality of Low Expectation*. London: Cassell.

Galtung, J. and Ruge, M. ([1965] 1981) Structuring and selecting news, in S. Cohen and J. Young (eds) *The Manufacture of News: Deviance, Social Problems and the Mass Media*. London: Constable.

Gamson, W.A. and Modigliani, A. (1989) Media discourse and public opinion on nuclear power: a constructionist approach, *American Journal of Sociology*, 95(1): 1–37.

Gentry, C. (1988) The social construction of abducted children as a social problem, *Sociological Inquiry*, 58(4): 413–25.

Giddens, A. (1991) *Modernity and Identity: Self and Society in the Late Modern Age*. Cambridge: Polity.

Giulianotti, R. (1997) Drugs and the media in the era of postmodernity: an archaeological analysis, *Media, Culture and Society*, 19: 419–39.

Goddard, C. and Liddell, M. (1995) Child abuse fatalities and the media: lessons from a case study, *Child Abuse Review*, 4: 356–64.

Golding, P. and Elliott, P. (1979) *Making the News*. London: Longman.

Golding, P. and Middleton, S. (1979) Making claims: news media and the welfare state, *Media, Culture and Society*, 1: 5–21.

Goode, E. (1969) Marijuana and the politics of reality, *Journal of Health and Social Behavior*, 10: 83–94.

Goode, E. (1990) The American drug panic of the 1980s: social construction or objective threat?, *The International Journal of the Addictions*, 25(9): 1083–98.

Goode, E. and Ben-Yehuda, N. (1994) *Moral Panics: The Social Construction of Deviance*. Oxford: Blackwell.

Gordon, A.F. (1993) Twenty two theses on social constructionism: a feminist response to Ibarra and Kitsuse's 'proposal for the study of social problems', in J.A. Holstein and G. Miller (eds) *Reconsidering Social Constructionism*. New York: Aldine de Gruyter.

Gould, A. (1994) Sweden's syringe exchange debate: moral panic in a rational society, *Journal of Social Policy*, 23(2): 195–217.

Grubin, D. (1998) *Sex Offending against Children: Understanding the Risk*. Home Office Police Research Series 99. London: Home Office.

Gusfield, J. (1963) *Symbolic Crusade: Status Politics and the American Temperance Movement*. Urbana, IL: University of Illinois Press.

Gusfield, J. (1967) Moral passage: the symbolic process in public designations of deviance, *Social Problems*, 15(fall): 175–88.

Gusfield, J. (1981) *The Culture of Public Problems*. Chicago: University of Chicago Press.

Hagell, A. and Newburn, T. (1994) *Young Offenders and the Media: Viewing Habits and Preferences*. London: Policy Studies Institute.

Hall, S., Critcher, C., Jefferson, T., Clarke, J. and Roberts, B. (1978) *Policing the Crisis: Mugging, the State and Law and Order*. London: Macmillan.

Halloran, J.D., Elliott, P. and Murdock, G. (1970) *Demonstrations and Communication: A Case Study*. Harmondsworth: Penguin.

Harris, M. (1984) The strange saga of the Video Bill, *New Society*, 26 April.

Hartley, J. (1998) Juvenation: news, girls and power, in C. Carter, G. Bransdon and S. Allen (eds) *News, Gender and Power*. London: Routledge.

Hawdon, J.E. (2001) The role of presidential rhetoric in the creation of a moral panic: Reagan, Bush and the war on drugs, *Deviant Behavior*, 22(5): 419–45.

Henderson, S. (1993) Luv'dup and de-lited: responses to drug use in the second decade, in P. Aggleton, P. Davies and G. Hart (eds) *AIDS: Facing the Second Decade*. London: Falmer.

Henderson, S. (1997) *Ecstasy: Case Unsolved*. London: Pandora.

Henningsen, G. (1996) The child witch syndrome: Satanic child abuse of today and child witch trials of yesterday, *The Journal of Forensic Psychiatry*, 7(3): 581–93.

Henriksson, B. and Ytterberg, H. (1992) Sweden: the power of the moral(istic) left, in D.L. Kirp and R. Bayer (eds) *AIDS in the Industrialized Democracies: Passions, Politics and Policies*. Montreal: McGill-Queen's University Press.

Herzlich, C. and Pierret, J. (1989) AIDS in the French press, *Social Science and Medicine*, 29(11): 1235–42.

Hetherington, K. (1992) Stonehenge and its festival: spaces of consumption, in R. Shields (ed.) *Lifestyle Shopping*. London: Routledge.

Hier, S.P. (2001) Risk and panic in late modernity: implications of the converging sites of social anxiety. Unpublished paper, Department of Sociology, McMaster University, Canada.

Hier, S.P. (2002) Rave, risk and the ecstasy panic: a case study in the subversive nature of moral regulation, *Canadian Journal of Sociology*, 27(1): 33–57.

Hilgartner, S. and Bosk, C.L. (1988) The rise and fall of social problems: a public arenas model, *American Journal of Sociology*, 94(1): 53–78.

Hill, A. (2001) Media risks: the social amplification of risk and the media violence debate, *Journal of Risk Research*, 4(3): 209–25.

Hill, C. (1985a) Historical background to the video enquiry, in G. Barlow and A. Hill (eds) *Video Violence and Children*. Sevenoaks: Hodder and Stoughton.

Hill, C. (1985b) Conclusion, in G. Barlow and A. Hill (eds) *Video Violence and Children*. Sevenoaks: Hodder and Stoughton.

Hill, M. (1990) The manifest and latent lessons of child abuse inquiries, *British Journal of Social Work*, 20(2): 197–213.

Holland, P. (1992) *What is a Child? Popular Images of Childhood*. London: Virago.

Hollway, W. and Jefferson, T. (1997) The risk society in the age of anxiety: situating a fear of crime, *British Journal of Sociology*, 48(2): 255–66.

Home Office (1998) *Trespass and Protest: Policing under the Criminal Justice and Public Order Act 1994*. Home Office Research Study 190. London: Home Office.

Hood, R., Shute, S., Frilzer, M. and Wilcox, A. (2002) Sex offenders emerging from long-term imprisonment, *British Journal of Criminology*, 42: 371–94.

Hunt, A. (1997) 'Moral panic' and moral language in the media, *British Journal of Sociology*, 48(4): 629–48.

Hutchinson, R. (1986) The effect of inquiries into the cases of child abuse upon the social work profession, *British Journal of Criminology*, 26(2): 178–82.

Ibarra, P.R. and Kitsuse, J. (1993) Vernacular constituents of moral discourse: an interactionist proposal for the study of social problems, in J.A. Holstein and G. Miller (eds) *Reconsidering Social Constructionism*. New York: Aldine de Gruyter.

Illsley, P. (1989) *The Drama of Cleveland*. London: Campaign for Press and Broadcasting Freedom.

Jackson, S. and Scott, S. (1999) Risk anxiety and the social construction of childhood, in D. Lupton (ed.) *Risk and Sociocultural Theory*. Cambridge: Cambridge University Press.

Jacobs, R.N. (1996) Producing the news, producing the crisis: narrativity, television and news work, *Media, Culture and Society*, 18: 373–97.

James, A., Jenks, C. and Prout, A. (1999) *Theorizing Childhood*. Cambridge: Polity.

Jenkins, P. (1992) *Intimate Enemies: Moral Panics in Contemporary Great Britain*. New York: Aldine de Gruyter.

Jenkins, P. (1998) *Moral Panic: Changing Concepts of the Child Molester in Modern America*. New Haven, CT: Yale University Press.

Jenkins, P. (1999) *Synthetic Panic: The Symbolic Politics of Designer Drugs*. New York: New York University Press.

Jenkins, P. (2001) *Beyond Tolerance: Child Pornography on the Internet*. New York: New York University Press.

Jenkins, P. and Maier-Katkin, D. (1992) Satanism: myth and reality in a contemporary moral panic, *Crime, Law and Social Change*, 17: 53–73.

Jenks, C. (1994) Child abuse in the postmodern context: an issue of social identity, *Childhood*, 2: 111–21.

Jenks, C. (1996) *Childhood*. London: Routledge.

Johnson, J.M. (1985) Symbolic salvation: the changing meanings of the child maltreatment movement, *Studies in Symbolic Interaction*, 6: 289–305.

Jones, P. (1997) Moral panic: the legacy of Stan Cohen and Stuart Hall, *Media International Australia*, 85(November): 6–16.

Kelly, L. (1996) Weasel words: paedophiles and the 'cycle of abuse', *Trouble and Strife*, 33: 44–9.

Kempe, C.H., Silverman, F.N., Steele, B.F., Droegemuller, W. and Silver, H.K. (1962) The battered-child syndrome, *Journal of the American Medical Association*, 181(July): 17–24.

Kepplinger, H.M. and Habermeier, J.H. (1995) The impact of key events upon the presentation of reality, *European Journal of Communication*, 10(3): 371–90.

Kidd-Hewitt, D. (1995) Crime and the media: a criminological perspective, in D. Kidd-Hewitt and R. Osborne (eds) *Crime and the Media: The Post-Modern Spectacle*. London: Pluto.

Kirp, D.L. and Bayer, R. (eds) (1992) *AIDS in the Industrialized Democracies: Passions, Politics and Policies*. Montreal: McGill-Queen's University Press.

Kitzinger, J. (1993) Understanding AIDS: researching audience perceptions of Acquired Immune Deficiency Syndrome, in J. Eldridge (ed.) *Getting the Message Across: News, Truth and Power*. London: Routledge.

Kitzinger, J. (1996) Media representations of child abuse, *Child Abuse Review*, 5: 301–9.

Kitzinger, J. (1999) The ultimate neighbour from hell? The media representation of paedophilia, in B. Franklin (ed.) *Social Policy, the Media and Misrepresentation*. London: Routledge.

Kitzinger, J. (2000) Media templates; patterns of association and the (re)construction of meaning over time, *Media, Culture and Society*, 22: 61–84.

Kitzinger, J. and Miller, D. (1998) Conclusion, in D. Miller, J. Kitzinger, K. Williams and P. Beharrell, *The Circuit of Mass Communication: Media Strategies, Representation and Audience Reception in the AIDS Crisis*. London: Sage.

Kitzinger, J. and Reilly, J. (1997) The rise and fall of risk reporting: media coverage of human genetics research, 'false memory syndrome' and 'mad cow disease', *European Journal of Communication*, 12(3): 319–50.

Kitzinger, J. and Skidmore, P. (1995) Playing safe: media coverage of child sexual abuse prevention strategies, *Child Abuse Review*, 4: 47–56.

Kohn, M. (1997) The chemical generation and its ancestors: dance crazes and drug panics across eight decades, *The International Journal of Drugs Policy*, 8(3): 137–42.

Kress, G.R. (1985) *Linguistic Processes in Sociocultural Practice*. Geelong, Victoria: Deakin University Press.

La Fontaine, J.S. (1990) *Child Sexual Abuse*. Cambridge: Polity.

La Fontaine, J.S. (1994) *The Extent and Nature of Organised and Ritual Abuse*. London: HMSO.

Lang, K. and Lang, G. (1955) The inferential structure of political communications, *Public Opinion Quarterly*, 19(summer).

Lauderdale, P. (1976) Deviance and moral boundaries, *American Sociological Review*, 41: 660–76.

Lawler, S. (2002) Mobs and monsters: *Independent* man meets Paulsgrove woman, *Feminist Theory*, 3(1): 103–13.

Lemert, E.M. (1967) *Human Deviance, Social Problems and Social Control*. Englewood Cliffs, NJ: Prentice Hall.

Lippert, R. (1990) The construction of Satanism as a social problem in Canada, *Canadian Journal of Sociology*, 15(4): 417–35.

Livingstone, S. (1998) Mediated childhoods: a comparative approach to young people's changing media environment in Europe, *European Journal of Communication*, 13(4): 435–56.

Lupton, D. (1994) *Moral Threats and Dangerous Desires: AIDS in the News Media*. London: Taylor & Francis.

Lupton, D. (1999) *Risk*. London: Routledge.

Lupton, D. (2001) Constructing 'road rage' as news: an analysis of two Australian newspapers, *Australian Journal of Communication*, 28(3): 23–6.

Lyttle, T. and Montagne, M. (1992) Drugs, music and ideology: a social pharmacological interpretation of the Acid House movement, *The International Journal of the Addictions*, 27(10): 1159–77.

McDermott, P., Matthews, A. and O'Hare, P. (1993) Ecstasy in the UK: recreational drug use and social change, in N. Heather, A. Wodak, E. Nadelmann and P. O'Hare (eds) *Psychoactive Drugs and Harm Reduction*. London: Whurr.

McDevitt, S. (1996) The impact of news media on child abuse reporting, *Child Abuse and Neglect*, 20(4): 261–74.

McC Miller, P. and Plant, M. (1996) Drinking, smoking and illicit drug use amongst 15 and 16 year olds in the United Kingdom, *British Medical Journal*, 313: 394–7.

MacGregor, S. (1999) Medicine, custom or moral panic: policy responses to drug misuse, in N. South (ed.) *Drugs: Culture, Controls and Everyday Life*. London: Sage.

McNeish, D. and Roberts, H. (1995) *Playing it Safe: Today's Children at Play*. Ilford: Barnardo's.

MacRae, D. (1974) *Weber*. London: Fontana.

McRobbie, A. (1994) Moral panics in the age of the postmodern mass media, in A. McRobbie, *Postmodernism and Popular Culture*. London: Routledge.

McRobbie, A. and Thornton, S.L. (1995) Re-thinking 'moral panic' for multi-mediated social worlds, *British Journal of Sociology*, 46(4): 559–74.

Manoff, R.K. (1986) Writing the news (by telling the story), in R.K. Manoff and M. Schudson (eds) *Reading the News*. New York: Pantheon.

Marsh, D., Gowin, P. and Read, M. (1986) Private Members' Bills and moral panic: the case of the Video Recordings Bill, *Parliamentary Affairs*, 39(2): 179–96.

Marsh, D., Read, M. and Myers, B. (1987) Don't panic: the Obscene Publications Bill 1985, *Parliamentary Affairs*, 40(1): 73–9.

Marshall, P. (1998) *The Prevalence of Convictions for Sexual Offending*. Home Office Research Paper 55. London: Home Office.

Martin, J. (1993) *The Seduction of the Gullible*. Nottingham: Procrustes.

Mayall, B. (1994) Children in action at home and school, in B. Mayall (ed.) *Children's Childhoods: Observed and Experienced*. London: Falmer.

Measham, F., Newcombe, R. and Parker, H. (1994) The normalisation of recreational drug use amongst young people in N.W. England, *British Journal of Sociology*, 45(2): 287–312.

Meldrum, J. (1990) The role of the media and the reporting of AIDS, in B. Almond (ed.) *AIDS: A Moral Issue, the Legal Ethical and Social Aspects*. London: Macmillan.

Merchant, J. and McDonald, R. (1994) Youth and the rave culture, ecstasy and health, *Youth and Policy*, 45(summer): 16–38.

Miller, D. and Beharrell, P. (1998) AIDS and television news, in D. Miller, J. Kitzinger, K. Williams and P. Beharrell, *The Circuit of Mass Communication: Media Strategies, Representation and Audience Reception in the AIDS Crisis*. London: Sage.

Miller, D. and Kitzinger, J. (1998) AIDS, the policy process and moral panics, in D. Miller, J. Kitzinger, K. Williams and P. Beharrell, *The Circuit of Mass Communication: Media Strategies, Representation and Audience Reception in the AIDS Crisis*. London: Sage.

Miller, D. and Williams, K. (1993) Negotiating HIV/AIDS information: agendas, media strategies and the news, in J. Eldridge (ed.) *Getting the Message Across: News, Truth and Power*. London: Routledge.

Miller, D. and Williams, K. (1998a) The AIDS public education campaign, in D. Miller, J. Kitzinger, K. Williams and P. Beharrell, *The Circuit of Mass Communication: Media Strategies, Representation and Audience Reception in the AIDS Crisis*. London: Sage.

Miller, D. and Williams, K. (1998b) Sourcing AIDS news, in D. Miller, J. Kitzinger, K. Williams and P. Beharrell, *The Circuit of Mass Communication: Media Strategies, Representation and Audience Reception in the AIDS Crisis*. London: Sage.

Miller, D., Kitzinger, J., Williams, K. and Beharrell, P. (1998) *The Circuit of Mass Communication: Media Strategies, Representation and Audience Reception in the AIDS Crisis*. London: Sage.

Mills, S. (1997) *Discourse*. London: Routledge.

Misztal, B.A. and Moss, D. (eds) (1990a) *Action on AIDS: National Policies in Comparative Perspective*. New York: Greenwood.

Misztal, B.A. and Moss, D. (1990b) Conclusion, in B.A. Misztal and D. Moss (eds) *Action on AIDS: National Policies in Comparative Perspective*. New York: Greenwood.

Mitchell, J. (2001) The moral panic about raves: newspaper transmission and legislation. Unpublished MA thesis, Humboldt State University, Arcata, CA.

Moerkerk, H. and Aggleton, P. (1990) AIDS prevention strategies in Europe: a comparison and critical analysis, in P. Aggleton, P. Davies and G. Hart (eds) *AIDS: Individual, Cultural and Policy Dimensions*. London: Falmer.

Molotch, H. and Lestor, M. (1974) News as purposive behaviour: the strategic use of routine events, accidents and scandals, *American Sociological Review*, 39: 101–12.

Moss, D. and Misztal, B.A. (1990) Introduction, in B.A. Misztal and D. Moss (eds) *Action on AIDS: National Policies in Comparative Perspective*. New York: Greenwood.

Mugford, S. (1992) Policing euphoria: the politics and pragmatics of drug control, in P. Moir and H. Eijkman (eds) *Policing: Old Issues, New Perspectives*. Melbourne: Macmillan.

Mugford, S. (1993) Social change and the control of psychotropic drugs – risk management, harm reduction and 'postmodernity', *Drug and Alcohol Review*, 12: 369–75.

Murdock, G. (1997) Reservoirs of dogma: an archaeology of popular anxieties, in M. Barker and J. Petley (eds) *Ill Effects: The Media/Violence Debate*. London: Routledge.

Murray, T. and McClure, M. (1996) *Moral Panic*. London: Cassell.

National Council for Civil Liberties (NCCL) (1986) *Stonehenge: a Report into the Civil Liberties Implications of the Events Relating to the Convoys of Summer 1985 and 1986*. London: NCCL.

Nava, M. (1988) Cleveland and the press: outrage and anxiety in the reporting of child sexual abuse, *Feminist Review*, 28: 103–22.

Nelson, B. (1984) *Making an Issue of Child Abuse*. Chicago: University of Chicago Press.

O'Donnell, C. and Craney, J. (1982) The social construction of child abuse, in C. O'Donnell and J. Craney (eds) *Family Violence in Australia*. Melbourne: Longman Cheshire.

Orcutt, J.D. and Turner, J.B. (1993) Shocking numbers and graphic accounts: quantified images of drug problems in the print media, *Social Problems*, 40(2): 190–206.

Osgerby, B. (1998) *Youth in Britain since 1945*. Oxford: Blackwell.

Palmer, J. (1998) News values, in A. Briggs and S. Cobley (eds) *The Media: An Introduction*. London: Addison Wesley Longman.

Parker, H., Measham, F. and Aldridge, J. (1995) *Drug Futures: Changing Patterns of Drug Use Amongst English Youth*. London: Institute for the Study of Drug Dependency.

Parker, H., Aldridge, J. and Measham, F. (1998) *Illegal Leisure: The Normalization of Recreational Drug Use*. London: Routledge.

Parkin, F. (1982) *Max Weber*. London: Tavistock.

Parris, M. (1998) Call off the lynch mob, *The Times*, 10 April.

Parton, N. (1979) The natural history of child abuse: a study in social problem definition, *British Journal of Social Work*, 9(4): 431–51.

Parton, N. (1981) Child abuse, social anxiety and welfare, *British Journal of Social Work*, 11(4): 391–415.

Parton, N. (1985) *The Politics of Child Abuse*. London: Macmillan.

Parton, N. (1996) The new politics of child protection, in J. Pilcher and S. Wagg (eds) *Thatcher's Children? Politics, Childhood and Society in the 1980s and 1990s*. London: Falmer.

Pearson, G. (ed.) (1995) *Scare in the Community*. London: Community Care.

Petley, J. (1984) A nasty story, *Screen*, 25(2): 68–74.

Petley, J. (1994) In defence of video nasties, *British Journalism Review*, 5(3): 52–7.

Petley, J. (1997) Us and them, in M. Barker and J. Petley (eds) *Ill Effects: The Media/ Violence Debate*. London: Routledge.

Peyrot, M. (1984) Cycles of social problem development: the case of drug abuse, *Sociological Quarterly*, 25: 83–96.

Pfohl, S.J. (1977) The 'discovery' of child abuse, *Social Problems*, 24: 310–23.

Pilcher, J. and Wagg, S. (eds) (1996) *Thatcher's Children? Politics, Childhood and Society in the 1980s and 1990s*. London: Falmer.

Plant, M.A. and Plant, M.L. (1992) *Risk-takers: Alcohol, Drugs, Sex and Youth*. London: Routledge.

Pollack, M. (1990) AIDS Policies in France: biomedical leadership and preventive impotence, in B.A. Misztal and D. Moss (eds) *Action on AIDS: National Policies in Comparative Perspective*. New York: Greenwood.

Potter, J. and Wetherell, M. (1987) *Discourse and Social Psychology*. London: Sage.

Pritchard, C. and Bagley, C. (2001) Suicide and murder in child murderers and child sexual abusers, *Journal of Forensic Psychiatry*, 12(2): 269–86.

Putnam, F.W. (1996) The satanic abuse controversy, *Child Abuse and Neglect*, 15: 175–9.

Quam, M. and Ford, N. (1990) Aids policies and practice in the United States, in B.A. Misztal and D. Moss (eds) *Action on AIDS: National Policies in Comparative Perspective*. New York: Greenwood.

Rayside, D.M. and Lindquist, E.A. (1992) Canada: community activism, federalism, and the new politics of disease, in D.L. Kirp and R. Bayer (eds) *AIDS in the Industrialized Democracies: Passions, Politics and Policies*. Montreal: McGill-Queen's University Press.

Redfern, L. (1997) The paedophile as 'folk devil', *Media International Australia*, 85(November): 47–55.

Redhead, S. (1991) Rave off: youth subcultures and the law, *Social Studies Review*, 6(3): 92–4.

Reeves, J.L. and Campbell, R. (1994) *Cracked Coverage: Television News, the Anti-Cocaine Crusade and the Reagan Legacy*. Durham, NC: Duke University Press.

Reiner, R. (1998) Media made criminality: the representation of crime in the mass media, in M. Maguire, R. Morgan and R. Reiner (eds) *The Oxford Handbook of Criminology*. Oxford: Clarendon.

Reinarman, C. and Levine, H.G. (1989) The crack attack: politics and media in America's latest scare, in J. Best (ed.) *Images of Issues: Typifying Contemporary Social Problems*. New York: Aldine de Gruyter.

Richardson, J. (1997) The social construction of satanism: understanding an international social problem, *Australian Journal of Social Issues*, 32(1): 61–85.

Richardson, J.T., Best, J. and Bromley, D. (1991a) Satanism as a social problem, in J.T. Richardson, J. Best and D. Bromley (eds) *The Satanism Scare*. New York: Aldine de Gruyter.

Richardson, J.T., Best, J. and Bromley, D. (eds) (1991b) *The Satanism Scare*. New York: Aldine de Gruyter.

Roberts, H., Smith, S. and Bryce, C. (1995) *Children at Risk? Safety as a Social Value*. Buckingham: Open University Press.

Rocheron, Y. and Linné, O. (1989) AIDS, moral panic and opinion polls, *European Journal of Communication*, 4: 409–34.

Roe, K. (1985) The Swedish moral panic over video 1980–1984, *Nordicom-Information*, 2–3: 13–18.

Saunders, N. (1995) *Ecstasy and Dance Culture*. London: Saunders.

Schlesinger, P. (1990) Re-thinking the sociology of journalism: source strategies and the limits of media-centrism, in M. Ferguson (ed.) *Public Communication: The New Imperatives*. London: Sage.

Schlesinger, P. and Tumber, H. (1994) *Reporting Crime: The Politics of Criminal Justice*. Oxford: Clarendon.

Scott, D. (1995) The social construction of child abuse: debates about definitions and the politics of prevalence, *Psychiatry, Psychology and Law*, 2(2): 117–26.

Scott, S., Jackson, S. and Backett-Milburn, K. (1998) Swings and roundabouts: risk anxiety and the everyday worlds of children, *Sociology*, 32(4): 689–705.

Scraton, P. (ed.) (1997) *Childhood in Crisis?* London: UCL Press.

Shapiro, H. (1999) Dances with drugs; pop music, drugs and youth culture, in N. South (ed.) *Drugs: Culture, Controls and Everyday Life*. London: Sage.

Shiner, M. and Newburn, T. (1999) Taking tea with Nowell: the place and meaning of drug use in everyday life, in N. South (ed.) *Drugs: Culture, Controls and Everyday Life*. London: Sage.

Shoemaker, P., Chang, T. and Brendlinger, N. (1987) Deviance as a predictor of newsworthiness: coverage of international events in the US media, in M.L. McLaughlin (ed.) *Mass Communication Yearbook*. Thousand Oaks, CA: Sage.

Shuker, R. (1986) 'Video nasties': censorship and the politics of popular culture, *New Zealand Journal of Sociology*, 1(1): 64–73.

Silverman, J. and Wilson, D. (2002) *Innocence Betrayed: Paedophilia, the Media and Society*. Cambridge: Polity.

Skidmore, P. (1995) Telling tales: media power, ideology and the reporting of child sexual abuse in Britain, in D. Kidd-Hewitt and R. Osborne (eds) *Crime and the Media: The Post-Modern Spectacle*. London: Pluto.

Smart, C. (1989) *Feminism and the Power of the Law*. London: Routledge.

Smelser, N.J. (1962) *Theory of Collective Behaviour*. London: Routledge.

Soothill, K. and Francis, B. (1998) Poisoned chalice or just desserts? (The Sex Offenders Act 1997), *Journal of Forensic Psychiatry*, 9(2): 281–93.

Soothill, K. and Walby, S. (1991) *Sex Crime in the News*. London: Routledge.

Soothill, K., Francis, B. and Ackerley, E. (1998) Paedophilia and paedophiles, *New Law Journal*, 12 June: 882–3.

Soothill, K., Francis, B., Sanderson, B. and Ackerley, E. (2000) Sex offenders: specialists, generalists – or both?, *British Journal of Criminology*, 40: 56–67.

South, N. (1999a) Debating drugs and everyday life: normalisation, prohibition and 'otherness', in N. South (ed.) *Drugs: Culture, Controls and Everyday Life*. London: Sage.

South, N. (ed.) (1999b) *Drugs: Culture, Controls and Everyday Life*. London: Sage.

Sparks, R. (1995) Entertaining the crisis: television and moral enterprise, in D. Kidd-Hewitt and R. Osborne (eds) *Crime and the Media: The Post-Modern Spectacle*. London: Pluto.

Spector, M. and Kitsuse, J.L. (1977) *Constructing Social Problems*. Menlo Park, CA: Cummings.

Stainton Rogers, R. and Stainton Rogers, W. (1992) *Stories of Childhood: Shifting Agendas of Child Concern*. Toronto: University of Toronto Press.

Steffen, M. (1992) France: social solidarity and scientific expertise, in D.L. Kirp and R. Bayer (eds) *AIDS in the Industrialized Democracies: Passions, Politics and Policies*. Montreal: McGill-Queen's University Press.

Stevens, P. (1991) The demonology of Satanism: an anthropological view, in J.T. Richardson, J. Best and D. Bromley (eds) *The Satanism Scare*. New York: Aldine de Gruyter.

Stockwell, S. (1997) Panic at the Port, *Media International Australia*, 85(November): 56–61.

Strong, P. and Berridge, V. (1990) No one knew anything: some issues in British AIDS policy, in P. Aggleton, P. Davies and G. Hart (eds) *AIDS: Individual, Cultural and Policy Dimensions*. Bristol: Falmer.

Sumner, C. (1981) Race, crime and hegemony: a review essay, *Contemporary Crises*, 5: 277–91.

Sumner, C. (1990) Rethinking deviance; towards a sociology of censure, in C. Sumner (ed.) *Censure, Crime and Criminal Justice*. Buckingham: Open University Press.

Sutherland, E. (1950) The diffusion of the sex psychopath laws, *American Journal of Sociology*, 56: 142–8.

Taylor, I. (1987) Violence and video: for a social democratic perspective, *Contemporary Crises*, 11: 107–28.

Thompson, K. (1998) *Moral Panics*. London: Routledge.

Thompson, W. (1990) Moral crusades and media censorship, *Franco-British Studies*, 9: 30–41.

Thornton, S. (1995) *Club Cultures: Music, Media and Subcultural Capital*. Cambridge: Polity.

Toolan, M. (2001) *Narrative: A Critical Linguistic Introduction*. London: Routledge.

Ungar, S. (2001) Moral panic versus the risk society: the implications of the changing sites of social anxiety, *British Journal of Sociology*, 52(2): 271–92.

Victor, J.S. (1998) Moral panics and the social construction of deviant behavior: a theory and application to the case of ritual child abuse, *Sociological Perspectives*, 41(3): 541–65.

Waddington, D., Critcher, C. and Jones, K. (1989) *Flashpoints: Studies in Public Disorder*. London: Routledge.

Waddington, P.A.J. (1986) Mugging as a moral panic, *British Journal of Sociology*, 37(2): 245–59.

Walker, A. (1984) The latest intruders on official morality, *The Listener*, 1 March.

Walker, A. (1996) Suffer the little children, in K. French (ed.) *Screen Violence*. London: Bloomsbury.

Warner, M. (1994) *Managing Monsters: Six Myths of our Time*. London: Vintage.

Watney, S. (1988) AIDS, 'moral panic' theory and homophobia, in P. Aggleton and H. Homans (eds) *Social Aspects of AIDS*. London: Falmer.

Weber, M. ([1904] 1949) 'Objectivity' in social science and social policy, in M. Weber, *The Methodology of the Social Sciences*, trans. and edited by E.A. Shils and H.A. Finch. New York: Free Press.

Webster, D. (1989) Who dunnit? America did: Rambo and post-Hungerford rhetoric, *Cultural Studies*, 3(2): 173–93.

Webster, R. (1998) *The Great Children's Home Panic*. Oxford: Orwell Press.

Weeks, J. (1985) *Sexuality and its Discontents*. London: Routledge.

Weeks, J. (1989) AIDS: the intellectual agenda, in P. Aggleton, G. Hart and P. Davies (eds) *AIDS: Social Representations, Social Practices*. Bristol: Falmer.

Weeks, J. (1993) AIDS and the regulation of sexuality, in V. Berridge and P. Strong (eds) *AIDS and Contemporary History*. Cambridge: Cambridge University Press.

Welch, M., Fenwick, M. and Roberts, M. (1997) Primary definitions of crime and moral panic: a content analysis of experts' quotes in feature newspaper articles on crime, *Journal of Research in Crime and Delinquency*, 34(4): 474–94.

White, S. (1998) Inter-discursivity and child welfare: the ascent and durability of psycho-legalism, *Sociological Review*, 46(2): 264–92.

Wilczynski, A. and Sinclair, K. (1999) Moral tales: representations of child abuse in the quality and tabloid media, *Australia and New Zealand Journal of Criminology*, 32(3): 262–83.

Wilkins, L.T. (1964) *Social Deviance: Social Policy, Action and Research*. London: Tavistock.

Wilson, A.W. and Duncan, S.P. (1985) Child sexual abuse; a study of prevalence in Great Britain, *Child Abuse and Neglect*, 4: 457–67.

Woolgar, S. and Paluch, D. (1985) Ontological gerrymandering: the anatomy of social problems explanations, *Social Problems*, 32(February): 213–27.

Wyre, R. and Tate, T. (1995) *The Murder of Childhood*. Harmondsworth: Penguin.

Young, J. (1971) *The Drug Takers: The Social Meaning of Drug Taking*. London: Paladin.

Young, J. (1974) Drugs and deviance, in P. Rock and M. Macintosh (eds) *Deviance and Social Control*. London: Tavistock.

INDEX

MEDIA, RISK AND SCIENCE

Stuart Allan

- How is science represented by the media?
- Who defines what counts as a risk, threat or hazard, and why?
- In what ways do media images of science shape public perceptions?
- What can cultural and media studies tell us about current scientific controversies?

Media, Risk and Science is an exciting exploration into an array of important issues, providing a much needed framework for understanding key debates on how the media represent science and risk. In a highly effective way, Stuart Allan weaves together insights from multiple strands of research across diverse disciplines. Among the themes he examines are: the role of science in science fiction, such as *Star Trek*; the problem of 'pseudo-science' in *The X-Files*; and how science is displayed in science museums. Science journalism receives particular attention, with the processes by which science is made 'newsworthy' unravelled for careful scrutiny. The book also includes individual chapters devoted to how the media portray environmental risks, HIV-AIDS, food scares (such as BSE or 'mad cow disease' and GM foods) and human cloning. The result is a highly topical text that will be invaluable for students and scholars in cultural and media studies, science studies, journalism, sociology and politics.

Contents

Series editor's foreword - Introduction: media, risk and science - Science fictions - Science in popular culture - Science journalism - Media, risk and the environment - Bodies at risk: news coverage of AIDS - Food scares: mad cows and GM foods - Figures of the human: robots, androids, cyborgs and clones - Glossary - References - Index.

256pp   0 335 20662 X (Paperback)   0 335 20663 8 (Hardback)

VIOLENCE AND THE MEDIA

Cynthia Carter and C. Kay Weaver

- Why is there so much violence portrayed in the media?
- What meanings are attached to representations of violence in the media?
- Can media violence encourage violent behaviour and desensitise audiences to real violence?
- Does the 'everydayness' of media violence lead to the 'normalisation' of violence in society?

Violence and the Media is a lively and indispensable introduction to current thinking about media violence and its potential influence on audiences. Adopting a fresh perspective on the 'media effects' debate, Carter and Weaver engage with a host of pressing issues around violence in different media contexts – including news, film, television, pornography, advertising and cyberspace. The book offers a compelling argument that the daily repetition of media violence helps to normalise and legitimise the acts being portrayed. Most crucially, the influence of media violence needs to be understood in relation to the structural inequalities of everyday life. Using a wide range of examples of media violence primarily drawn from the American and British media to illustrate these points, *Violence and the Media* is a distinctive and revealing exploration of one of the most important and controversial subjects in cultural and media studies today.

Contents

192pp   0 335 20505 4 (Paperback)   0 335 20506 2 (Hardback)